THE STATE OF THE NATION'S PUBLIC SCHOOLS

A CONFERENCE REPORT

*Sixteen Distinguished Authorities
Assess the Present and Offer Visions
of the Future*

*Plus the Report of a Conference Based on These
Assessments and Their Meaning for Tomorrow*

Stanley Elam, Editor

A project combining the resources of Phi Delta Kappa,
the Institute for Educational Leadership,
and the Educational Excellence Network

Published by
Phi Delta Kappa
Bloomington, Indiana

Cover design
by
Victoria Voelker

Library of Congress Catalog Card Number 93-84746
ISBN 0-87367-461-8
Copyright © 1993 by Phi Delta Kappa
Bloomington, Indiana

TABLE OF CONTENTS

INTRODUCTION

Phi Delta Kappa, the Institute for Educational Leadership, and the Educational Excellence Network joined together to sponsor a conference on the state of America's public schools. Held in Washington, D.C., on February 4-5, 1993, the conference brought together leaders from a variety of fields to discuss and to debate the issues surrounding the schools. Both school critics and defenders were represented.

Pre-planning for the conference was designed to insure a productive discussion. Sixteen papers were commissioned, with the authors being asked to comment on what's right and what's wrong with the public schools and to offer a vision for the future. The papers were distributed in advance of the conference. The opening presentation at the conference was by Harold Hodgkinson and was intended as a background to support the envisioning discussion. From that point forward, the participants were the program; and their comments and reactions were the substance of the conference.

The purpose of this book is to try to capture as much of the flavor and substance of the proceedings is possible. Stanley Elam, editor emeritus of the *Phi Delta Kappan*, served as reporter for the conference and as editor of this book. He has tried to report, summarize, and interpret what transpired. He also conducted a post-conference survey of participants to try to measure the degree of agreement on the issues identified. For the reader who desires to go directly to the source, the 15 commissioned papers are presented in full.

The sponsors of this conference believed that it was important to initiate discussion on the state of America's public schools. How people feel about their schools will have a direct impact on changes that are proposed and on the kinds of solutions that are offered. The conference provided a vehicle for a range of views to be expressed and for many issues to be discussed. Phi Delta Kappa is pleased to contribute to the continuing discussion through the publication of this book. We hope readers will find the information interesting, useful, and provocative.

In closing, I would like to express appreciation to the EXXON Education Foundation for its support of the conference. The funding provided made the conference possible and contributed to broad dissemination of the conference proceedings.

Jack Kosoy
International President
Phi Delta Kappa

PART ONE: BACKGROUND PAPERS

STRENGTHS AND WEAKNESSES OF AMERICAN EDUCATION

Michael W. Kirst

Taking the time to examine the strengths of the U.S. education system helps to put our problems in perspective, Mr. Kirst suggests. There is no evidence that abandoning our public schools will improve the situation.

The public education system in the United States has served this nation well. Today and in the future, it must meet unprecedented challenges. However, arguments about whether the performance of our students has declined over time miss the point. The 1990 Oldsmobile was better than any Olds made before. But was it good enough to meet worldwide competition in 1990? A similar question faces U.S. education: Are we good enough to stand up to worldwide competition?

The time is right to assess the strengths and weaknesses of the U.S. public education system. We need to build on its strengths and shore up its weaknesses. We know more than ever about how to do this, but serious questions remain about the resources we are willing to devote to the task and about our political will to get the job done.

What Is Right

Inclusiveness. The U.S. K-12 education system as we know it today was created in the mid-20th century to serve all pupils for 12 years and not weed them out at an earlier age. Until very recently, this policy provided high retention rates compared to those of other nations. Since 1970, however, other industrialized nations (for example, Great Britain, Australia, and Japan) have increased their retention rates dramatically. The inclusiveness of our system through high school is no longer

Michael W. Kirst is co-director of Policy Analysis for California Education and a professor in the Department of Administration and Policy Analysis, School of Education, Stanford University, Stanford, Calif.

3

the competitive edge it once was, although 88% of our young people have earned high school diplomas or the equivalent by age 25.

Nevertheless, we should strengthen our efforts at dropout prevention and expand the second-chance opportunities we offer to dropouts who wish to resume their schooling. The GED (General Education Development) program, broad access to community colleges, and high school adult education programs are parts of the U.S. system that are frequently overlooked. Moreover, their curricular standards are a concern and need to be reviewed; but the role they play in the U.S. education system should not be underestimated.

Postsecondary education. The most commonly cited indicators of the health of education in the United States − international assessments, the National Assessment of Educational Progress (NAEP), scores on college entrance exams, scores on standardized achievement tests, and the results of state assessment programs − all ignore the value added by the postsecondary education system. However, in the international arena, the U.S. system of postsecondary education − including community colleges, trade schools, and universities − is one of our chief strengths.

For example, in 1988 the United States spent a higher percentage of its gross national product on public and private higher education than any other country in the world. Moreover, U.S. spending on higher education as a percentage of all education spending was 39.4%, compared to 20.8% for West Germany and 21.4% for Japan.[1] The principal reason for the high level of U.S. spending on higher education is that the proportion of the population participating in higher education is greater here than in any other large nation.[2] But the U.S. per-student expenditure on public and private higher education is also high. For example, in 1988 the United States spent about $9,844 per pupil for higher education while Japan spent $6,105 and France spent $4,362.[3]

We also should be pleased with the *total* years or days of schooling that young people in the United States accumulate through age 25. Much is made in the press about our 180-day school year, compared to a school year of 240 days in Japan. But it is rarely mentioned that in the United States the highest percentage of 24-year-olds in the world graduate from a four-year college or university. Our particular advantage is in the percentage of females who graduate from colleges and universities. The United States graduates 24% of its 24-year-old females; Japan, 12.4%; West Germany, 10%.

Many studies have emphasized that U.S. students complete little homework and do not work hard on academic subjects in high school.[4] But U.S. students are often confronted with a demanding academic regimen in college. The adjustment to the academic pressures of the university in freshman year can be difficult for many U.S. students, but they do make up for the ground lost in high school.

The difficulty of the postsecondary experience in the United States contrasts sharply with the situation in Japan, where the university years are viewed as a time to take it easy between the intense academic pressure of high school and the demands of Japanese business. Japanese universities are not as challenging as those in the United States, especially for many Japanese women, who often take a less-rigorous academic curriculum that prepares them for homemaking.[5] A 1988 study of teacher education students in the United States and Japan concluded:

> Although American students seem to know less about global issues than Japanese students at the beginning of college, by graduation they are performing as well. This is attributable to a considerable positive difference between U.S. freshmen and seniors, and a small difference between Japanese freshmen and seniors. This finding corroborates recent statements by Japanese scholars expressing concern about the quality of higher education.[6]

The pre-eminence of U.S. graduate schools is widely recognized. The United States attracts a large number of foreign students, and our most prestigious research universities are certainly competitive by world standards — many consider them to be the best in the world. Is there a better technical university in Japan or Germany than MIT, Cal Tech, or Stanford? Given the overall quality of all U.S. research universities, it is likely that some of the international academic gap is closed at this final stage, at least for our most outstanding science and math students.

Content standards and assessment. A recent international study concluded that U.S. 9- and 14-year-olds compared quite favorably with their counterparts in other industrialized nations in reading.[7] While basic reading looks relatively good, we still have a long way to go before the majority of U.S. students can comprehend complex passages and grasp the tone and mood of the author. Moreover, math and science appear very weak in international comparisons. The U.S. math and science curricula do not expose the mass of students to very much problem solving, statistical inference, chemistry, or physics.[8]

Some help appears to be on the way. For example, by the end of the 1990s, the United States probably will have national curriculum standards and subject-matter frameworks, though not a detailed national curriculum. Currently, de facto national "policies" are all around us — set by the school accreditation agencies, such as the North Central Association of Schools and Colleges, the College Entrance Examination Board, and the National Collegiate Athletic Association.

The movement toward national content standards in various curricular areas is justified by several concerns.

• Current state and local standards for pupil achievement and teacher performance are lacking in rigor and do not provide uniform data on outcomes — data crucial for interstate or local comparisons.

• Commonly used multiple-choice tests are excessively oriented to low-level basic skills that inappropriately emphasize single right answers. Moreover, local education agencies tend to choose commercial tests that do not adequately emphasize analysis, statistical inference, mathematical problem solving, experimental science, synthesis, expository writing, and complex reading. Many widely available standardized tests — such as the Comprehensive Tests of Basic Skills, the Stanford Achievement Tests, and the Metropolitan Achievement Tests — are not geared to the high curricular standards of our economic competitors in Europe and Asia. Since the United States is involved in worldwide economic competition, complete local control of tests and curricula is a luxury we can no longer afford.

• Since the commonly used standardized multiple-choice tests are pitched at such low levels, parents and the general public receive a "phony story" that exaggerates what U.S. pupils know and can do today — compared to prior decades or to students in other nations. The "Lake Wobegon" effect, in which all the students are above average, then becomes the reality.

• U.S. tests and exams often do not have "high stakes" for the pupils who take them. Few employers look at the transcripts of high school graduates, and state assessments are not used for college entrance. The Scholastic Aptitude Test is not aligned with the high school curriculum and purports to measure "aptitude" rather than achievement.

A coalition of policy leaders has concluded that national subject-matter curricular standards that meet world-class benchmarks are needed.[9] This coalition contends that a nationwide system of exams should be developed and aligned to these world-class standards in five core subjects: English, mathematics, science, social studies, and foreign languages. Moreover, the results should be reported for individual students; and "high-stakes" decisions should be based largely on student performance. Specifically, the coalition contends that employers should use the results of national exams when hiring high school graduates and that universities should consider scores on national exams as well as high school grades. Furthermore, these initiatives for national standards need to be part of any state-level strategy for systemic reform, especially in the areas of staff development and teacher training.

Local flexibility. Despite the likely evolution of national standards, the locally based education system in the United States is flexible and can innovate without feeling the heavy hand of national control. The 15,000 school districts provide the United States with the ability to adapt to diverse local contexts. While many districts are stuck in political gridlock, others are increasingly on the move. Citizens with the resources to relocate can find many educational choices to suit their tastes. Despite growing state control, there is still a large range of options in local education. Districts differ in their mix of secondary school curricula and in their stress on extracurricular activities. They also differ in their local tax burdens.

Socialization and the common school. The U.S. system of public education has been a crucial element in unifying a nation of immigrants, producing the *unum* from the *pluribus*. More immigrants entered the United States in the two decades between 1970 and 1990 than in any previous 20-year period. Consequently, the need to teach community values and concepts is just as urgent as it was during the rise of common schools at the turn of the century. If the public schools do not include the vast majority of our children, the only other common transmitter of our culture will be television. And so far, television does not seem to have had a positive influence on American youth.

We have lost much of the national cohesiveness that the common school crusaders helped to create. Today, powerful and well-organized interest groups — whether labor, business, or agriculture — have no inclination to unite with other segments of the community to explore differences and work toward the common good. Although the leaders of these interest groups are not irresponsible, they have developed attitudes that make collaboration with others almost impossible. Since each group feels that it is not getting what it deserves, the leaders are in no mood to work with others to shape a constructive future.

7

Problems with U.S. Schools

The bottom half. The United States is particularly weak in providing higher-order skills to those students — roughly half — who do not go on to postsecondary education. In part, this failure is caused by the declining conditions of children and the relative lack of support here for children, compared to other nations in the industrialized world.

Today, more than 20% of children in the United States live in poverty, up from 14% in 1969.[10] The median income of families in the bottom income quintile (lowest 20%) has eroded over time, and the gap between the incomes of the poorest and wealthiest families has grown.[11] The decline in real income for those in the lowest quintile has been accompanied by gains for those in the top 40% of the income distribution. Race and ethnicity, gender, and family structure are strongly associated with the likelihood of living in poverty. In 1992, half of families headed by single women lived in poverty, compared to only 11.4% of two-parent families.[12]

While many children fare well in low-income households, studies have shown that children in such circumstances are more likely to die in infancy and early childhood, suffer serious illnesses, become pregnant during their teen years, or drop out of school. They are also less likely to continue education beyond high school.[13] Despite the statistical association of these outcomes with poverty, the direction of causality is less clear. The diminished life chances of the poor may be linked to the lack of access to adequate health care and nutrition, the often lower quality of schooling in low-income neighborhoods, the stress of poverty on family relationships, or a variety of other elements.

Family structure. Traditionally, most institutions that serve children and youths make the implicit assumption that children live with two biological parents, one working in the home and the other working in the formal labor market. This traditional family type now accounts for less than one-third of all families. Forty-six percent of children live in homes in which both parents (or the only parent) work outside the home.[14] Because of an increase in divorce and in the number of births to single mothers, about 60% of all children and youths will live in a single-parent family for some period of their lives.[15]

Teachers. While the United States is developing challenging and better-conceived curricula and exams, there is no commensurate effort under way to improve the training or the working conditions of teachers. Teachers still work in a structure that inhibits collaboration and professional growth. Staff-development programs are typically one-shot affairs with scant follow-up and coaching. The United States has no national strategy for staff development that provides depth and breadth for its 2.2 million teachers. The United States also lacks levers to improve teacher preparation, which is largely controlled by independent universities and driven by state requirements. The probable result will be minimal classroom implementation of the high-level national content standards.

Fragmentation and gridlock. In the 1950s and 1960s, the politics of education was a "closed system" that was unresponsive to communities and political constituencies. Now the situation is quite different. Numerous actors and constituencies have created a sense of fragmentation and have led to complaints that no one is in charge of U.S. education policy. This fragmentation of interests inhibits coherent reform. For example, it is very difficult to align categorical programs with the standards developed by the National Council of Teachers of Mathematics. Moreover, it is difficult to sustain education reform over a long period of time because newly elected politicians generally do not want to continue reforms that they did not originate.

Most of the social movements of the 1990s differ from those of the 19th century that led to the creation of such social institutions as the public schools. Today, social movements are interested in challenging public institutions and trying to make them more responsive to forces outside the local administrative structure. Some would even assert that these movements help fragment decision making so that schools cannot function effectively. This conclusion is reinforced by the almost unremitting litany of the media suggesting that violence, vandalism, and declining test scores are the predominant conditions of public education.

In California, for example, this situation has become so serious that the schools increasingly suffer from shock and overload characterized by poor morale and too few resources to operate all the programs that the society expects schools to offer. The issue then becomes how much change and agitation a public institution can take and still continue to function effectively. Californians have confronted numerous initiatives, such as Proposition 13, vouchers, and spending limits. Citizens in California and elsewhere go to their local school boards and superintendents expecting redress of their problems only to find that the decision-making power rests with the state. The impression grows that *no one* is in charge of public education.

All of this does not mean that local school authorities are helpless. Rather, it means that they cannot control their agendas or shape outcomes as much as they could in the past. Superintendents must deal with shifting and ephemeral coalitions that might yield some temporary local advantages; but many important policy items on the local agenda arise from external forces, such as state and federal governments or the pressures of interest groups, including teachers.

There is a feeling abroad in the land that the education system *cannot* be restructured on a massive scale. According to this view, the most that we can expect is incremental improvement, along with a few show-case anomalies of structural change. More "projects" do not seem to be the answer. But national exams on their own are not a sufficient policy either. Perhaps our biggest weakness is our uncertainty about what to do next in pursuit of comprehensive and systemic change.

The weaknesses of U.S. education are most evident in big cities, and the strengths are clearest in suburbs with high incomes and high levels of education. NAEP results, however, highlight significant weaknesses even in the upper ranges of achievement in terms of problem solving, synthesis, analysis, statistical inference, and comprehension of complex passages of prose.

Despite a century of education reforms, nothing much has changed at the classroom level. Reforms that have lasted have usually been structural additions that are monitored easily and create a long-term influential constituency. Some examples are vocational education and the use of Carnegie units. But overcoming the weaknesses discussed above will require reform at the lowest unit — teachers and teaching — in addition to systemic restructuring. It also will require the political will to stick with a coherent strategy directed toward improving student outcomes in all parts of the education system. Our democracy leads us to make frequent changes in leadership, and new policy makers must overcome the tendency to throw out their predecessors' approaches automatically.

Analyses on a national scale mask urgent problems that specific U.S. regions confront. In the Southwest, for example, students with limited facility in English are a large and growing portion of the population. One of every eight schoolchildren in the nation lives in California, but more than 20% have limited proficiency in English; and by the year 2000, half of California children will be Hispanic or Asian. The educational problems of these children never make the top of national lists, which suggests that a nationwide analysis may not always lead to the right approach in specific regions.

It is probable that the Clinton Administration will focus on job creation through policies that emphasize the transition between high school

10

and the workplace. However, it is doubtful that apprenticeships will provide a complete answer to the problems of the bottom half outlined above. It seems more likely that apprenticeship initiatives will have but scattered and limited impact. Other strategies to meet this challenge may be even less effective. Some proponents of national exams contend that, if employers ask for national exam scores, students will be motivated to work harder in school. This theory has never been tested in the United States and will require large-scale mobilization of employers.

Taking the time to examine the strengths of the U.S. education system helps to put our myriad problems in perspective. There is no evidence that abandoning our public education system will improve the situation. A great deal of rhetoric and numerous theories surround the alleged panacea of choice. But the strengths of the U.S. education system are embedded in our culture and history, and we should not discard them easily or without better data about what choice would actually accomplish. The U.S. education system is gigantic, with roughly $250 billion spent annually, 2.6 million employees, and 44 million pupils. Untested schemes, such as vouchers, are dangerous and represent a plunge into unknown waters. We already know quite a bit about systemic education reform and school improvement.

Footnotes

1. Arthur Hauptman, Eileen O'Brien, and Lauren Supena, *Higher Education Expenditures and Participation: An International Comparison* (Washington, D.C.: American Council for Educational Research, 1991).
2. *Education at a Glance* (Paris: Organisation for Economic Cooperation and Development, 1992), p. 77.
3. Ibid., p. 57.
4. Joseph Murphy, *The Education Reform Movement of the 1980s* (Berkeley, Calif.: McCutchan, 1990), pp. 10-19.
5. Michael W. Kirst, "Japanese Education: Its Implications for Economic Competition in the 1980s," *Phi Delta Kappan* 62 (June 1981): 707-708. For a critique of U.S. higher education, see Ray Marshall and Marc Tucker, *Thinking for a Living* (New York: Basic Books, 1992).
6. John Cogan, Judith Torney-Purta, and Douglas Anderson, "Knowledge and Attitudes Toward Global Issues: Students in Japan and the U.S.," *Comparative Education Review* 32 (1988): 282-97.
7. Warwick B. Elley, *How in the World Do Students Read?* (New York: International Association for the Evaluation of Educational Achievement, July 1992).
8. For direct comparisons of achievement in the United States with that in other nations, see *Education at a Glance*.

9. See *Raising Standards for American Education* (Washington, D.C.: National Council on Education Standards and Testing, 1992).

10. See Harold Hodgkinson, *A Demographic Look at Tomorrow* (Washington, D.C.: Institute for Educational Leadership, 1992), p. 4.

11. Ibid., pp. 7-10.

12. Ibid., pp. 4, 7, 8.

13. Ibid.

14. Ibid., p. 4.

15. Ibid; see also Marshall and Tucker, op. cit.

AMERICAN EDUCATION: THE GOOD, THE BAD, AND THE TASK

Harold Hodgkinson

Mr. Hodgkinson discerns a clear message amid the data on shifting populations, on test scores, and on students' socio-economic status. The figures are telling us that we must turn our attention to the students who are at the highest risk of school failure.

My aims in this brief article are to describe the unique diversity of the American student body and the magnitude of the demographic changes that are to come, to consider our accomplishments with this student body by looking at test data, to point out the failures of the system in working effectively with certain students, and to indicate what needs to be done to make the system work more effectively for *all* young Americans.

Diversity

While the national population grew 9.8% during the 1980s, certain groups grew very rapidly, and others posted only small increases. The number of non-Hispanic whites grew by 6%; of African-Americans, by 13.2%; of Native Americans, by 37.9%; of Asian-Pacific Islanders, by 107.8%; of Hispanics of all races, by 53%.

While about 22% of the total population can be described as minority, 30% of school-age children are minority, a number that will reach 36% shortly after the year 2000. A look at immigration rates can give us a clue as to why this is so. Between 1820 and 1945, the nations that sent us the largest numbers of immigrants were (in rank order): Germany, Italy, Ireland, the United Kingdom, the Soviet Union, Canada, and Sweden. The nations that send us the most immigrants now and

Harold Hodgkinson is director of the Center for Demographic Policy, Institute for Educational Leadership, Washington, D.C.

that are projected to do so through the year 2000 are (in rank order): Mexico, the Philippines, Korea, China/Taiwan, India, Cuba, the Dominican Republic, Jamaica, Canada, Vietnam, the United Kingdom, and Iran.

It is clear from the former list that we have not really been a "nation of nations," as both Carl Sandburg and Walt Whitman proclaimed; rather, we have been a nation of Europeans. There was a common European culture that the schools could use in socializing millions of immigrant children. The latter list indicates that we face a brand-new challenge: the population of American schools today truly represents the world. Children come to school today with different diets, different religions (there were more Moslems than Episcopalians in the United States in 1991), different individual and group loyalties, different music, different languages. The most diverse segment of our society is our children. While these children bring new energy and talents to our nation, they also represent new challenges for instruction.

In the 1990 Census, for the first time in history, only three states accounted for more than half of the nation's growth in a decade. These states were California, Florida, and Texas. They also picked up a total of 14 seats in the U.S. House of Representatives, while New York, Pennsylvania, Ohio, Indiana, and Illinois lost an equivalent number of seats. California will have to prepare for a 41% increase in high school graduates by 1995, with 52% of them being "minority," a term that loses its meaning in such a situation. By the year 2010, the number of minority young people in the United States will increase by 4.4 million, while the number of non-Hispanic white young people will decline by 3.8 million.

The states that are growing fastest have high percentages of "minority" youth. If the large minority population of New York is added to the large and fast-growing minority populations of California, Texas, and Florida, these four states will have more than one-third of the nation's young people in 2010; and the youth population of each state will be more than 52% "minority." In 2010 about 12 states will have "majority minority" youth populations, while Maine's youth population will be 3% minority. It makes little sense to focus solely on the national changes when the states are becoming much more diverse in terms of ethnicity, age of population, job production, population density, family types, and youth poverty.[1]

Children at Risk and Schools

In 1993 more than 23% of America's children were living below the poverty line and thus were at risk of failing to fulfill their physical and mental promise. This is one of the highest youth poverty rates in the "developed" world and has shown little inclination to decline. Most of these children live in our nation's inner cities and rural areas, in about equal numbers. (The issue of youth poverty in rural America has not been addressed seriously by the nation's leaders.) Because these children bring the risks with them on the first day of kindergarten, it becomes a vital job of the schools to overcome these risks. Schools should be assessed on how well they and other agencies responsible for youth development meet the challenges posed by these children.

Since the publication of *A Nation at Risk* in 1983, there has been a general impression that American students have slumped from a previous position of world leadership to near the bottom in terms of academic achievement. (Of course, we have had similar waves of criticism of public school standards in previous decades; Arthur Bestor's *Educational Wastelands*, James Bryant Conant's reform movement, and the many responses to Sputnik I — suggesting that American students were hopelessly behind those of the Soviet Union — spring immediately to mind, along with a long list of books suggesting that American education is "falling behind.")

Behind what? That question is seldom voiced, though its implied answer is clear to readers of the literature of decline: schools are falling behind some previous Golden Age during which American public school students were the world's best in every aspect of the curriculum. In reality, if you look at the data from 30 years of international achievement testing, you will find *no* period during which American students led the world in school achievement.

Anyone who questions the methodology of the international comparisons on which much of the literature of decline is based usually will be accused of advocating "complacency." Those who ask such questions are thus shown to be enemies of excellence. However, a variety of data suggest that the picture is not as universally bleak as it is sometimes painted.

A report from the Sandia National Laboratories, carefully assessing a wide variety of data sources, concluded that American education has done well in most areas of performance. That report has never formally seen the light of day. The largest-ever international study of reading, directed by a distinguished U.S. researcher, tested thousands of students in more than 30 countries. It found that U.S. students were among the best in the world in reading, surpassed only by Finland. Only *USA Today* covered the story; and the U.S. Department of Education immediately discredited the results by saying that higher levels of difficulty were not assessed, and therefore the United States was not interested in the findings. Actually, the data were politically unacceptable rather than cripplingly flawed.

The fact is that all the international studies of educational achievement have a number of built-in flaws. First, translation is an art, not a science; and an item in one language can seldom be translated into another language with the identical set of culturally derived meanings. All items have a cultural "spin" based on the values behind the words. If a student can correctly identify a harpsichord as a musical instrument, we learn little about that student's intelligence but a lot about his or her family and social class. Moreover, there is no way to control for the differing motivations of the students who take the tests.

In addition, international comparisons are not diagnostic: they don't help students (or nations) understand their mistakes in order to improve performance. They don't help policy makers figure out what is wrong with an education system in order to improve it. Outside of a major preoccupation with finding out who's "number one" in some vague terms, it is hard to see how any education system in any nation has been helped by these tests. It's hard to tell from these test scores what specifically needs to be fixed in American education. One can wonder what the return has been on this considerable investment.

Test Data in the United States

Let's look at test data from our own country and see what we can make out of them, starting with the performance of younger children and ending with that of graduate students. For this purpose I'll rely on an excellent compendium, titled *Performance at the Top*, recently issued by the Educational Testing Service (ETS).[2]

With regard to reading, the data show that one 9-year-old in six can search for specific information, relate ideas, and make generalizations — the same fraction as in 1971. But we also learn that whites do much better and that Hispanics actually do a little better than blacks, despite the complications associated with English as a second language for many Hispanic children. Most important, there are spectacular differences in reading that are associated with parents' level of education: 22% of children whose parents have had some college can read at this higher level of comprehension, but only 6% of the children of high school dropouts can. Indeed, parents' level of education is one of the very best predictors of students' educational achievement.

16

The implications of the importance of parents' education for our education reform efforts are huge, and they have been largely neglected by the reform initiatives that issued from the Bush White House under the banner of the America 2000 strategy. Poverty would seem to be the root cause of educational deficiency (college graduates being unusually low on poverty measures), yet the reforms suggested as part of America 2000 seldom mention poverty or disadvantage.

If a child who was poor and a member of a minority group is allowed to enter the middle class — as happens if the parents become college graduates and move to the suburbs — then that child will tend to perform in school like other children whose parents are college graduates living in suburbs. This means that we should not let go of the American Dream just yet; if given the chance, it still works.

In math, slightly more 9-year-olds (20%) can perform at intermediate levels. Again, there has been no change over the years, although the first data are from 1978. But whites still do far better, and the scores of blacks are slightly lower than those of Hispanics. Geographically speaking, the Southeast and the West do not do as well as the Northeast and the Central United States. But again, differences in parents' level of education reveal much: 29% of the children of college graduates perform at the intermediate level, while only 6% of the children of high school dropouts do so.

In science, about one-fourth of 9-year-olds can apply basic scientific information, a figure unchanged since 1977. Here, racial and ethnic differences are somewhat smaller, and blacks do a little better than Hispanics. Regional differences are also smaller. But once again, the differences between the children of college graduates and the children of high school dropouts are the greatest: 36% of the former do well in science versus only 9% of the latter. (Oddly enough, children whose parents had some additional education past high school do better than the children of college graduates, but only by 3%.)

The data on the performance of 13-year-olds in reading reveal patterns similar to those of 9-year-olds. Again, whites do better than minorities; but the differences have narrowed among the 13-year-olds, and the scores of blacks are slighter higher than those of Hispanics. Regional differences are also smaller. However, differences associated with parents' level of education remain quite large: 15% of 13-year-old children of college graduates read at the "figuring out" level, but only 6% of the children of high school dropouts can. (Other subjects use different comparisons and therefore are not included. Among 17-year-olds, the data for comparing regions and parents' education are not comparable, although there is no evidence of systematic declines in subject areas.)

As we look past high school, some fascinating numbers are present. The Advanced Placement (AP) testing program has grown rapidly since its inception — jumping by more than 500% in the last two decades. The numbers of minority test-takers also have shown large increases, reaching about one-fifth of all test-takers in 1990, though Asian-Americans make up about half of all the minority students tested. The program has become very popular in a variety of schools, ranging from the inner cities to the wealthy suburbs; the number of test-takers grew from about 100,000 in 1978 to 320,000 in 1990.

In most testing situations, expanding the pool of test-takers lowers the average scores. The AP program proves to be the exception, as the scores have remained virtually stable for the past two decades. One interpretation in the ETS report suggests that the limits of the pool have not been reached and that many more students could successfully complete college work in high school through AP-type programs. (This is particularly exciting for low-income and minority youths, as I have contended that inner-city students often will rise to a challenge, no matter how depressed their background may be.) The data certainly suggest that the consistency of AP scores cannot be explained by the conventional wisdom that all schools are terrible and getting worse.

When we finally get to scores on the Scholastic Aptitude Test (SAT), we find that the declines of the 1970s were largely recouped during the 1980s in terms of the percentage of students scoring 600 or above on either the verbal or the math sections. (The percentage of students achieving high scores in math has been about twice as large as the percentage achieving high verbal scores, which could have some useful implications for high schools.) Even more interesting with regard to the "high end" scores are those for the College Board's Achievement Tests, which are designed to test what is actually taught in high school courses. About 8% of high school seniors take these tests. Their average SAT verbal and math scores have steadily increased since 1977, and their average scores on the Achievement Tests have increased since 1979. It seems clear that the performance of our top students is, in some senses, improving over time.

If we look at issues of equity with regard to college attendance and graduation, we find that about 23% of all white high school graduates in the classes of 1972 and 1980 received a bachelor's degree, while the corresponding figure for black high school graduates actually declined

18

from 17.5% for the class of 1972 to 13.9% for the class of 1980. The rate at which Hispanics earned college degrees actually improved a little, from 10.7% in 1972 to 11.2% for the 1980 class, even though Hispanics' percentages of college completion were consistently below those of blacks. The 1992 *Almanac* of the *Chronicle of Higher Education*, however, shows an increase in college enrollment for all minorities during the 1980s, although degree data are not given.

It seems that during the 1980s, when minority scores were improving on many K-12 measures, *access* to higher education was slipping for many minority groups. Whether this was a result of shifts in financial aid policies (converting grant programs to loans) or of other factors is not clear. However, half of our graduating seniors enter college, and about one-fourth of them receive bachelor's degrees. Two percent then enter graduate school, and 3% enter professional schools. While minorities were steadily increasing their numbers through high school graduation, their participation in the higher education pipeline showed some disturbing trends. In 1992 minorities represented about 30% of public school students, 20% of college students, and 14% of recipients of bachelor's degrees. (Note that an increase in the number of high school diplomas earned by minorities will take five or more years to show up as an increase in bachelor's degrees.)

Even more striking is a look at the ETS data on high-ability students. While half did earn a bachelor's degree, 10% of high-ability seniors did not attend *any* higher education program after high school; and 40% of those who did so attended a community college, from which some transferred later to four-year programs. Given our stereotype that community colleges have virtually none of the high-ability students, it appears that they actually enroll about two-fifths of them, which may explain why students who transfer to four-year programs do quite well.

When we come to the question of entrance to graduate school and consider scores on the Graduate Record Examination, we find even more interesting issues. From 1981 to 1990, the number of test-takers increased 16%, from 135,000 to 157,000, while the mean verbal score rose 16 points, the mean quantitative score rose 36 points, and the mean analytical score rose 30 points. The average score on the Graduate Management Admissions Test has gone from 481 in 1982 to 503 in 1990, while the number of test-takers surged from 114,000 in 1984 to 160,000 in 1990. Scores on the Medical School Admissions Test and on the Law School Admissions Test also have shown great stability (and some score increases), even with a more diverse group of test-takers. From these data it appears that both the diversity and the quality of our future scientists, researchers, and professional workers have increased simultaneously.

An Explanation

We now need to try to find some way of explaining all the data we have examined. Below, I offer a brief summary, and then I propose one explanation that fits all the data.

First, the top 20% of our high school graduates are world class — and getting better. However, talented minority youths do not get as far in the educational pipeline as they should. (The production of black Ph.D.s declined by more than one-third during the 1980s, a factor that cannot be explained in terms of declining test scores for blacks or declining numbers of blacks in the pool.)

As Iris Rotberg and others have pointed out, 40% of all research articles in the world are published by U.S. scholars; no other nation produces more than 7%.[3] There seems to be little doubt that the American intellectual elite, particularly in math and the sciences, is retaining its dominant position. The problem is that, if all public schools are doing such a miserable job, how do colleges make up for that loss and produce the world's best graduate students? (Note that the vast majority of U.S. graduate students are U.S. citizens, not Asian citizens; only at the doctoral level in the areas of engineering and computer science are U.S. students not holding their own.) The data on the AP tests and graduate school admissions tests certainly suggest that our best are already world class, have been improving, and probably will continue to improve, despite more diversity in the examinees.

Second, the 40% right behind the top 20% are mostly capable of completing a college education, although some will need remediation in writing and science. A large number of minorities are probably now in this group, the first generation in their families to get a crack at a college education. Many students from low-income backgrounds also are in this group. We have colleges that serve a wide range of student abilities in the United States, which explains the large American middle class. Having a wide range of undergraduate institutions that specialize in different kinds of students from different backgrounds is vital to success in a highly diverse nation.

Third, the lowest 40% of students are in very bad educational shape, a situation caused mostly by problems they brought with them to the kindergarten door, particularly poverty, physical and emotional handicaps, lack of health care, difficult family conditions, and violent neighborhoods. (Using indicators of these conditions, it is very easy to predict in the early grades which children will be at risk of school failure.) Because many of these children stay in our schools until age 18, while in most other countries they would be on the streets, our test scores reflect our commitment to try to keep them in school. These are the children who are tracked into the "general" curriculum in high school, which prepares them neither for college nor for a job. We know exactly where most of these very difficult students reside — in our inner cities and in our rural areas.

If we can locate the young people who need help the most, why do we not target our resources and focus our concern on improving the entire system by working on the students who are at the highest risk of school failure? Most of our top students are going to do well with very little effort from the school system. But the students in the bottom 40% have few resources they can bring to the school; their parents often are high school dropouts, and they know very few people who have benefited from education. Without assistance and concern from the school, they are destined for failure. If half of the students in the bottom third of U.S. schools were stimulated to do well, developed some intellectual and job skills, and moved into the middle class, everyone in the nation would benefit.

The best way to deal with this problem is to provide a "seamless web" of services, combining education, health care, housing, transportation, and social welfare. Such efforts represent an attempt to reduce the vulnerability to school failure of the lower 40% of students. Head Start and follow-up programs can give very young children a sense of their own accomplishment and potential and can help in building a supportive and enthusiastic home environment. Chapter 1 can continue the battle in the early grades, while TRIO, Upward Bound, and Project Talent can keep the achievement level up through the high school years and on into college, where other programs are available to improve graduation rates.

On the health-care front, one of the best ways to improve education would be to make sure that every pregnant woman in America received at least one physical exam during the first trimester of her pregnancy (which would reduce births of handicapped infants by around 10%); a second way would be to make sure that every child is immunized against polio, diphtheria, and measles before entering school. All the components of the "seamless web" of services are in place, but it's not clear that we know how to coordinate these services in the best interests of young people. That would make a fine agenda for the next decade.

It also is clear that American students have regained any ground lost during the 1970s and that students are doing approximately as well as when the National Assessment of Educational Progress began more than two decades ago. Some might say that that level of achievement is not high enough for today's world, and that's a reasonable position. But then one must specify what level is needed and why. The idea of making America "number one in math and science" is meaningless unless we understand what skills and habits of mind we wish to develop and *why*. Certainly becoming numero uno on the existing international tests would not necessarily increase the number of graduate students in science and math, would not increase the scholarly output of our universities, and would not increase the number of patents or inventions (indeed, we might see a reduction in creativity, since these tests do not reward innovative or divergent thinking). Broadening the educational pipeline to include more disadvantaged students with an interest in science might work, but no one has proposed that.

So where should the United States spend its energies and talents in education? It seems very clear to me: We should focus on the students who are at greatest risk of school failure, numbering close to one-third of the children born in 1992. These children will become the college freshmen of 2010. We know where these children are; we know that they are smart and energetic, even when doing illegal things; we know what they need in order to become successful students; and, generally, we have the resources they need (although local, state, and federal programs are largely uncoordinated). What we lack is the will to make this a national direction. Yet if we were told that an unfriendly foreign power had disabled one-third of our youth, rendering them incapable of reasonable performance in school, we would view it as an act of war. We don't need to imagine a foreign enemy; by systematically neglecting the needs and potential of disadvantaged children, we have done the damage to ourselves.

Footnotes

1. For a complete discussion of diversity, see Harold Hodgkinson, *A Demographic Look at Tomorrow* (Washington, D.C.: Center for Demographic Policy, Institute for Educational Leadership, 1992); and Harold Hodgkinson, Janice Hamilton Duttz, and Anita Obarakpor, *The Nation and the States* (Washington, D.C.: Center for Demographic Policy, Institute for Educational Leadership, 1992).

2. Paul E. Barton and Richard J. Coley, *Performance at the Top: From Elementary Through Graduate School* (Princeton, N.J.: Educational Testing Service, 1991).
3. Iris Rotberg, "Measuring Up to the Competition: A Few Hard Questions," *Technos* (Winter 1992): 12-15.

AMERICAN SCHOOLS: GOOD, BAD, OR INDIFFERENT?

Denis P. Doyle

As important as criticism is, it is only a call to arms, Mr. Doyle points out. It is necessary but not sufficient. Constructive critics know that the time has come for American education to move on — toward solutions.

Attempting to assess the temper of our times, historians of the next century will no doubt fall back on Dickens' memorable opening of *A Tale of Two Cities*: "It was the best of times, it was the worst of times." That at least captures the spirit of the fevered revisionism now unfolding. On the one hand, there are analysts, such as *Kappan* contributor Gerald Bracey, who argue that contemporary critics of education — myself included — are simply myopic naysayers who are attacking public schools for personal or ideological reasons. Luckily, there is nothing ideological about Bracey.

Then there is Jonathan Kozol. He believes that American education has gone to hell in a handcart (unlike Bracey, who appears to believe that reports of its decrepitude are greatly exaggerated). But Kozol's demonology turns out to be much the same as Bracey's: dread conservatives. In Kozol's world, however, we are not just carping critics, misanthropes, and misguided methodologists; we are starving public schools into submission.

That the critics of the critics are themselves divided suggests the emergence of a modern scholasticism, in which fierce pleasure is taken in playing with the statement of the problem rather than with the problem itself. Numbers are marshaled to demonstrate that we critics have either over- or under-reached: that is, things are not really as bad as they seem or, as Kozol would have it, things are a lot worse. No matter, the crit-

---

Denis P. Doyle, a senior fellow with the Hudson Institute, Indianapolis, writes about education and human capital from his office in Washington, D.C.

ics are wrong. No doubt the next step will be to estimate the number of critics that can dance on the head of a pin. (In the case of angels, the scholastics contrived an appealing answer: an infinite number, because angels are immaterial. So too with critics?) One is reminded of Mark Twain's observation about Richard Wagner's music: "It is not as bad as it sounds."

Still, 10 years after the release of *A Nation at Risk*, it would be disingenuous not to admit that there is a powerful − and understandable − desire to assert that all is well. People do need a break. In particular, teachers and principals feel, with some justification, that they have been treated unkindly.

By and large, educators do not embrace the politicians' adage that the only thing worse than bad news is no news; and in fairness to educators, it must be noted that the Eighties were not a pleasant decade in which to be an educator. But is it equally the case that educators have not, on balance, seized on the events of the Eighties as an opportunity to make things better? That, of course, was the reason for all the criticism to begin with.

As it happened, however, after the release of *A Nation at Risk* in 1983, most of the important books and reports of the Eighties did not dwell on a litany of complaint and criticism. We didn't need to. The projects with which I was associated − the Committee for Economic Development's 1985 report, *Investing in Our Children: Business and the Schools*; the book I co-authored with former Deputy Secretary of Education David Kearns, *Winning the Brain Race*; and the 175-page *Business Week* white paper, *Children of Promise* − deliberately steered away from the sorry state of public education, except for the briefest reprise to set the stage. My collaborators on these projects and I were convinced that a catalogue of horrors was not the way to stimulate change. Equally to the point, we believed that any description of how bad things are can be justified only if it is accompanied by constructive ideas about reform and renewal.

Not to put too fine a point on it, even in the best of times criticism serves only one legitimate function: to stimulate change. Without that objective, it is both cynical and counterproductive. Yet the recent spate of revisionist arguments strikes me as equally cynical. Is it meant to suggest that we should leave well enough alone? Or that the only hope is a socialist workers' paradise? Attempting to unscramble the omelet is not only time-consuming, but it also diverts attention from real issues. We do have problems to solve.

25

And what might they be? The simple fact is that American education faces a productivity crisis. This assertion is neither name-calling nor carping criticism. It does not represent fantastical claims about either the problem or its solution. It is both an analytic perspective and a simple statement of fact with powerful policy implications. To date, its absence as an analytic perspective has been a source of disappointment and great mischief, because that absence makes it almost impossible to answer such sensible questions as, "How well are American schools doing in light of their expenditures?" or "What is the value added by schooling?" or "How great are the returns on human capital investment?"

This view of education, of course, owes a debt to the dismal science, economics — particularly political economics — which is preoccupied with questions concerning the allocation of scarce resources. We never have as much of many things as we might like: education, fine wine, medical care, inexpensive transportation, leisure — select your own list. This proposition is self-evident. On occasion, however, the issue of relative scarcity becomes more important than at other times. In the Sixties, before Vietnam at least, we enjoyed both guns and butter. This is not to be in the Nineties.

President Clinton and the Congress face deficits — current accounts, trade, and budget — so large that there is little room to maneuver. Without reciting the numbers in detail, suffice it to say that there is not enough room in local, state, and federal budgets to buy our way out of the educational impasse. There may be some new money for education — but not much. Schools will simply have to work smarter.

Let us agree to the following propositions: Budgets for American education are necessarily limited, and American education is not as efficient — or as humane — as it must be if we are to face the next century with confidence. Does anyone really doubt these statements? It should be clear that this is not solely an economic argument, though it includes an economic component.

By "productivity crisis," I mean that schools must learn to do more with less — or, better yet, much more with a little bit more. I do not mean that schools as they once were failed; indeed, historically they have met their purposes reasonably well. So, too, did Detroit, at least through the era of "muscle cars." Remember the movie *A Man and a Woman*? The story line's centerpiece was a Mustang, the American car that was to catapult Lee Iacocca to fame and fortune. Imagine the French glorifying an American car in the 1990s. How times have changed. The point is that Detroit's problem over the past few decades is not that it forgot how to make muscle cars or that someone else made them better or cheaper. Muscle cars are out. Period. Detroit didn't get it. Detroit couldn't figure out how to make the transition into the modern era. So, too, with schools.

But a problem remains. To most educators, no matter how the terms are defined or explained, such words as *efficiency* and *productivity* are verboten when talking about schools. They conjure up images of time-and-motion studies — of white-jacketed efficiency experts with stop-watches and clipboards, who understand the cost of everything and the value of nothing. But in the postindustrial world (or the postcapitalist world, as Peter Drucker now describes it), productivity has a very different meaning. It means the most efficient deployment of resources in the most effective work environment that can be designed.

Mine is not an argument for more or less spending on schools; it is an argument on behalf of better use of whatever we've got. The modern productivity model for schools is not Frederick Taylor's factory, but the symphony orchestra; Drucker's well-run, not-for-profit organization (for example, the Red Cross or Girl Scouts); or the modern high-tech, high-performance firm. What do these modern organizational forms have in common with schools? In the days when the factory was king, when the gate clanged shut at night, the capitalist's wealth was locked securely inside. At the end of the workday in these modern organizations, when the door swings closed behind the last worker, the organization's wealth, its capital (human in this case), has gone home for the evening.

Consider another analogy. Remember the days of the early mainframe computers? Not only did they produce great amounts of heat, but they were extremely sensitive to changes in temperature and humidity. As a consequence, the rooms that housed them were the first parts of an organization to be fully air-conditioned, 24 hours a day, 365 days a year. Workers should be so lucky. Yet, in modern high-performance organizations, they are. Indeed, it is a matter not of luck but of good sense. Today's managers — at least those with their wits about them — recognize that their most valuable resource is their workers. And it is more often the case today that employees are not considered workers at all, but associates. The employer is the manager of production.

Before I consider the implications of "productivity" as the central concern of the modern firm, however, let me turn briefly to the two questions that must be dealt with if we are to reform education rationally: What is good about American education? And what is bad about American education?

In important respects, the questions are not empirical but normative. True, test scores and other quantitative indicators can be marshaled in support of the schools' performance; but they are largely empty indicators, because they do not relate to an accepted metric. Such research can answer questions that ask, "How much?" But those that ask, "How much is enough?" can be answered only in the domains of philosophy and politics.

So how do I answer them? What is good about American education? What is bad? The two themes intertwine. American education is democratic, egalitarian, and meritocratic. It is robust, dynamic, and resilient. It is responsive — at least to fads of the moment — and it is well financed, by any measure. It is radically decentralized, at least by world standards; and each component of the education system, from humble rural school districts to great research universities, stands on its own bottom. Attempts to centralize education have largely failed — save only the movement over the past 50 years to consolidate school districts. Yet even in this area, the 15,700 that remain (of more than 100,000 before World War II) are largely "independent."

Indeed, the marked sameness that characterizes American education — the fact that most of our schools look alike and behave similarly — is a commentary on the power of the culture of education, rather than a reflection of statutes or administrative regulations. The similarity of statutes from state to state is as much a product as a cause of that uniformity.

The consequence of this decentralization (at least as it appears to foreigners) is a system that is a system in name only. In fact, American education is most accurately described as "measured anarchy." What does this mean to the participants? Enormous freedom, including the freedom to fail. As long as they observe the rituals of the school and respect the privacy of their office or classroom, teachers and principals are largely free to do as they like. So, too, are students. In fact, in no other aspect of American education is the anarchic tendency so strong as among students. As long as they observe the minimum conventions of civility and behavior, students may do pretty much what they like — to the chagrin of teachers, parents, administrators, and serious students alike, I might add. But this has always been so.

The upside of this set of arrangements is schooling without equal for those who are disciplined, energetic, motivated, and supported by family and friends. And in our anarchic system, these traits may surface at any time in a student's career, even though, as a practical matter, surfacing early is to be preferred to surfacing late. But surface late they do in the case of many students, in which event the American passion for "second chances" comes into full play. America, of course, is a nation of second chances; that is what we are all about. We are a nation of immigrants. As Octavio Paz notes in his marvelous account, *One Earth, Four or Five Worlds*, America is the quintessential second-chance society. A new people in a new world, freed of the baggage of hereditary class, Americans invent themselves anew with each generation.

Not surprisingly, these habits extend well beyond school. America is a global scandal in terms of the rate of small-business failure; Europeans and Asians are simply aghast. But they are equally astonished and impressed by the rate of small-business formation, which is the flip side of failure. It is not too much to assert that small-business failure is the true school of hard knocks, in which entrepreneurs learn the ropes the hard way. So prevalent are such failures that, alone in the industrialized world, no stigma attaches to having failed in America — not as long as you get up and try again.

So, too, with school. The school dropout can, if sufficiently energetic, drop back in — if not to the school he left, then to another. Or he can earn an equivalency diploma or, on occasion, go straight to a community or four-year college. So "naturally" and so readily is this done that we take it for granted. Today, for example, the average age of postsecondary students hovers around 30; and it is the rare undergraduate who finishes a course of study in four consecutive years.

But if this fluid and dynamic system works well for some, it has a terrible downside for many. In particular, youngsters from disorganized backgrounds, broken homes, and poverty — and even more particularly, students who are members of microcultures that do not prize education — find themselves left out. Sadly, this lack of a support network too often characterizes poverty-stricken minority youths, students who need to capitalize on their first chance and who are unlikely to seek and find second chances.

As John Ogbu, a sociologist at the University of California, Berkeley, points out, profoundly disadvantaged Americans look like nothing so much as members of a lower caste: outcasts. This distinction helps explain why boat people — poor, dispossessed, speaking little or no English — can rise so rapidly and decisively in American public schools. They do not think of themselves as outcasts; they think of themselves as individuals who, through diligence and hard work, can significantly improve their life chances. And they are right. Ironically, it is they who best exemplify the American Dream.

This, then, is what is wrong with American education: It has no systematic and effective way to deal with youngsters who do not see themselves as part of the system — who, for whatever reason, are not *workers*. Neither American education nor the larger society motivates these youngsters. The enabling power that education confers is kept secret from them. Because they hate school, their lives become a cruel hoax. Unlike students in Japan and Europe — who know that their life chances will be decided by how well they do in school — American youngsters do not believe that their performance in school will have a great deal of impact on their later life. To many of these youngsters, education is not an opportunity but a burden, one to be tolerated at best or, more frequently, avoided altogether. When asked how he escaped Harlem's mean streets to become a Navy pilot, Drew Brown, son of boxing promoter Budini Brown, attributes his success to his devoted father's admonition: "College or death!"

However, the views of American education I have set forth raise the risk of two unwelcome interpretations. First, it is possible to indulge in the popular sport of blaming the victim. As the late, unlamented Gov. Lester Maddox of Georgia observed, when asked about improving his state prison system, "It can't be done without a better class of prisoner."

The second possible unwelcome interpretation would lead us to ask the schools to bear more weight than they can carry. Because schools are first and foremost educational institutions, they are poorly suited to deliver noneducational services, notwithstanding popular impressions to the contrary.

The view that schools should somehow be social service providers has, of course, gained wide currency because of its superficial plausibility. Kids have problems; kids are in school; ergo, solve the problems in the school. There is a rough justice in this notion, and in theory it makes administrative sense. Inoculations, well-baby screening, feeding programs, Norplant implants, condom distribution, contacts with case workers, and similar activities can, in fact, take place in school buildings. And it is surely the case that schools are a convenient place to track down young people, at least as long as compulsory attendance is the law of the land. Moreover, hungry, sick, and disoriented children do not make good students; and ameliorating their problems is both a good thing to do in its own right and good for the schools.

But if the problems presented by youngsters from disorganized backgrounds make it difficult for schools to go about their business, it is not clear that schools should enter the business of providing social services. Put plainly, if schools can't teach a youngster to read, can they minister to his or her social needs? While the question is no doubt in part empirical, management theory provides some guidance. As Peter Drucker observes, effective organizations *optimize*; they do not maximize. They do what they are good at and let others do what they are good at.

What does this have to do with schools? They, too, should optimize. And what they are good at − one hopes − is educating youngsters. That some of their charges are poor and dispossessed does not lead ineluctably to the idea that schools should attempt to fill the social service breach. It is self-evidently true that a wealthy society that cares about its future must care for its children. But children's social needs are not necessarily best met in school.

I belabor this obvious point because so many defenders of the public schools have begun to assert that the problems of the public schools are the problems of their clients. Indeed, the assertion is so often made that schools cannot deal with "these" children that it is a commonplace. That it is usually offered as a rationale for school failure is too often overlooked. So close to "blaming the victim" is this assertion that one wonders if it is a distinction without a difference. Be that as it may, I am convinced that we must draw a distinction between the social and educational needs of children and not use the former as an excuse not to fulfill the latter.

To return to Drucker's distinction, the schools must optimize. They must ask themselves what their mission is, who their clients are, how they are to deliver the service called education, how they measure its quality, and how they know when they have met their goals. If schools try to be all things to all students − if they try to maximize − they will serve no one well. If they decide that they are social service institutions first and educational institutions second, they are not likely to meet either objective successfully. But if they decide that they are first and foremost educational institutions, charged with the responsibility of educating children, there is at least a chance that they may succeed.

The sorry fact is that most schools are not doing what they should be doing. And what they are doing, they are not doing well. They remind me of the Woody Allen routine in which a little old lady complains to her companion about airplane food. "Isn't it awful?" she asks. "Yes," her companion responds, "it certainly is, and the portions are so small!"

The one thing schools can and should do about the issue of social services is best illustrated by a program unfolding in Charlotte, North

Carolina. No stranger to disadvantaged children, the schools in Charlotte are undertaking a comprehensive inventory of the needs of children; creating a catalogue of community resources, public and private; identifying the gaps in services; and bringing these gaps — deliberately, even provocatively — to the attention of the community as a whole. The superintendent, John Murphy, meets each month with representatives of the Charlotte Interfaith Council to coordinate a response. The Interfaith Council plans to build a countywide preschool network — the first facility opened in February 1993 — and the Charlotte schools are creating a pre-K parent/teacher organization to orient new parents. As evidence of how seriously it takes the issue, the school system will soon provide a brochure for mothers in the maternity ward. The objective: to welcome the newborns, but also to let parents know what their responsibilities are in helping their children get ready for school.

The strategy behind these programs stems from Charlotte's refusal to let its education budget hemorrhage in a futile attempt to *improvise* children's services. The school can sound the alarm, act as an honest broker, and make its facilities available. But responsibility for providing children's services lies with the community as a whole.

What, then, is my vision of the future for education? First, debating the question of the quality of American schools — Are they as bad as the critics say? Are they better? — is a sterile and counterproductive exercise. Truly, it is the intellectual equivalent of rearranging the deck chairs on the *Titanic*. No good purpose is served by the exercise. The only legitimate reason to raise the question of school quality is to improve the schools. The question we must ask is, Are schools good enough for the future? Does anyone truly believe that they are?

The list of what might be done to improve our schools is understandably long, and I propose to treat only two examples here. Earlier I suggested that we need a coordinated children's policy; schools cannot go it alone. But at the same time, American schools face a productivity crisis. That is, they expect too little of teachers and students; and expecting little gets little. Few penalties — other than the remote possibility of failure as an adult, an incomprehensible idea for most adolescents — attach to a failure to perform, and few rewards attach to academic success.

As to the first part of the problem, the details of a children's policy are simply beyond the scope of this essay. I note only that such a policy is desirable, probably necessary, and possible *only if* President Clinton, working with his domestic policy council and relevant Cabinet members, can actually bring about real — I emphasize *real* — collaboration among the federal Departments of Education, Health and Human Services, and Labor (he could even encourage Commerce, Defense, and Energy to play a role). As an opponent of the creation of the Department of Education, I am fascinated that the interest groups that insisted that President Carter create it now lament the lack of connection between education and children's services. Might they ask Mr. Clinton to put the "E" back into HEW?

Whatever the interest groups do or fail to do, Washington is a major part of the problem. Consider employment, welfare, and health policies for starters. Washington must become part of the solution, and that means employment, welfare, and health policy reform on a massive scale if any lasting improvements in the condition of children are to be made. And it should be clear to all that education reform will not reach the poorest of the poor unless their social conditions are ameliorated.

Let me close by returning to my initial assertion that the real problem of American schools is a productivity crisis. Yet this problem is also an opportunity. Ironically, inefficiency — slack in the system — provides opportunities to save and invest and to improve dramatically. As an analogy, consider Americans' profligate use of energy. Wasting as much as we do, it is relatively easy, through conservation, to save a great deal of energy. In this light, we can see that there is one thing that schools can do for themselves that would make a difference: They can "benchmark."

Benchmarking, originally a topographical and nautical practice of defining permanent reference points against which measurements are made, has been appropriated by U.S. business, first by the Xerox Corporation, now by most high-tech, high-performance organizations. Not widely understood among educators, it is worth describing briefly. First, it is a form of self-measurement; it cannot be imposed from the outside. It is not a club with which to beat an organization over the head; it is a tool to permit members of the organization to improve their own performance by better understanding how other successful organizations achieve their success.

By way of illustration, Xerox seeks and finds the best performers in industry — not just other copier manufacturers, though Xerox looks at them closely, but the best performers, period. For copiers and office equipment, Xerox looks first at its direct competitors. When Xerox discovered that the Japanese were designing, manufacturing, assembling, shipping, and retailing high-quality copiers for less than it took Xerox to manufacture them, the company recognized a clear message: restructure or collapse. Xerox chose the first course and remains one of the few American corporations to recapture market share from the Japanese.

In looking at generic processes, however, such as inventory control and management, the best performer Xerox could find was not Toyota or Kodak but L.L. Bean, the clothing and outdoor-wear catalogue house in Freeport, Maine. That's the standard of quality to which Xerox compares itself today. For customer response, in terms of both timeliness and courtesy, Xerox compares itself to Florida Light and Power.

Benchmarking is a form of accountability with special significance for public sector organizations — insulated as they are from the play of market forces — because, if it is to work, benchmarking must be self-imposed. It cannot be ordered up by a remote bureaucracy. Benchmarking forces organizations to rethink everything they do, from recruiting to compensation, from objectives to measurement, from assessment to management.

What kinds of things should benchmarking make schools think about? Outputs rather than inputs. The role of effort rather than innate ability. The importance of "mastery" as the appropriate measure of success in education. Making students workers and teachers managers of instruction. Using administrators as facilitators and superintendents as choreographers rather than autocrats. Using technology to increase output and not simply as glitz. These are only a few of the ideas that benchmarking will force schools to deal with.

That is precisely the challenge — and the opportunity — American schools face. If they begin to benchmark seriously, they will compare themselves to the best of the best, not just in public elementary and secondary schools, but also in high-performance organizations. The power of benchmarking is that it does internally what competition is supposed to do externally: It holds organizations to high standards of performance, measurement, and reporting. It accepts no excuses. It is continuous. There is no finish line.

What's right with American education? There's much that's right. It has a proud history and an honorable tradition; it is generously funded; it is staffed by men and women of good will; and it is resilient. What's wrong with American education? It misconceives its own best interests in the Nineties; it tries to maximize when it should optimize; it comes perilously close to playing Lester Maddox with its clients, hoping for a "better class of student" as its salvation; and it sees problems where it should see opportunities.

What are the prospects for the future of American education? They are good. Criticism — constructive criticism — is the lifeblood of healthy organizations, just as it is the keystone of democracy. With it, conditions may be improved; without it, progress never occurs. It is for that reason that closed societies will not tolerate criticism; they fear it because they know it is the engine of change and renewal. But as important as criticism is, it is only a call to arms. It begins, but does not end, the dialogue. It is necessary but not sufficient. Constructive criticism knows that the time has come for American education to move on — toward solutions.

MYTHOLOGY AND THE AMERICAN SYSTEM OF EDUCATION

David C. Berliner

Mr. Berliner sets out to identify — and shatter — the myths that have caused the American people to lose confidence in their public schools.

What is wrong with the American public school system is that it runs on myths. As we all know, myths are functional. Thus the myths about the American public school system must be serving the purposes of some, though not necessarily all, citizens. But the myths about the American public schools also may be misleading the majority of the citizenry and undermining the American people's confidence in one of their most cherished institutions.

What is right about the American education system is that the myths are so far off the mark. Contrary to the prevailing opinion, the American public schools are remarkably good whenever and wherever they are provided with the human and economic resources to succeed.

Let us examine a baker's dozen of these myths about U.S. education and see if they hold up. As we challenge the myths about what is wrong with our schools, we may learn what is right about them.

Myth 1. Today's youth do not seem as smart as they used to be.

Fact: Since 1932 the mean I.Q. of white Americans aged 2 to 75 has risen about 0.3 points per year. Today's students actually average about 14 I.Q. points higher than their grandparents did and about seven points higher than their parents did on the well-established Wechsler or Stanford-Binet Intelligence Tests.[1] That is, as a group, today's school-age youths are, on average, scoring more than 30 percentile ranks higher than the group from which have emerged the recent leaders of government and industry. The data reveal, for example, that the number of

---

David C. Berliner is a professor of education at Arizona State University, Tempe.

students expected to have I.Q.s of 130 or more — a typical cutoff point for giftedness — is now about seven times greater than it was for the generation now retiring from its leadership positions throughout the nation and complaining about the poor performance of today's youth. In fact, the number of students with I.Q.s above 145 is now about 18 times greater than it was two generations ago. If the intelligence tests given throughout the United States are measuring any of the factors the general public includes in its definition of "smart," we are now smarter than we have ever been before.

Myth 2. Today's youths cannot think as well as they used to.

Fact: The increased scores on intelligence tests throughout the industrialized world have *not* been associated with those parts of the tests that call for general knowledge or for verbal or quantitative ability. We could assume performance in those areas to be positively affected by the increase in schooling that has occurred throughout the industrial world during the last two generations. Rather, it turns out that the major gains in performance on intelligence tests have been primarily in the areas of general problem-solving skills and the ability to handle abstract information of a decontextualized nature.[2] That is, the gains have been in the areas we generally label "thinking skills."

If we look at statistics on the Advanced Placement (AP) tests given to talented high school students every year, we find other evidence to bolster the claim that today's American youths are smarter than ever. In 1978, 90,000 high school students took the AP tests for college credit, while in 1990 that number had increased 255% to 324,000 students, who took a total of 481,000 different AP tests. Although the population taking these tests changed markedly over this time period, the mean score dropped only 11/100 of a point. Meanwhile, the percentage of Asians taking the AP tests tripled, the percentage of African-Americans taking the examinations doubled, and the percentage of Hispanics quadrupled.[3] Something that the public schools are doing is producing increasingly larger numbers of very smart students, for those tests are very difficult to pass.

Myth 3. University graduates are not as smart as they used to be and cannot think as well as they did in previous generations.

Fact: When we look at objective data, such as the scores on the Graduate Record Examination (GRE), we discover that the talented students who take this exam are smarter and think better than students have for some time.[4] It is a myth to believe that today's college graduates are less talented than those from some previous time.

In the verbal area, these students perform at about the same level as graduates did 20 years ago. But in the area of mathematical skills, they far exceed the graduates of two decades ago. And in analytic skills — a measure of what we usually mean by "ability to think" — their performance has gone up during the decade that such skills have been measured.

Reliable data exist that appear to challenge the myth of poor performance by high school and college graduates. A very good data-based case can be made that the K-12 public schools and the colleges and universities are conferring many more degrees than in previous generations, and the products of all those schools are smarter than ever before.

Myth 4. The Scholastic Aptitude Test (SAT) has shown a marked decrease in mean score over the last 25 years, indicating the failure of our schools and our teachers to do their jobs.

Fact: To be sure, since 1965 the average SAT score has fallen. The *scaled* scores showed 70- or 90-point declines, a drop that frightened many government officials and the press. The scaled scores, however, are distorted records of performance. Not noted, for example, was the fact that, if we multiplied those scores by 10, the declines would have been 700 or 900 points — and we could have scared more people — while if we divided those scaled scores by 10, the decline would have been only 7 or 9 points over a 30-year period. If we use the *raw* score to judge performance over time, as we should, the decline has actually been only 3.3% of the raw score total — about five fewer items answered correctly over a period of 30 or so years.

Far from being ashamed of this loss, educators should celebrate it. Why? Because it is explainable by the fact that much greater numbers of students in the bottom 60% of their graduating classes have been taking the SAT since the 1960s.[5] As educational opportunities and higher education became available to rural Americans and to members of traditionally under-represented minorities, more of these students started taking the SAT. Since they were frequently from impoverished communities and from schools that offered a less-rigorous academic curriculum and fewer advanced courses than wealthier schools, it is not surprising that they tended to score lower than advantaged, suburban, middle-class, white students. This is why the mean number of items correct is less than it was. Most of the drop actually occurred between 1965 and 1975, not since. And the drop was primarily in the verbal, not the mathematics, measure.

Anyone rearing a child during the 1950s probably noticed an increase in television viewing. Associated with that change in the nature of childhood was a decrease in book reading and other verbal skills among the students who graduated from high school during the 1960s. Between the changes in the population taking the test and a changed pattern of child rearing because of TV, the decline we witnessed in SAT performance seems perfectly reasonable and not easily attributable to inadequate teachers or a failing school system. In fact, one might properly ask why we do not test our children on decoding information from complex audiovisual displays, or on remembering information presented in auditory or visual forms, or on comprehending extremely fast-changing video arrays of information, and so forth. The media through which our children learn about the world changed dramatically in the 1950s, and so did our children's cognitive skills. Our assessment instruments, however, have not changed at all; and therefore some decrease in measured verbal ability is to be expected.

Actually, as an educator, I am filled with pride that we have played a major role in the achievement of two of America's most prized goals of the 1960s − a higher high school graduation rate, particularly for minority children, and increased access to higher education. We accomplished both goals with a loss of only a few correct answers on the SAT.

This is a remarkable achievement, I think, particularly when we look at other data. For example, from 1975 to 1990 the mean SAT scores of white, African-American, Asian-American, Native American, Mexican-American, and Puerto Rican high school students went up.[6] Every one of the subgroups for which there are data has increased its average score on the SAT over the period during which the mean score dropped. The most likely cause of this nationwide increase in measured student achievement is an improvement in education. The decline of the average SAT score, used to bolster the myth that the schools are failing, seems meaningless in light of this increase in the scores of *every* subgroup that attends our public schools. These data can more easily be used to make the point that our public schools must actually be improving.

Myth 5. The bottom students now score better on achievement tests, but the performance of the better students has declined. Our top students are not as good as they were.

Fact: There has been some concern that, while the performance of underachieving students in the United States (primarily the poor, primarily those black and brown in color) has gotten better, it has been at the cost of underserving the better students (primarily the richer and whiter students). But that myth also appears not to be true. The SAT perform-ance of all test-takers between 1975 and 1990 was unusually stable. Whatever drops there were in performance occurred prior to 1975; since then, scores have remained steady. But if we look at the performance of only those students who match the profile of those who *used to* take the SAT (students who were primarily white, suburban, middle and upper-middle class, higher in high school class rank, and so on), we see an increase between 1975 and 1990 of more than 30 SAT points — more than 10 percentile ranks.[7] Among these advantaged, primari-ly white youths, who were supposedly achieving less because they suf-fered from harmful desegregation policies (including forced busing), low standards of performance, poor teachers, no homework, too much television, low morals, and a host of other plagues, we find considera-ble improvement in performance on the SAT. What boosts my pride as an educator even more is that the Educational Testing Service, the developer of the test items for the SAT, has admitted that the test today is more difficult than it was in 1975.[8]

What have we learned about our students when we look at the facts about SAT scores? Three things stand out. First, the supposedly great loss in America's intellectual capital, as measured by the average score on the SAT, is trivial, particularly since the average scores of every minority group went up for 15 years. Even the traditional college-bound students (those white, middle-class students more likely to have taken the examination in 1975) are doing dramatically better today than they did in the Seventies. Second, more American students are graduating from high school and thinking about college. That is why the mean SAT score did fall somewhat. Many of the students who took the SAT actu-ally did go on to college, with the United States achieving one of the highest rates of college attendance in the world.[9] Third, the data we have from this well-accepted indicator of educational achievement will not support the accusation that, overall, we have a failing school sys-tem and inadequate teachers. The public and many educators bought this spurious charge in the past, and they should not do so any longer.

Myth 6. The performance of American students on standardized achievement tests reveals gross inadequacies.

Fact: This myth can be examined first by looking at the data col-lected by the National Assessment of Educational Progress (NAEP). The NAEP tests are given to national samples of 9-, 13-, and 17-year-olds in the subjects of mathematics, science, reading, writing, geography, and computer skills. Since the 1970s, modest gains, at best, have been

40

the rule. But what is more important is that one group of scientists reviewing the data believe unequivocally that the "national data on student performance do not indicate a decline in *any* area" (emphasis in the original). They have concluded that "students today appear to be as well educated as previously educated students."[10]

Summaries of the NAEP test results, purporting to be the nation's report card, inform us only that our students are performing the same over time. But there are other data in which we can take greater pride. When you investigate the norming procedures used with the most commonly purchased standardized tests, you find that it takes a higher score now to reach the 50th percentile rank than it did in previous decades. For example, on average, students in the 1980s scored higher on the California Achievement Tests than they did in the 1970s. Similarly, on the venerable Iowa Tests of Basic Skills, at the time of the last norming of the test, the test developer said that achievement was at an all-time high in nearly all test areas. The same trend was found in the renorming of the Stanford Achievement Test, the Metropolitan Achievement Tests, and the Comprehensive Tests of Basic Skills.[11]

In both reading and mathematics we find meaningful annual gains in percentile ranks from one representative norming sample to the next. If a school district does not gain more than one percentile rank a year in reading or mathematics, it loses out in the subsequent norming of the test, because every other district is doing better than it did previously. If a district at the 60th percentile in reading and mathematics on the last set of norms kept the same program and teachers and had the same kinds of students, that district would be at about the 50th percentile on the new set of norms, without any change in performance having occurred. Each renorming sets the mean higher − clear evidence of the increased productivity of the American schools.

Major standardized tests are renormed, on the average, approximately every seven years. A reasonable estimate is that, over one generation, norms have been redone around three times. Thus we can estimate that about 85% of today's public school students score higher on standardized tests of achievement than the average parent did.[12] But, as in the high jump, the bar keeps getting higher; and it takes better performance today than it did around 1965 to hit the 50th percentile.

While on the subject of standardized test performance, we also should examine the social studies survey developed by Diane Ravitch and Chester Finn and discussed in their gloomy 1987 book, *What Do Our 17-Year-Olds Know?* Their answer was that 17-year-olds know embar-

41

rassingly and shockingly little! Their conclusions were part of a barrage of similar arguments showered on the American people by E.D. Hirsch in his book *Cultural Literacy* (1987), by Allan Bloom in his book *The Closing of the American Mind* (1987), and by William Bennett in his report *To Reclaim a Legacy* (1984).[13] The popular press, of course, promoted the claim that today's children know less than they ever did and, therefore, that we are surely a nation at risk. The authors and the editorial writers throughout the land seemed to see nothing but doom for America if we didn't return to our old ways as a nation and as a people, to those mythical halcyon days.

Dale Whittington decided to check the claim that the 17-year-olds of the 1980s knew less than their parents, grandparents, or great-grandparents.[14] She examined social studies and history tests administered from 1915 onward and found 43 items on the Ravitch and Finn test that corresponded to items from other tests given at other times. Today's students were less knowledgeable than previous generations on about one-third of the items. They scored about the same on about one-third of those items. And they scored better on about one-third of the items. When compared to historical records, the data in Ravitch and Finn's study do not support the charge that today's 17-year-olds know less than any previous generation. In fact, given the less-elitist composition of today's high schools, the case can be made that more 17-year-olds today know as much about social studies and historical facts as previous generations.

There may never have been any halcyon days to which to return. Every generation of adults has a tendency to find the next generation wanting. This social phenomenon has been recorded for about 2,500 years, since Socrates condemned the youths of Athens for their impertinence and ignorance. Ravitch and Finn, continuing this grand tradition, are merely disappointed that the next generation does not know what they themselves do.

What may we reasonably conclude from these studies of standardized tests? First, there is no convincing evidence of a decline in standardized test performance. This is true of intelligence tests, the SAT, the NAEP tests, and the standardized achievement tests used by local school districts. If any case for a change in these scores can be made, it is that the scores on standardized aptitude and achievement tests are going up, not down. Educators — working under almost intolerable conditions in some settings — have not failed society. It is incredibly difficult to keep academic achievement constant or to improve it with increasing numbers of poor children, unhealthy children, children from dysfunctional families, and children from dysfunctional neighborhoods.[15] Yet the public school system of the United States actually has done remarkably well as it receives, instructs, and nurtures children who are poor, who have no health care, and who come from families and neighborhoods that barely function. Moreover, they have done this with quite reasonable budgets.

Myth 7. Money is unrelated to the outcomes of schooling.

Fact: Current income can be predicted from the characteristics of the state school systems in which men received their education during the first half of the century. After the usual statistical controls are applied, it is found that teachers' salaries, class size, and length of the school year are significant predictors of future earnings. States that had spent the most on their schools had produced the citizens with the highest incomes.[16]

It also has been found that higher salaries attract teaching candidates with higher academic ability and keep teachers in the profession longer.[17] Clearly, both of those benefits pay off for students.

An unusual set of data from Texas looks at the effects of teacher ability, teacher experience, class size, and professional certification on student performance in reading and mathematics. Data on millions of students in 900 districts were examined longitudinally from 1986 to 1990. Two rather simple findings emerged. First, teachers' academic proficiency explains 20% to 25% of the variation across districts in students' average scores on academic achievement tests. The smarter the teachers, the smarter their pupils appeared to be, as demonstrated by results on standardized achievement tests administered to both groups. Second, teachers with more years of experience have students with higher test scores, lower dropout rates, and higher rates of taking the SAT. Experience counts for about 10% of the variation in student test scores across districts. The effects are such that an increase of 10% in the number of teachers within a district who have nine or more years' experience is predicted to reduce dropout rates by about 4% and to increase the percentage of students taking the SAT by 3%. Dollars appear to be more likely to purchase bright and experienced professionals, who, in turn, are more likely to provide us with higher-achieving and better-motivated students.[18]

The Texas data also show that, in grades 1 through 7, once class size exceeds 18 students, each student over that number is associated with a drop in district academic achievement. This drop is estimated to be very large — perhaps 35 percentile ranks on standardized tests — between a class size of, say, 25 and a class size of 18.

Furthermore, the percentage of teachers with master's degrees accounted for 5% of the variation in student scores across districts in grades 1 through 7. So we learn from the Texas study *and other data that support its conclusions* that academically more proficient teachers, who are more experienced, who are better educated, and who work with smaller classes, are associated with students who demonstrate significantly higher achievement.

It costs money to attract academically talented teachers, to keep them on the job, to update their professional skills, and to provide them with working conditions that enable them to perform well. Those districts that are willing and able to pay the costs attract the more talented teachers from neighboring districts, and they eventually get the best in a region. Those districts can improve their academic performance relative to other districts that are unable to pay the price, resulting in an education system that is inherently inequitable.

For those who point out that education costs have been rising faster than inflation, it is important to note that special education populations have been rising as well. It costs 2.3 times as much money to educate a child in special education as it does to educate a student in the regular education program.[19] Most of the real increases in educational expenditures over the last 20 years have been the result of increased costs for transportation, health care, and special education. They have not been connected with regular instruction or teachers' salaries.

Myth 8. The American public school system is a bloated bureaucracy, top-heavy in administrators and administrative costs.

Fact: The average number of employees that each administrator supervises in education is among the highest of any industry or business in America. With 14.5 employees for every one administrator, education is leaner than, for example, the transportation industry (9.3 to one), the food-products industry (8.4 to one), the utilities industry (6.6 to one), the construction industry (6.3 to one), and the communications industry (4.7 to one). Central office professionals plus principals, assistant principals, and supervisors in the public schools make up a mere 4.5% of the total employee population of the schools. If all these supervisory personnel were fired and their salaries given to teachers, the salaries of teachers would rise no more than 5%. And if those supervisors' salaries were redistributed to reduce class size, the size of classes nationwide would be reduced by an average of one student![20] The administration of education is not a major cost factor. That is a myth.

Myth 9. American schools are too expensive. We spend more on education than any other country in the world, and we have little to show for it.

Fact: Former Secretaries of Education William Bennett, Lauro Cavazos, and Lamar Alexander said we spend more on education than do our rivals Germany and Japan. Former Assistant Secretary of Education Chester Finn wrote in the *New York Times* that we "spend more per pupil than any other nation." And, just before the education summit of 1989, John Sununu, once President Bush's chief of staff and close advisor, declared that "we spend twice as much [on education] as the Japanese and almost 40 percent more than all the other major industrialized countries of the world."[21] But it appears that the people who made these claims, like David Stockman before them, made up the numbers as they went along.

The United States, according to UNESCO data, is tied with Canada and the Netherlands, and all three fall behind Sweden in the amount spent per pupil for K-12 education and higher education.[22] We look good in this comparison because we spend much more than most nations on higher education and have two to three times more people per 100,000 enrolled in higher education than most other countries do. When only the expenditures for preprimary, primary, and secondary education are calculated, however, we actually spend much less than the average industrialized nation.

In 1988 dollars we rank ninth among 16 industrialized nations in per-pupil expenditures for grades K-12, spending 14% less than Germany, 30% less than Japan, and 51% less than Switzerland. We also can compare ourselves to other countries in terms of the percentage of per-capita income spent on education. When we do that comparison, we find that, out of 16 industrialized nations, 13 of them spend a greater percentage of per-capita income on K-12 education than we do. If we were to come up just to the *average* percentage of per-capita income spent on education by the 15 other industrialized nations, we would have to invest an additional $20 billion per year in K-l2 education![23] The most recent report by the Organisation for Economic Cooperation and Development on education in the European Community and some other industrialized nations also finds the United States low in its commitment to education. That report places the United States behind 12 other industrial nations in the percentage of Gross Domestic Product devoted to public and private education.[24]

Perhaps we do not teach as much in the K-12 schools as some would like. But we do not have to. A relatively large percentage of our students go on to postsecondary studies, where they can acquire the learning the nation needs them to have. Our nation has simply chosen to invest its money in higher education. Consequently, our education system ultimately provides about 25% of each year's group of high school graduates with college degrees, and it is the envy of the world. We run a costly and terrific K-16 school system, but we must acknowledge that we run an impoverished and relatively less good K-12 school system.

Moreover, in many of the countries that spend more per capita than we do, the funding is relatively even across regions and cities. But in our nation, we have, to use Jonathan Kozol's scathing formulation, "savage inequalities" in our funding for schools.[25] Even though the national *average* for per-pupil expenditures in the primary and secondary schools is relatively low, included in the calculation of that figure are the much, much lower annual per-pupil expenditures of those school districts at the bottom of the income distribution. To our shame, conditions in many of those districts resemble conditions in the nonindustrialized nations of the world.

Former President George Bush perpetuated the myth we address here when he declared at the education summit of 1989 that the United States "lavishes unsurpassed resources on [our children's] schooling."[26] What he should have said was that we are among the most cost-efficient nations in the world, with an amazingly high level of productivity for the comparatively low level of investment that our society makes in K-12 education.

Myth 10. Our high schools, colleges, and universities are not supplying us with enough mathematicians and scientists to maintain our competitiveness in world markets.

Fact: There are solid data to suggest that the supply of mathematicians and scientists is exceeding the demand for them! First of all, we now exceed or are at parity with our economic competitors in terms of the technical competence of our work force — for example, in the number of engineers and physical scientists we have per hundred workers.[27] So, if we have lost our economic edge in the world marketplace, it may well be because of poor business management and faulty government economic policies, but it is certainly not because of the lack of a technically skilled work force. But that is the present situation. Projections of the future supply in these fields do look gloomy, but that is true only as long as the economy's demand for such individuals is not examined. When demand and supply are examined together, it turns out that the economy is not now able to absorb all the scientists and engineers that we produce. With no increase in the rate of supply of scientists and engineers, we will accumulate a surplus of about one million such individuals by the year 2010. Given the probable reduction in military spending during the next few years, the glut of trained scientists is likely to be even more serious than was forecast a year or two ago. Moreover, the National Science Foundation recently apologized to Congress for supplying it with phony data a few years back. That agency now admits that its predictions of shortages in supply were grossly inflated.

In my most cynical moments, I think that the business community and the politicians are demanding that the schools produce even more engineers and scientists because the labor of these individuals is currently so expensive. An oversupply will certainly drive down the salaries of such workers.

The myth of the coming shortage of technically able workers has been debunked by many economists.[28] In fact, it has been estimated that, if the entering workers had an average of only one-fourth of a grade level more education than those now retiring from the labor force, all the needs of the future economy would be served.

How can this be? The answer is in the mix of jobs available in the future. The five most highly skilled occupational groups will make up only about 6% of the job pool by the year 2000. On the other hand, service jobs, requiring the least technical skill, will actually grow the fastest overall in the next few years; and they will constitute about 17% of the job pool by the year 2000. Apparently this nation is not in any danger of failing to meet its technological needs.

Furthermore, research has found that, during the first eight years on the job, young adults without a college education receive no rewards from the labor market for their abilities in science, mathematical reasoning, or language arts.[29] The fact that so many American high school students avoid rigorous mathematics and science courses may actually be a rational response to the lack of rewards for these skills in the labor market.

Myth 11. In our science laboratories and our graduate schools, we train foreign students who leave us to return to their native lands.

Fact: Many of our graduate degrees in mathematics and the natural sciences do go to foreign-born students. But we are blessed with the good luck that more than half of these enormously talented individuals choose to stay in the United States.[30] We are draining the world of its talent, which is a moral problem; but our good fortune serves the national interest just fine. These individuals — Pakistanis, East Indians, Asians, Latin Americans — become law-abiding, relatively high-salaried American citizens, who increase our international competitiveness. Opposition to such students is probably based more on xenophobia and racism than on any economic argument that could be made.

Myth 12. The United States is an enormous failure in international comparisons of educational achievement.

Fact: I would ask some questions about international comparisons before I would worry about our students' relative performance. First, I would like to know if we Americans want our children to experience a childhood like those of Japanese, Korean, Israeli, or East Indian children. I do not think so. Other countries rear children in their ways, and we rear them in our way. As you might expect, we have a vision of what constitutes a "normal" childhood that is uniquely American.

My middle-class neighbors seem to agree that their children should be able to watch a good deal of TV; participate in organized sports such as Little League, basketball, and soccer; engage in after-school activities such as piano lessons and dance; spend weekends predominantly in leisure activities; work after school when they become teenagers; have their own cars and begin to date while in high school; and so forth. To accomplish all of this, of course, children cannot be burdened by excessive amounts of homework. This kind of American consensus about childhood produces uniquely American youths. According to many visitors to the United States, we have some of the most creative and spontaneous children the world has ever seen. And these students do go on to more challenging schooling at the college level, in numbers that are the envy of the world.

It is clear that our system is not designed to produce masses of high-achieving students before the college years. You cannot have both high levels of history, language, mathematics, and science achievement for great numbers of students and the conception of childhood that I have just sketched. But our nation is certainly not at risk because of that conception. Enough able workers are being trained to meet our national needs.

Second, I would like to know whether the students tested in international comparisons have all spent the same amount of time practicing the skills that are to be assessed. It is not clear that this is so. Given the additional school days in the Japanese school year, multiplied by 10 years of schooling, we find by the simplest arithmetic that the typical Japanese student has the equivalent of more than two years' more schooling than the typical American student when they are both 16 years old. Moreover, with the additional time they spend in private "after-school" schools and in Saturday schools (the *juku* schools, attended by a large percentage of the Japanese school-age population), Japanese children accumulate still greater amounts of education, such that by age 16 they have more than three years' more schooling than their American counterparts. Furthermore, the immense (at least by American standards) amount of homework assigned to and completed by Japanese students means that they accumulate huge quantities of extra time practicing school subjects at home and on weekends. Suppose you now compare these groups in terms of their mathematics and science achievement in the 10th grade. It would be truly newsworthy if the results were any different from what they are now. The results we get are exactly what we should expect.

Third, before taking the international comparisons at face value, I would want to make sure that the samples of students who take the test are somehow equivalent. It is easy for the United States to produce a representative sample of 13- or 16-year-olds for an international comparison. Is that also true of some of our international competitors? Some of the nations in these studies have neither an accurate census nor a school system that attempts to keep everyone in school. We have a larger percentage of our school-age population in school than most other nations. Thus our representative sample is culturally and economically more heterogeneous.

In the first international assessment conducted by the International Association for the Evaluation of Educational Achievement, from which we learned how awful the United States was doing, the average performance of 75% of the age group in the United States was compared with the average scores of the top 9% of the students in West Germany, the top 13% in the Netherlands, and the top 45% in Sweden.[31] Could the results have been predicted? In the most recent international comparisons of science and mathematics achievement, the United States did not do as well as Korea and Taiwan. But in our sample we had more children at lower grade levels for their age than they did. All other things being equal, when around 10% of our sample has attained one or two fewer grade levels of schooling than the sample of the same age from Korea and Taiwan, we have a sampling problem.[32] What could be newsworthy about differences in achievement when the samples are not equivalent?

49

Fourth, I would like to be sure that the different groups in the international comparisons all had the opportunity to learn the same things. We should note that school systems that do not hold as many children as we do until high school graduation and that have fewer students continuing on to higher education need to teach many things at an earlier point in the curriculum — calculus and probability, for example. Because we are a nation that is rich enough and democratic enough to attempt to retain our youngsters longer in school and because we send a comparatively large number of them on to college, we often look weak in the international comparisons. Many of our students learn what they need to learn later than do students in other countries.

We need to remember that students will not do well on any content to which they have not been exposed. Opportunity to learn a subject is probably the single best predictor of achievement that we have. If you cannot control for it, you have no basis for comparing achievement. The findings of the Second International Mathematics Study are a case in point.[33] Do we see, in the performance of the Japanese and others, evidence of efficiency and effectiveness in education — or merely evidence that national curricula differ?

If we look at the 273 eighth-grade math classes that made up the U.S. sample, we find that they were actually labeled as remedial, typical, pre-algebra, and algebra classes. To no one's great surprise, only the pre-algebra and algebra classes — about 25% of the U.S. sample — had had nearly the same amount of exposure as the Japanese classes in the sample to the algebra items that made up the test. Three-quarters of the classes in the U.S. sample were simply not exposed to the same curriculum as were the Japanese! Can you guess what the result might be in such a comparison? If we look only at the eighth-grade algebra classes among our sample, we find that American performance in algebra meets or exceeds the performance of the Japanese eighth-graders.

The differences in achievement between nations are most parsimoniously explained as differences in national curricula, rather than as differences in the efficiency or effectiveness of a particular national system of education. International comparisons such as these make us realize that American students, including the most ordinary ones, are capable of learning more mathematics at earlier ages — if that is what we want them to learn.

But while we should wrestle with these legitimate curriculum issues, we need not blame our students and castigate their teachers for gross failure. Our nation, particularly at state and local levels, has made curricular decisions that are in accord with prevailing views of childhood and of education. We can change those decisions if we want. But the system has actually been serving the nation well for decades; and, as noted, it is producing all the mathematicians and scientists this economy can use for the foreseeable future.

Finally, in considering the results of international comparisons, I would like to be assured that the motivation of the students who took the tests was similar across different nations. It is not clear that this is the case. The Koreans, for example, take the tests for the honor of the nation.[34] The American students often use the test to rest for two hours, knowing that neither their teachers nor their parents will see the results.

I cannot find much to worry about in the international comparisons. Every nation has its visions of childhood, development, schooling, equality, and success. While our nation heatedly debates and gradually modifies these visions, as a dynamic society must, let us just note that the system we created has been remarkably successful for a large number of the children and parents it serves.

Myth 13. American productivity has fallen, and a major factor in that decline is the education of the work force.

Fact: According to the 1992 report of McKinsey and Company, one of our nation's most prestigious management consulting firms, there has been no decline in American productivity.[35] It is true that productivity in other countries has grown at a faster rate than ours; but since their productivity was historically much lower, that is not surprising. Their rates of increase are not nearly as steep as they approach our rate of productivity. McKinsey and Company estimates that overall economic productivity is lower in Germany by 14% and in Japan by 28%. In the service areas, where the United States is beginning to lead the world, our productivity rates are even higher when compared with those of other nations.

When we examine the various factors that can influence the productivity of a nation — market conditions, labor unions, government regulations, behavior of management, available capital, skill of the labor force, and so on — only one variable predicts productivity in the service sector across nations. That factor is the behavior of management. The educational level of the labor force is unrelated to productivity. As we now realize, it was the management of General Motors, the management of Sears, and the management of Pan American Airlines (remember them?) that caused the economic hardships those companies have undergone. The educational level of the labor force was not an issue, though that makes a nice target when arrogant and intransigent managers are looking for scapegoats for their billion-dollar blunders.

Let me be clear. We have failing schools in this nation. But where they fail we see poverty, inadequate health care, dysfunctional families, and dysfunctional neighborhoods. Where our public schools succeed — in Princeton, New Jersey; in Grosse Pointe, Michigan; in Manhasset, New York — we see well-paying jobs, good health care, functional families, and functional neighborhoods. Families that can live in dignity send the schools children who have hope. Those children we can educate quite well. Families that have lost their dignity function poorly. They send us children with no hope for the future. Those children we cannot easily educate.

The agenda America should tackle if we want to improve schooling has nothing to do with national tests, higher standards, increased accountability, or better math and science achievement. Instead, we should focus our attention and our energies on jobs, health care, reduction of violence in families and in neighborhoods, and increased funding for day care, bilingual education, summer programs for young people, and so forth. It is estimated that 100,000 handguns enter the schools each day. It seems to me that this is a greater problem than the nation's performance in international mathematics competitions.

Footnotes

1. J.R. Flynn, "Massive IQ Gains in 14 Nations: What IQ Tests Really Measure," *Psychological Bulletin* 101 (1987): 171-91.
2. Ibid.
3. Paul E. Barton and Richard J. Coley, *Performance at the Top: From Elementary Through Graduate School* (Princeton, N.J.: Educational Testing Service, 1991).
4. Ibid.
5. C.C. Carson, R.M. Huelskamp, and T.D. Woodall, "Perspectives on Education in America," Third Draft, Sandia National Laboratories, Albuquerque, N.M., May 1991.
6. Ibid.
7. Ibid.
8. Ibid.
9. Organisation for Economic Cooperation and Development, *Education at a Glance* (Paris: Centre for Educational Research and Innovation, 1992).
10. Carson, Huelskamp, and Woodall, op. cit.
11. Robert L. Linn, M. Elizabeth Graue, and Nancy M. Sanders, "Comparing State and District Test Results to National Norms: The Validity of Claims

That 'Everyone Is Above Average'," *Educational Measurement: Issues and Practice* (Fall 1990): 5-14.

12. Robert L. Linn, personal communication, February 1991.

13. Diane Ravitch and Chester E. Finn, Jr., *What Do Our 17-Year-Olds Know?* (New York: Harper & Row, 1987); E.D. Hirsch, Jr., *Cultural Literacy: What Every American Needs to Know* (Boston: Houghton Mifflin, 1987); Allan Bloom, *The Closing of the American Mind: How Higher Education Has Failed Democracy and Impoverished the Souls of Today's Students* (New York: Simon & Schuster, 1987); and William J. Bennett, *To Reclaim a Legacy: A Report on the Humanities in Higher Education* (Washington, D.C.: National Endowment for the Humanities, 1984).

14. Dale Whittington, "What Have 17-Year-Olds Known in the Past?" *American Educational Research Journal* 28 (1991): 759-83.

15. National Commission on Children, *Beyond Rhetoric: A New American Agenda for Children and Families* (Washington, D.C.: U.S. Government Printing Office, 1991).

16. David Card and Alan B. Krueger, "Does School Quality Matter? Returns to Education and the Characteristics of Public Schools in the United States," Working Paper No. 3358, Bureau of Economic Research, Washington, D.C., 1990.

17. Charles F. Manski, "Academic Ability, Earnings, and the Decision to Become a Teacher: Evidence from the National Longitudinal Study of the High School Class of 1972," in David A. Wise, ed., *Public Sector Payrolls* (Chicago: University of Chicago Press, 1987); and Richard J. Murnane and R.J. Olsen, "The Effects of Salaries and Opportunity Costs on Duration in Teaching: Evidence from Michigan," *Review of Economics and Statistics* 71 (1989): 347-52.

18. Ronald F. Ferguson, "Paying for Public Education: New Evidence on How and Why Money Matters," *Harvard Journal on Legislation* 28 (1991): 465-98.

19. Glen Robinson and David Brandon, *Perceptions About American Education: Are They Based on Facts?* (Arlington, Va.: Educational Research Service, 1992).

20. Ibid.

21. Both Finn and Sununu are quoted in M. Edith Rasell and Lawrence Mishel, *Shortchanging Education: How U.S. Spending on Grades K-12 Lags Behind Other Industrialized Nations* (Washington, D.C.: Economic Policy Institute, 1990).

22. Ibid.

23. Ibid.

24. Organisation for Economic Cooperation and Development, op. cit.

25. Jonathan Kozol, *Savage Inequalities* (New York: Crown, 1991).

26. George H. Bush, speech delivered at the Education Summit, University of Virginia, Charlottesville, 28 September 1989.

27. Carson, Huelskamp, and Woodall, op. cit.

28. Lawrence Mishel and Ruy A. Texeira, *The Myth of the Coming Labor Shortage: Jobs, Skills, and Incomes of America's Workforce 2000* (Washington, D.C.: Economic Policy Institute, 1991).

29. John H. Bishop, "The Productivity Consequences of What Is Learned in High School," *Journal of Curriculum Studies* 22 (1990): 101-26.

30. Carson, Huelskamp, and Woodall, op. cit.

31. Iris C. Rotberg, "I Never Promised You First Place," *Phi Delta Kappan* 72 (December 1990): 296-303.

32. Archie E. Lapointe, Janice M. Askew, and Nancy A. Mead, *Learning Science* (Princeton, N.J.: Educational Testing Service, 1992); and Archie E. Lapointe, Nancy A. Mead, and Janice M. Askew, *Learning Mathematics* (Princeton, N.J.: Educational Testing Service, 1992).

33. Ian Westbury, "Comparing American and Japanese Achievement: Is the United States Really a Low Achiever?" *Educational Researcher* (June/July 1992): 18-24.

34. Lapointe, Askew, and Mead, op. cit; and Gerald W. Bracey, "Why Can't They Be Like We Were?" *Phi Delta Kappan* 73 (October 1991): 104-17.

35. McKinsey Global Institute, *Service Sector Productivity* (Washington, D.C.: McKinsey and Company, 1992).

WHAT'S IN? WHAT'S OUT? AMERICAN EDUCATION IN THE NINETIES

John Murphy

Technology has changed almost every aspect of our lives. But our schools, Mr. Murphy argues, are still stuck in the last century. Continuing along the same course, he warns, will put the United States at a serious disadvantage with respect to its economic competitors.

American public schools were once ranked with the world's best. No longer. We have lost our edge, and that poses dire consequences for our country's future. Evidence from international comparisons is consistent and alarming. Data show that American schools do not begin to approach the standards of the rest of the developed world.

Some educators maintain that the performance of American schools has not gotten worse over the decades, that graduates of our schools today are better educated than graduates of a century ago. They may be right, but that news is hardly comforting. The fact remains that today's students are not learning nearly enough to meet present-day demands. Moreover, standing still while much of the rest of the world makes giant strides has put us sorely behind. We must reclaim our education legacy or relinquish our world pre-eminence. It's that simple.

The odds are with us, however. Education is a national icon. We are not likely to sit by and watch it drive itself — along with our collective future — into the ground. Think of it: growing up in America is synonymous with going to school. Everyone does it. Everyone is expected — indeed, required — to do it. School is so much a part of our culture that high school graduation has become a chief rite of passage into adulthood. The local football team, the student band, student achievement — all have become community emblems.

As a nation, we understand that much more is at stake than matters of industry and commerce. Good schooling is every citizen's ticket to

John Murphy is superintendent of the Charlotte-Mecklenburg (N.C.) Schools.

the good life and does much to secure the vigor of our culture, the vitality of our neighborhoods, and the collective wisdom of our nation. Education is the hallmark of a free and thriving society. It is an enterprise in which everyone has a stake; something to be revered and protected. That's what makes it strong.

Curiously, that's also the problem. Times have changed, yet we are reluctant to remodel what has become, in our mind's eye, a grand old institution. The schools of the 1990s are the schools of the 1890s with a fresh coat of paint. They are pony express institutions trying to make it in a high-tech world. Technology, instantaneous worldwide communications, and improved transportation have revolutionized almost every aspect of our lives, except for what happens in schools. Low standards, too little time, anemic content, and irrelevant tests make for a dull system these days. We cling tightly to arcane structures and practices, despite the fact that American education is choking on mediocrity.

We have spent the better part of the last century battling to improve access to schools. We should take heart in the fact that we largely accomplished what we set out to do. Today, children of every race, class, ethnic background, or handicapping condition can get a primary and secondary education free of charge. So completely have our norms changed that, while we used to celebrate the few who finished school, we now expect every child to graduate.

The inclusiveness of our school system is one of its greatest strengths and augurs well for the future of our nation. But somewhere along the line we confused "more" with "better" education. They are not equivalent. They are not even close. In fact, more of the same is a recipe for disaster.

The imperatives are clear. If our schools are to provide us with a modern work force prepared to excel in a postindustrial, knowledge-based society, we must transform the design and structure of education; we must make a fundamental change that strikes at the core of current operations. No strategy, no style of administration, no power allocation can be seen as off-limits. The bottom line is that we must translate the passion for improving access to schools into an insistence that something better should happen to children once they get there.

Standards and Expectations

The sad fact is that for too long far too little has been expected of American students. American education made a major blunder in earlier decades by organizing thresholds around the lowest common denominator — usually defined as what every sixth-grader should know. We wanted everybody to feel good, but we created those good feelings at the expense of excellence. Minimum requirements quickly turned into maximum goals. We forgot that young people, like most adults, do just enough to get by.

Most students have not learned very much because we have not expected very much. It's high time to push youngsters hard and ask them to master a body of knowledge and skills that they will need if they are going to make it in the new world order. If we don't raise standards, reform will have no purpose. We live in a world of determined, well-educated competitors. Our students must match the competition in Bonn, Stockholm, Paris, Seoul, and Osaka.

Focusing on Outcomes

For as long as anyone can recall, we have judged the quality of schools by what goes into them rather than by what comes out of them. A good school, we said, is one with ample facilities and resources, low student/teacher ratios, well-stocked library shelves, lots of specialists, and numerous programs and activities. By the same token, we grant diplomas to students who rack up enough Carnegie units to graduate. The rationale goes something like this: What students study and for how long can stand as a rough proxy for what they actually learn. But we know better now. Most high school diplomas mean only that a student has accumulated seat time in an approved location. These diplomas are described more accurately as evidence of patience than as evidence of authentic academic achievement.

The infatuation with inputs in education has created an administrative logjam. Legions of highly paid personnel in our school systems — from the local to the national level — hold nonteaching jobs and are unaccountable to the people in whose behalf they ostensibly labor. Classroom teachers and students rarely see them. Taxpayers are unaware of their existence. Yet their grip on the schools is tight.

Central administrators churn out an inexhaustible supply of prose and policy about how to teach. They touch every facet of schooling: testing, time, textbooks, curriculum, compensation, credentials, competence, staff training, attendance, and graduation requirements. Little is left to the imagination or to the discretion of those on the front lines. And the numbers of these administrators are growing. Practically one-half of all educational expenditures are spent on things outside the classroom — a jump from one-third only 25 years ago.

57

Perhaps most important, though, rules don't teach. If children are not learning, it doesn't much matter that the regulations and guidelines were followed or that the public's money was spent in accordance with the law. In fact, rules and formulas tend to make staff members focus on the wrong things and furnish the wrong resources. Moreover, when legislatures, school boards, and central office staff dictate every move, teachers and principals are not responsible for the results. With others calling all the plays, they have a perfect excuse for poor performance.

Put in simple terms, inputs are a fraud. Look around the nation: Spending is up, course-taking is up, grades are up, college admissions are up, but learning is down. Lacking clear goals and reliable feedback, we risk wandering aimlessly about, unsure whether we are headed in the right direction, whether we need to adjust our course, or whether we are advancing at all. Being certain of our destination is the only sure way to find our way. Outcomes are all that really matter. A good school is one that produces knowledgeable students. Competency in challenging subject matter, enrollment in demanding classes, good citizenship, low suspension and expulsion rates, and strong connections between home and school must become the prime indicators of our success.

Ability Versus Effort

I wish to call attention to this point because it is an important one. The prevailing American attitude is that innate ability determines school success. Although we rarely admit it outright, we believe that we cannot educate everyone of normal intelligence to high levels. Yet we built this nation on an opposite belief: that anything is possible for those who work long and hard enough.

The current system of curricular tracking, which gives the "good" students one curriculum and the "poor" students a watered-down version, is a prime example of the ability-equals-success philosophy in action. Students are sorted out at an early age and relegated to separate tracks for fast, medium, and slow learners. Once consigned to a track, there is no escape. Students tend to remain in a given track through high school.

What does this do to the children? Being uninspired is one thing. That's curable. Being labeled innately unable, on the other hand, is terminal; and children respond accordingly. Why work harder if success is not related to effort? This presents a problem for those of "high ability"

58

as well. The message to them is that they can simply rely on their talents and "breeze through."

This system works a cruel hoax on students in the low tracks. Those unfortunate enough to be dumped into the general or vocational tracks — characterized by unchallenging courses and the accumulation of low-level skills — find themselves wholly unprepared for either postsecondary education or meaningful work.

Let's be forthright. It is the achievement of the poor, the disadvantaged, the disaffected, and racial minorities that we have been willing to sacrifice all these years. They have disproportionately filled the ranks of the lower tracks.

If the moral affront of this situation does not convince the people of this nation that a change in attitude is essential, then we must rely on good old-fashioned self-interest. In the days of the industrial economy, when semiskilled jobs were a dime a dozen, our approach could be tolerated from a purely economic standpoint. But no longer. The new knowledge-based economy is desperate for employees who are broadly and deeply educated, steeped in the traditions of a liberal education. Modern companies need a host of workers who know how to think, how to solve problems, and how to use the lessons of science, history, math, language, and geography to good effect.

The bottom line is that everyone deserves — and the nation needs everyone to have — a hefty dose of the very best learning, and it is up to schools to deliver it. Good teaching must reach every child. We must vary the means — not the ends — of education in ways that respect the particular differences of children.

Individualizing

Currently, we seem to take pride in teaching all young people in the same way. We believe that doing so promotes equality. It does the opposite. What is fair about creating just one kind of school with one kind of teaching when children's interests, learning styles, and developmental levels differ so dramatically?

School assignments made on the basis of geography presume that children are interchangeable and that parents have no stake in the individuality of their children. Why not tap into the particular educational and career aspirations of students and offer them choices in the form of a variety of distinctive specialty schools? What better way to capture the minds of young people than to enroll them in schools they want to attend, tailored to their particular interests?

59

Some argue that creating distinctive schools — special centers of competence — creates inequalities. However, because all people do not learn in the same way, to run schools of only one kind is profoundly prejudicial. If a school fits like a glove, you're in luck. The school feels relevant, and studies come easily. If the fit is poor, tough luck. Hang in there, or drop out — psychologically if not physically.

Choice celebrates the differences among children and uses those differences to good effect. Standards of accomplishment are held firm, while curricular emphases and the means and style of teaching change. Youngsters and schools are matched on the basis of their individual strengths and preferences.

Choice works for teachers, too. Now teachers are shunted around the system on the basis of seniority, without regard to their skills or preferences. Time in the saddle determines school assignment. Teachers are told where and how to teach. Imagine the difference in attitude if teachers had some choice of venue and some say-so over who would teach alongside them. The voluntary nature of such new relationships would make people instant partners, collaborators from the start.

Breaking the Age/Grade Link

Grade levels are another absurdity of current practice. We hold tight to grades, we say, because all children of a certain age are somehow alike. Treat all seventh-graders the same. Teach them the same stuff in the same way at the same time. To the untrained eye of the noneducator, this practice seems to defy common sense. Youngsters grow at different rates — intellectually, physically, and emotionally — with unpredictable starts, stops, and surges along the way. In fact, there is no body of knowledge that experts can point to as age- or grade-specific. Let's be honest: Grades and classrooms are the way we keep track of students; they are an administrative convenience embraced for the sake of the grownups in the system. The practice creates a mirage of homogeneity and allows teachers to develop a single lesson plan. But if we value learning above all else, the current structure of grades segregated by age with 25 children per classroom must go.

We need a system that can flex to accommodate the fact that individual students learn some subjects quickly and others slowly and that there are some days when information comes more quickly than others. This means that we will have to break the arbitrary age/grade link, let go of the traditional 12 grades of school, and allow students to advance as they master the material, without regard to age.

It makes sense to enable students at relatively similar levels of accomplishment in a particular subject area to study together, especially since all students will be held to the same high standard in order to graduate. They will just reach those standards at different rates. The point is to tailor instruction to the learning needs of each child. If students cannot learn algebra or geometry in one year, they should be given two years, three years, or however long it takes, with all the help necessary to ensure that students are prepared to pursue any future ambitions.

Seniority Versus Competence

Treating everyone alike in schools is not limited to the students. The enterprise of schooling treats all its staff exactly alike, too — no matter how they perform. By and large, whether teachers do a good job of educating students or not, nothing different happens to them either way.

Salaries are determined by arbitrary measures. A dedicated and successful inner-city teacher receives no more pay than a disgruntled or inept colleague. Pay is awarded solely on the basis of paper credentials and seniority. If a teacher takes college courses — almost any courses, relevant or not — we'll pay a higher salary. If a teacher works longer and doesn't get fired, we'll pay more, too. Job performance is irrelevant; incompetents are rarely fired. High achievers are penalized, while the low achievers are rewarded. Such a system hardly inspires people to great accomplishment. Any way you look at it, it's profoundly demoralizing.

To be effective inducements for change, any honors and rewards must be evident in advance. They must be simple, clear, and certain — as must be the interventions in cases of failure. Salaries must be based on performance and must be sensitive to the market. That means higher pay for good teachers and for those who assume extra duties. Teachers who perform "above and beyond" the call of duty deserve a payoff in status, in role, and in compensation. Being sensitive to the market also means paying more to those certified to teach in shortage areas (for example, science and mathematics) than to those in overstocked fields.

In addition to rationalizing pay among the ranks, attention must be paid to justifying district pay scales up and down the line. We need to keep the best teachers in the classroom, where they belong. How can we blame our best teachers for making a beeline for the greener pastures of the central office, where the pay is decidedly higher and the working conditions befit their status as professionals? It's time to pay the most proficient teachers salaries equal to those of the most proficient school administrators.

Year-Round Learning

Here's a sobering thought: As long as young people in other nations commit a far greater share of their lives to learning, it is doubtful that our students' academic accomplishment will equal theirs. Moreover, with ambitious new exit standards, virtually every student will need to spend substantially more time learning each year, though how much more will vary for each child.

In stark contrast to the two-day weekends and long summer vacations that interrupt the learning of current generations, year-round schooling provides for shorter holidays, spaced more evenly throughout the year. As a result, learning becomes a seamless process, buoyed by the momentum of continuous instruction: The shorter the breaks, the more children remember of what they learned before. One caveat is necessary: A longer school year that translates into more of the same will be a curse, not a blessing. More of something bad does not make it good. We need to fix what we have first. Then we can give priority to lengthening the school year for students who are not doing particularly well and for those who learn more slowly.

Beginning at Birth

Children certainly don't wait for formal instruction to speak, think, and write. In fact, there is universal agreement that the learning that takes place in the first five years of children's lives — before they ever darken a schoolhouse door — is some of the most consequential learning they will ever do. Why must we wait until a child is five and on our doorstep?

We need to forsake the mindset that education means formal schooling — that what happens in the earlier years is none of our business — and strike while the iron is hot. If children do not have a good beginning, it is difficult to compensate fully for that failure in later years. According to recent estimates, nearly 35% of the nation's children come to school not fully ready to be successful in kindergarten.

In addition to improving and expanding preschool programs, why not contact new parents to let them know how best to prepare their children for school? The emphasis would be to encourage parents to enrich the home environment so that their children have a decided edge when they enter grade school. Individual schools could keep close track of each child's progress, with community agencies standing by, ready to kick in when their assistance is needed.

Vesting Authority in Teachers

As long as goals for student learning are reached, professionals at the school level deserve our trust to do right by their students. Teaching is one of the learned professions, yet the work feels more "blue collar" than "white." Professionals are supposed to be distinguished from other workers by their command of a special body of knowledge and skills, by the unique contributions they make, by their greater freedom to organize their time, and by the autonomy to direct their own work. The working lives of teachers bear none of these characteristics; they are drab, difficult, often demeaning.

Punch a clock. Sign in and out of the building. Thirty minutes for lunch. Scheduled bathroom breaks. No access to the school building unless the students are there. No private offices. No phones for private calls. No time to confer with colleagues. Bus duty, corridor duty, cafeteria duty, and playground duty. Imagine asking lawyers, doctors, or even college professors to put up with such conditions for one week, let alone a lifetime.

Despite nearly a decade of agitation, change in the field is barely perceptible. That's because those at the heart of the system — the schools and the individual classrooms within them — have had little say-so. The game is still being played by the old rules. Teachers — people in general — do not work harder in places that they feel are hostile. That's human nature. Yet reform requires that teachers work harder and smarter. Reform also requires a fresh cast of characters — some new blood in the ranks. That means we will need to lure a whole new contingent of bright, capable students away from other professions and into teaching. But if conditions stay as they are, we might as well forget about a revitalized teaching force.

Teaching is a job that requires judgment. Yet a teacher's world is governed by someone else's rules. We can hardly expect teachers to exercise judgment or to take responsibility for the result when they have little power to shape their work. For that matter, how can we expect teachers to excel when there is no time outside of class to prepare lessons? We want teachers to retain a sense of their own scholarly development, but we give them no time to confer with colleagues and little opportunity to observe and learn from skilled practitioners.

Think of the other professions, and the absurdity of the situation in education is difficult to ignore. It is hard to conceive of a hospital, for instance, denying its physicians time to consult with other staff members and patients. Indeed, hospitals expect collaboration in the diagnosis of problems and the selection of therapies. In glaring contrast, the only people who have time to sit around contemplating the future and proposing remedies in education are nonclassroom personnel. That's not altogether unlike giving hospital administrators — who never lay eyes on the patients — the responsibility for determining the course of treatments. It is unfair, unwise, and a shameful waste of valuable human resources to lock out talented professionals who know firsthand what the real problems are and what really works. We must free teachers from regulations and red tape and give them time during the school day to meet and talk about their students, their schools, and their visions of education.

If the school is the right location for making decisions, the central office must become a service center. School staffs should have sole discretion to buy or not to buy textbooks, training, and services. If central office services do not fill the bill, schools should have control of the resources necessary to secure outside services that meet their needs. The central office would then have to respond to keep its customers. No customers, no work. No work, no jobs. Either the central operation reconfigures to meet demands, or it goes out of business.

The Full-Service Schools

Schools represent neutral ground, and the entire community has a connection to them in one way or another. Tragically, this strategic real estate — so well-suited to meet family needs — remains vastly underused. With a few notable exceptions, schools are open for six hours on weekdays and closed tight all weekend and during vacations. We need to change that and keep as many schools as we can open for business 12 hours a day, seven days a week, 12 months a year.

Community schools are a cure for educational irrelevance. By linking school with real-world activities, the educational experience could be far more pertinent for most children — especially for those from distressed communities, who most clearly recognize the disparity between their school lives and the stark realities of their worlds. Moreover, parents and children struggling to overcome the untold hardships of poverty need safe, welcoming places for learning, for health care, for socializing, and for recreation.

The notion that a school might serve as something more than just a place where children are educated has long been a tradition in Great Britain. About half of the local education agencies there have community schools. While they are sources for continuing education for some adults, they also function as full-service social support systems for all residents. To meet community needs, a wide range of public services is offered — from day care and literacy development to health services, parent counseling, and job placement. At certain times of the day and evening, adults far outnumber children. These schools have become the dynamic hearts of their communities and a proving ground for innovation.

To make such schools a reality in American communities, social and health agencies must drop their bureaucratic boundaries, inject flexibility into their funding streams, and stop focusing on their narrow service jurisdictions. (All of these changes are far more difficult to accomplish than they sound.) These agencies need to set up shop in schools, and schools must welcome them as partners.

Education: Everyone's Business

Students don't just appear at school from nowhere and then disappear again at night. They come from and go home to adults — their parents or guardians. They grow up and spend time in neighborhoods. Both the adults they live with and the neighborhoods they live in have more impact than some of us in education like to admit.

School occupies only 9% of children's lives. The rest is spent outside of school. Parents, churches, social welfare organizations, employers, and a variety of other institutions and influences are the custodians of children during 91% of their lives. It is time that the schools stopped confining their activities to what is traditionally thought to be their domain: six hours a day in grades K-12. We must reach down, out, and beyond the school walls — down to those not yet in school, out to parents and the community, and beyond the 9% of the time that children are in our direct custody. We must engage the resources of the broader community to assist us.

It all boils down to this: much of learning depends on students' willingness to learn and excitement about learning. The beliefs, principles, and values by which the community lives set the tone for much of what goes on inside of schools. The young watch their elders to gather clues about what's important, about how to live. If communities do not value learning, children rarely do either. A community that holds scholastic achievement in high regard, on the other hand, encourages youngsters to excel in learning despite the many competing pressures (TV, sports, clothes, cars, the cute kid across the hall) that impede schoolwork and distract students from the goals of education. This is not to say that young people should be denied recreational activities, for recreation has a legitimate and salutary purpose. But as teachers struggle to capture their students' attention, the battle is already lost if the community denigrates scholarship.

It's all quite logical. We try hard when it seems worthwhile and when people we respect care that we learn. We learn best when the community in which we live signals in everyday ways that learning is valuable — and that there are consequences if we don't learn.

Right now, young people know that, no matter how poorly they do in school, they can still get hired or get into college. Though a high school diploma remains a necessary credential for employment, it's a rare employer who pores over the transcripts of prospective entry-level employees. And students are not stupid. They learn early on that it doesn't much matter what courses they take or how well they do in them. If there are no real-life consequences for poor performance, few students are moved to put forth much effort. And if there are no benefits to the struggle, why hustle?

Tangible rewards and sanctions are two of the surest ways to boost student learning, and those tools lie in the hands of business and the colleges. Entry requirements for jobs and for further study are the "real life" exit requirements for elementary and secondary schooling. Schools have tried to act as proxies for these two institutions by manufacturing their own set of consequences, but young people are too smart. They know a contrived policy without serious implications when they see one.

Instead of ignoring academic performance, business and colleges must make school performance central to their hiring and selection practices. For instance, business and industry could issue a list of courses or a list of competencies that they require future employees to have mastered. Why not pay high achievers a dollar more per hour? Why not make it clear that those with the strongest transcripts and best test scores will get the better jobs and working conditions? Why not reduce college tuition for good students? Alternatively, why not deny degree credit for remedial courses taken in college? Once it is clear that prospective employees or college students will be treated according to their success in school, word will spread quickly.

The responsibility for the education of children does not begin and end at the schoolhouse door. Education must be part of the public's mission if schools are to succeed with all the children who come to them.

AMERICAN PUBLIC EDUCATION: THE RELEVANCE OF CHOICE

Nathan Glazer

Mr. Glazer describes three of the key features of "trans-formative" choice — the kind of choice that he thinks can help the largely minority central-city schools.

American public education, like Gaul and so many other things, can be divided into three parts, even if only roughly and approximately. The first part consists of the schools of rural, small-town, small-city, and suburban America. These sectors constitute by far the greater part of the United States; and it is in this broad belt of America that we find the people who give high marks to their schools on the whole, much to the dismay of researchers who know that the schools and the children can do better. In these areas, for the most part, school districts are small; school bureaucracies are modest; it is possible for parents to have a direct relationship with teachers, principals, other school officials, and superintendents; school board members may be known to many parents; and, perhaps most important, a substantial homogeneity prevails — in race, culture, language, and values.

If we ask what is right about American education, it is in these broad reaches of small-town and small-city America that we can say that much is right — that the original vision of the common school prevails — and that what is wrong is that the social life in schools often dominates academic objectives. It is this America that would be distraught, as happened in Texas, if school reformers decreed that minimal academic objectives would have to be reached before a student would be allowed to play on the football team.

The second great division of American public education is made up of the schools of the inner cities of our large and medium-sized metropolitan areas, in which the majority of students tend to be black or Hispan-

---

Nathan Glazer is a professor of education and sociology at Harvard University, Cambridge, Mass.

ic, even if the cities do not have majorities of these minorities. Here the number of students from single-parent families, from poor families, and from families with problems is large. As is necessary in large school systems containing scores of thousands of students, school bureaucracies are large. The major obstacles to reaching high levels of academic achievement stem less from the competition of social life than from the drain of social problems that affect children from poor and troubled homes — the threat of violence, the presence of drugs, and all the other ailments so familiar from accounts of inner-city schools. It is these schools that we generally see portrayed in television specials and that make the news about American public education.

The third part of American public education consists of the schools that are situated in sections of our large central cities in which social problems are not concentrated — the urban areas occupied by the stable working class, the lower-middle class, and the middle class. For these groups, the chief threat in public education in recent years has been the possibility that their children will be bused to inner-city schools and that they will be barred from their neighborhood schools in order to promote racial integration. And their chief response has been to move off to the suburbs, where they will be protected from these threats.

For both kinds of urban schools, the question of values education is a steady problem. What does one do about street language in the schools, street dress in the schools, and the frequent challenging of teachers and other authorities? How does one teach about AIDS and homosexuality, in what grades and with what specificity; and what is one to do about condoms? And parents of students in both kinds of city schools find themselves to be just some of many constituents of a large and distant bureaucracy, which frustrates them as often as any large public bureaucracy does.

In the absence of a sufficient sense of urgency, I fear that not much can be done to change the pattern of public education in those broad stretches of the United States in which there is general satisfaction. National commissions tell us that we are not doing well compared to other nations. Businesspeople are not happy with the skills and work attitudes of high school graduates. Yet it is hard to raise sights where satisfaction is general and where admission to community colleges and state colleges, for those who want to attend, is easy. Sights can be raised; but it requires a difficult process of state-level reform, developing new curricula for elementary and secondary schools, raising standards for high school completion, raising standards for admission to community and state colleges, and raising standards for teachers.

On all these fronts there is a good deal of activity, but progress is necessarily slow. We have no ministry of education to decree new national standards, and even state departments of education hesitate to act like ministries of education. When they do, their decrees are not automatically implemented in the hundreds of school districts and thousands of schools they oversee.

But in the central cities — and in the smaller industrial cities that abut them and are often extensions of them — discontent is widespread, reaching high levels of frustration and anger. Under these circumstances, change is possible; and indeed, substantial change has occurred.

In fact, we could be seeing the beginning of the largest change in a hundred years in American public education: the break-up of the powerful central school bureaucracies that came into being around the turn of the century in all our large cities. The big-city bureaucracies were successful for decades in placing schools outside local partisan politics, in protecting them with an ethos of professionalization, and in educating great numbers of immigrant and working-class children to standards that were considered acceptable at the time. The idea of "choice," which now threatens these bureaucracies, means many things to different people; and it has been implemented in multifarious ways. But the key point is that it offers an alternative model for American public education. It is a model that frightens many schoolpeople and supporters of public schools; but if the schools of the central cities, the schools that deal with the black and Hispanic children who make up a large and growing part of our school population, are to improve, it is hard to see any other alternative that can be effective.

But to say "choice" alone is to say little. Just what is the problem, and how would a reform incorporating choice address it?

Here, of course, one must acknowledge great divergences in diagnoses and prescriptions. One diagnosis says that the curriculum has been dumbed down. The prescription: Make it more demanding, and students will respond, their levels of achievement will show improvement, fewer will drop out, and more will go to college. This is an attractive approach, and many states are trying to implement it. But the stories teachers tell convince me that relatively few of the children in our inner-city schools will respond to what is simply a harder and more demanding curriculum.

Another diagnosis tells us that the curriculum is irrelevant to these children. The prescription: Find a curriculum that speaks to them and takes their culture into account. In the context of prescribing what the

69

schools must address, culture is broadly construed to mean the history of the group from which the students come and their experiences in the inner city, including such characteristics of life there as broken families, street violence, drugs, and crime. In addition, the curriculum should present successful role models from the students' ethnic or racial groups. In short, what is being prescribed is the whole complex of "multiculturalism." This complex is being implemented in many inner-city schools; but one wonders how successful it can be in training students for either of the two real-life tests they will have to face: suitability for employment at the level of skills they currently possess (or can show the potential of possessing with on-the-job training) and admission to postsecondary education.

A third prescription consists of more money — for better-compensated teachers, more supplies, smaller classes, more social workers. In large measure this prescription has been carried out — expenditures for schools rose rapidly until the recent recession — just as the two previous approaches referred to have been implemented in some substantial measure. At some level, an increase in expenditure does have effects — for example, when classes drop below 15 children or when social services saturate the schools — but sufficient resources are rarely available to urban schools. Too many other causes compete for support: crime prevention, aiding the homeless, family support, infrastructure, and all the rest.

A fourth prescription — school integration — has been for the most part abandoned, though litigation continues, as in the current court case to integrate Hartford and its suburbs, and busing programs implemented one or two decades ago are still in effect here and there. Whatever its effects for black children (and research has documented some good effects), the major effect of integration on the central cities has been to speed the departure of white and middle-class families. The resulting higher concentration of minorities makes integration of schools in our larger cities an unattainable objective, short of exercising the kind of public authority that one cannot imagine in a democracy.

And then there is choice. What does it propose, what does it promise, and why is it suddenly so popular? Choice today comes in many forms: choice among schools within large-city school districts, choice that permits transfer to schools in other districts, choice within limits to protect racial and ethnic diversity, choice at the middle school level or at the high school level, choice with transportation assistance or without, choice with state compensation to districts that lose children, choice

70

including private schools or not, choice including religious schools or not. All these permutations have been proposed, and many have in part been implemented.

If all of this is choice, then choice, standing alone, means nothing and promises nothing. The kind of choice that is both meaningful and that threatens big-city school bureaucracies incorporates a distinctive analysis of what is wrong with big-city schools. Let us call this kind of choice "transformative" and describe three of its key features.

The first feature of transformative choice is that it finds in big-city school bureaucracies themselves the main problem in public education. The first choice movement of the late 1960s and early 1970s — under which independent but state-supported black schools were established in Boston, a program to bus inner-city black children to Boston suburbs was begun, and the Alum Rock (California) experiment was launched — was motivated by the belief that big-city school bureaucracies, as they existed in the 1960s and 1970s (and still exist), could not educate black children effectively.

What had happened to make the big-city school bureaucracy, which even as late as the 1950s was admired as an achievement of American democracy, so unpopular? One thing that happened was that a wide divergence developed between the ethnic and racial composition of school professional staffs and that of student populations. Another was that the school bureaucracies, in their commitment to a formal colorblindness, resisted racial censuses, school integration policies that would replace the norm of neighborhood schools, and affirmative action in employment and promotion. A third was that, in the heady days of the 1960s and the poverty program, *all* urban public bureaucracies were seen as sclerotic and inadequate — after all, the poverty program funded community action groups whose main function was to pressure and attack these bureaucracies.

It would be an interesting exercise in historical and social analysis to trace how these big-city school bureaucracies — once admired for their imperviousness to politics, their adherence to abstract and uniform rules of action, and their independence (their superintendents often stayed in office for decades) — became subjects of obloquy. In my judgment, this happened not because the bureaucracies became worse — or even the teachers — but because the conditions they had to deal with changed radically.

The second important feature of transformative choice is that it requires and demands the establishment of new schools to broaden the

71

kinds of education available, which means that teachers must have a degree of freedom to create them and parents must have a degree of freedom to choose them. To use the language of the free market, it requires free entrance. This was also a feature of the choice movement of the late 1960s and early 1970s, which hoped to see new schools established; but choice advocates in those days did not see the parallel between what they were proposing and the free market.

The third feature of transformative choice, and perhaps the sternest, is that it must have a way not only of rewarding success but of recognizing failure and requiring exit from the market. This principle means that schools would have to close because they do not attract students; that principals would lose their principalships, not for any gross dereliction in office, but because their schools simply do not attract students; that perhaps even teachers would lose their jobs, not because the money runs out, but because they are not good enough!

Others would posit additional features as being necessary to make choice effective and transformative. A system of choice must include private schools, some say, for only in this way will the market for choice be wide enough. The system will have to abandon racial guidelines, others propose, because only in this way will the range of choices be wide enough for it to be effective. It will have to include religious schools, because one of the main bases on which parents choose schools for their children is religion and attitude toward religion, and most private schools are religious schools. The latter two conditions are hardly likely to be attained under current constitutional requirements, and thus choice in the public sector will always have to be constrained.

Clearly choice is a chameleon. It has come to us at different times under at least three very different and widely divergent ideologies: the ideology of community control, the ideology of equity for Catholic schools, and the ideology of the free market. Advocates of community control led the first choice movement of the early 1970s; advocates of equity for Catholic schools led the second choice movement, the voucher proposals of the late 1970s; and advocates of the free market, buoyed by its new prestige in the wake of the collapse of communism, are the chief supporters of choice today.

What can choice be, then, if it finds support in so many different, ordinarily antagonistic quarters? The common element — for community organizers, for Catholics, for free marketers — is that in each case proponents of choice are arguing for the creation and support of *communities*. This may seem far-fetched with regard to the current choice movement — after all, the free market dissolves communities, it doesn't create them. But free choice in a free-market environment for schooling does indeed permit the expression, creation, and maintenance of communities. And if choice is effective, as its advocates hope, in raising academic achievement, the primary reason will be because it re-creates community in schools in which the maintenance of community had become difficult or impossible.

This factor, to my mind, is far more important in explaining the potential effectiveness of schools under a choice plan than is the competition among them. It is true that schools will have to compete, that some will succeed and some will fail, and that we will have to consider what a successful school may be allowed to do, as well as what will happen to an unsuccessful school. This is no easy task. Will a successful school be allowed to raise tuition or to select only the brightest students — the kind of practices that present-day successful private schools engage in? Will an unsuccessful school be given more money and more assistance, or will it be allowed to close? Another hard call.

But these issues are not as important as the ability of the school to become a community. A community is a complex of people and rules linked by common values. The concept is amorphous, but we know it when we see it. When James Coleman talks about community in schooling, he has in mind such characteristics as a degree of control over who enters, sanctions if rules are broken, acceptance of authority, some principle of government, and constraints on what is allowed in school — not only those constraints that are codified into law but also those arising naturally from the wish not to incur the disapproval of other members of the community. In a community there is a voluntary agreement among those who join to accept its rules, its constraints, its culture. That is what offers the promise of making schools effective.

This underlying commonality in all views of effective choice reflects a rejection of what has happened in inner-city public schools: the widespread disrespect of the authority of principals and teachers; the resistance to school rules; the use of outside forces to maintain order; the difficulty in disciplining or expelling the breakers of rules; the basic conflicts over curriculum, recently exemplified in the conflicts over the place of AIDS and gay/lesbian issues in the curriculum in New York City. I recall a comment from a Japanese teacher observing American schools. Why, he asked the principal and teachers, were the children out in the cold school yard, waiting to get into the school, when the doors were open and teachers and other staff members were arriving?

Because, he was told, if children were to enter the school before the official school hours and something were to happen to them, the city's liability would be greater! "I was embarrassed for them," the Japanese teacher wrote — embarrassed that the expansion of laws and liability made it impossible for them to act as teachers and principals.

Of course, the notion of "community" raises as many questions as "choice" does with regard to what it means, what is intended, and how it is implemented; and any reader will have a host of such questions. Yet the model of choice that was developed in East Harlem* — a system of small schools created by groups of teachers with the sympathetic support of higher authorities, who found them space and planning money and whatever else was needed to start up a school — seems to me a convincing picture of what choice, properly understood, can do to help that third, difficult sector of U.S. education, the largely minority central-city schools.

---

*See Seymour Fliegel, *Miracle in East Harlem* (New York: Times Books, 1993).

FROM TINKERING TO TRUE REFORM

Keith Geiger

If they are to realize their golden promise, there must be systemic and systematic change in four key dimensions of America's public schools: structure and organization, teaching and learning, curriculum, and assessment and accountability. So says the president of the nation's largest teacher organization. He outlines the transformations he believes necessary in each of these areas.

The year is 2043. The scene is a learning center, a place designed for people — not just children but adults as well — to meet and learn together.

All the people here understand that this is only one of the places where learning goes on. They understand that learning is a part of life; it is something everyone does, from birth to death, at home, outdoors, in work places.

The world these mid-21st-century people inhabit is quite different from the world of their parents and grandparents. Here, all people — young, old, rich, poor, and in-between — are provided the tools of learning.

In this 21st-century world, every person has a PDC — a personal digital computer, hand-held, about the size of a videocassette tape. The PDC links people to friends and learning partners, to work places, to networks and databases. Having a PDC is a right, not a privilege.

Textbooks are not used much any more. People have found that it is a lot less expensive — and better for the environment — to store information electronically. And since everyone has access to electronic information, it is more efficient as well. The texts of 10,000 books can be stored on a chip the size of a 20th-century credit card. Distance learning technologies — just beginning to be used by schools back in the 1990s — have been carried to new, almost magical dimensions. If these 21st-century learners want to study the Great Depression of the 1930s,

---

Keith Geiger is president of the National Education Association.

if they want to explore the inside of an atom or the floor of an ocean, if they want to discuss relativity with Einstein or sonnets with Shakespeare, they can just go there — traveling by way of virtual reality — to the time or place or person they want to study.

Most learning in the 21st century is cooperative — people working together and sharing their diverse talents and expertise. And learning is interactive. The computer does not tell people where to go; it gives them choices. The mid-21st century is not a world of smart machines and stupid people. It is a world of humans who use intelligent machines wisely. Working with each other and with the assistance of teachers, the students — not the computers — are the agents of thinking and learning.

Yes, teachers are still around, but not in the same role, or even with the same name they had in the 20th century. All-purpose teachers for every 30 students are creatures of the past. Today's learners work with instructional designers, curriculum managers, tutors, mentors, coaches.

Every youngster has one adult who guides him or her through the early learning years. This person sees to it that the child masters the fundamentals — the basic skills of reading, math, writing, decision making, and, most important, the skill of learning itself. Learners also work with tutors and other specialists on particular learning projects.

The 21st century has discovered about teachers what teachers learned about students in the late 20th century: One size does not fit all. Just as there are different ways to learn, there are different ways to guide learning. Teachers are no longer the dispensers of knowledge; they are guides to learning. People learn by discovery — by doing, by building, by creating. Teachers are there to help people learn to ask the right questions. To help them learn where and how to find answers. To guide them in applying knowledge.

The traditional school — the building where children come to sit in a classroom with a teacher from 9 to 3 — is a relic of history. There are many places for young people to get together for learning, for play, for both. The learning centers have organized group activities, as well as spaces for individuals to learn on their own. And there are specialized centers for different kinds of play and learning.

We may be indulging in fantasies here, but these are more than idle dreams. The teaching and learning we envision for the future, and the best work that educators and students are doing in schools today, are guided by a genuine respect for the different talents of children and adults. We recognize that not all children are — or learn — alike. We understand that diversity is a source of our strength.

The Current Scene

In this last decade of the 20th century, we are at the beginning of a time of change in the ways that learning, teaching, and schooling are conceived and carried out. In communities all across the country, the traditional patterns of schooling are being questioned. Faculties are examining and reshaping the structures, the schedules, and the cultures of their schools as places for students and teachers to work and learn together. With research support, teachers and principals are reworking curriculum content, revising instructional methods, and redefining the roles of teachers. They are exploring the ways in which students learn. And they are working to forge stronger links between schools, parents, and communities.

For years, exceptional teachers have challenged the timeworn conventions of schooling. Individually, and often at their own risk in a rule-bound school culture, they have arranged schedules and student groupings to organize interdisciplinary programs of study and cooperative learning teams. They have worked as coaches, mentors, and guides to involve students actively in the learning experience. They have found ways to engage the different learning styles and multiple intelligences of children. They have worked with other community agencies and businesses to develop apprenticeships and work-study projects, connecting school learning to the real worlds of work and art.

Taken singly, however, none of these changes will produce the schools our students and this society require. In fact, random implementation could result in even less-effective schools. Schools are *systems*; and adding a new program here, an improved teaching strategy or a new way of assessing growth there, is like prescribing aspirin for a serious illness.

What is needed is systemic change in the four key dimensions of American schools: structure and organization, teaching and learning, curriculum, and assessment and accountability.

Within each of these vast topics, literally hundreds of shifts in thinking and action are required if we are to re-create our schools systemically and systematically for the 21st century. Here are five examples within each of these topics that point to that future:*

---

*For a more complete description of this view of systemic reform, see Robert McClure, "From Reform to Transformation," *Doubts and Certainties* 6, no. 3 (Washington, D.C.: National Education Association, November 1991).

A CONTINUUM OF CHANGE

From a Traditional School System	To a Learning Community

Structure and Organization

• Teacher isolation	• Teacher collaboration
• Centralized decision making	• Site-based decision making inclusive of faculty and staff
• Parents, business people, and others as visitors	• Parents, business people, and others as partners and decision makers
• External "expert" staff-development programs	• Internal shared professional development
• Teacher role viewed as time with students	• Teacher role expanded to include planning, decision making, other professional duties

Teaching and Learning

• Teacher as worker; student as product	• Teacher as leader or facilitator; student as worker
• Students in passive (instructional) settings	• Students in active (constructional) settings
• Isolated, competitive setting for students and teachers	• Cooperative, collegial settings for students and teachers
• Four classroom walls, 50 minutes per subject	• Learning environment flexible as to time and place
• Homogeneous grouping	• Flexible, heterogeneous groups

Curriculum

• Learning in a "school only" context	• Learning in a life context
• Focus on covering content	• Focus on understanding concepts
• Fragmented, separate subjects	• Integrated, holistic learning
• Emphasis on "knowing"	• Emphasis on "learning"
• Standardized content for all	• Individualized programs

Assessment and Accountability

• Priority placed on standardized testing	• Multiple, authentic assessment options for students
• Evaluative reporting systems emphasizing "can't do"	• Descriptive reporting systems emphasizing "can do"
• Judgments based on bell curve	• Every child can and will learn
• Faculty assessment as once a year, top down	• Faculty assessment as continual, collegial, professional development
• School accountability based on standardized test scores	• Accountability measured by meeting output standards

The National Education Association is deeply involved in all of these aspects of school renewal. Through our National Center for Innovation, our National Foundation for the Improvement of Education (NFIE), and our Education Policy and Professional Practice unit, we are working directly in more than 150 participating school communities around the country. Our National Center has three interconnected school reform initiatives: The Mastery in Learning Consortium, involving six school-based reform sites; Learning Laboratories, involving 20 district-wide renewal programs; and the Teacher Education Initiative, which brings universities and colleges together with three state departments of education in programs uniting K-12 and teacher education reforms.

The various NEA and NFIE projects, and the school reforms initiated by our state affiliates across the nation, are all "home-grown." They all have different emphases and specializations, but throughout our work there is a shared vision of the directions that public schools should be taking to provide quality education for all children.

The Legacy

In considering the future of public education, it is instructive to remember that it has been only in the last half-century that America finally established a unitary, universal system of public education offering 12 years of free schooling to children in every state.

Since the *Brown* school-desegregation decisions of 1954-55, our public schools — not only in the South and not only for race-related reasons — have been at the center of the social, economic, and technological changes that have swept across the United States. Every decade has brought new crises; every decade has brought new reforms.

Russia's launching of Sputnik near the end of the Eisenhower era sent shock waves through the nation's defense establishment. With a major infusion of federal funding and federally designed curricula, the public schools initiated a number of innovative programs in math, science, and social studies education during this period; but the reformers showed little awareness that the knowledge and experience of teachers might be helpful either in developing the new materials or in offering feedback about their effectiveness.

The desegregation struggles of the 1960s and 1970s made a battleground of many schools, but they also prompted a greatly increased level of federal investment to promote school mergers and to compensate for generations of neglect of segregated black schools. Head Start, created in the mid-Sixties, is surely one of the most fully documented education success stories of our time.

In the 1960s and 1970s, students, their parents, and many teachers urged a broadening of curriculum to reflect the multicultural nature of our society. And, it turned out, during these years the civil rights movement was contagious, inspiring organized action by various groups — students, faculty, women and girls, disabled students and their parents — to assert their rights to equitable treatment in the schools. Teachers accelerated their campaign to win collective bargaining rights in most areas of the country. Their successes in improving the conditions of teaching and learning had beneficial ripple effects that spread to school districts in nonbargaining states as well.

With the publication of *A Nation at Risk* in 1983, an abrupt halt was called to the so-called "frills" — to "loosening up" curricula and "dumbing down" instruction. The report beckoned the schools back to basics in no uncertain terms. In essence, this was not so much an education report as it was an *economic manifesto*; the most critical issue it seemed to raise was the need for an educated *work force*, not an educated *people*. It ushered in a period of top-down, market-driven school reform proposals. Public debate at this time resounded with calls for "more of the same, screwed down tighter" — greater school accountability, more rigorous curricula, more competency testing for teachers, and higher student scores on standardized tests. "Competition" became the rallying cry of those whose prescription for public school improvement was educational "choice" — tax-supported school vouchers that purportedly would empower students by enabling them to choose their school, public or private, secular or sectarian, and have taxpayers pick up at least part of the tab.

Because this first wave of 1980s reform was driven more by political and economic than by educational imperatives, and because it was led and legislated from the state level and carried out for the most part without teacher involvement, its impact on faculties and students and schools was neither positive nor permanent.

In a *Harvard Educational Review* article in 1987, Harold Howe wrote:

> I doubt that educational excellence can truly be legislated. Instead, I believe that excellence has to be patiently *grown* in schools that are given the resources to nurture that process. . . . These building blocks are teacher morale, student motivation, parental interest, and a humane school environment supportive of learning.[1]

What is our legacy from these last four decades of crisis and reform? Undoubtedly, each wave of change has made its mark.

We have progressed well past the time when multicultural education meant decorating the school with the pictures of dead African-American heroes in an annual celebration of Black History Week. To a far greater degree than a generation ago, textbooks and school curricula today reflect the racial and ethnic diversity of our society, which, with the massive immigration of Hispanic and Asian populations, is vastly more diverse than it was a generation ago. But provincialism and prejudice die hard. In too many schools the history of people of color is still treated as a special, isolated part of the curriculum. We have never succeeded in the full integration of schools, but we can create an integrated curriculum — one that helps students develop a genuine understanding of the experience and achievements of the many races and cultures that inhabit this small planet.

The empowerment of the teaching profession has been sustained, though not without opposition from obdurate anti-unionists. Over the years the development of mature bargaining relationships between employee organizations and school districts has created more democratic school-governing structures throughout the country.

In recent years states and local school districts have struggled to compensate for continuing sharp declines in federal support, coupled with budget crises brought on by recession. The effects are painful for schools everywhere — and ruinous for schools in the most impoverished inner-city and rural areas. Head Start programs, despite their success, serve less than half of our income-eligible 3- to 5-year-old children. The tax inequities that make possible a $12,000 annual per-pupil expenditure in one district and, from the same tax effort, produce only a $3,200 expenditure in another, are unfair and irrational. In essence, we retain a system in which geographic location and local tax base, rich or poor, shape the educational destiny and life chances of our children.

Many teachers and students in the predominantly black and Hispanic schools of the nation's inner cities are living with the "savage inequalities" described so well by Jonathan Kozol: schools without libraries, science labs with little or no lab equipment, windowless rooms, leaking ceilings, peeling paint, layoffs of teachers, elimination of course offerings, classes being held in storage rooms, coat rooms, converted coal bins.

Increasingly, schools are being pressured (and rightly so) to teach higher-order thinking skills, the ability to analyze, reason, synthesize,

81

and apply knowledge in creative, problem-solving ways. And yet the predominant method of student assessment continues to be the standardized multiple-choice test, an instrument that not only fails to measure higher-order thinking skills but may actually impede their development. Teachers do not dispute the need to assess students and hold schools accountable. But they want alternative methods of assessment, procedures that actually advance learning rather than narrow its scope to a rigid, rote skills curriculum. Teachers would like to see assessments based on actual performance, such as portfolios of students' work, instead of multiple-choice and short-answer tests.

In Transition Toward Transformed Schools

The shifting currents of education reform over the past 40 years reveal the stresses of institutional response to the constant push and pull of often opposing forces in our society.

What we have inherited in our public school system is a national treasure — a vast, sprawling, outdated, but still resilient institution. As we work to make it better for all children who are going to live out their lives in the 21st century, we are building upon strength, not weakness.

We also are building upon lessons learned from the successes and failures of the past. One lesson that teachers have long understood is that "legislated learning" and top-down reforms are doomed to failure.

No reform measure, no matter how well intended or how brilliant in theory, can be successfully "grafted on" to the education system by outside authorities without regard for the unique culture of each school. No reform measure will endure as an organic part of the school program without the leadership and commitment of teachers in all stages of its design and implementation.

And no reform measure will be effective if its aim is to impose uniformity on teaching and learning. Students come in infinite variety; few of them will be responsive to standard-issue instruction. This is not to say that the curriculum should be watered down for some students; nor is it an endorsement of tracking — a practice that in the long term intensifies and entrenches learning deficiencies, rather than remedying them. Individualized instruction takes more time than tracking. It demands sensitivity to the diverse interests, strengths, weaknesses, and learning styles of different students. It also requires classes small enough to make possible a supportive learning environment for each student.

What is needed, and what is emerging today, is an authentic approach to school renewal — one that is *school-based, faculty-led*, and *student-centered*.

The following basic operating principles are key to this approach to educational change:

1. *Shifting Authority*: All education, like politics, is local; and all education reforms must be responsive to the unique needs of the local community. The individual school is the appropriate center of authority for development of the educational programs it is responsible for delivering.

2. *Shared Leadership*: Teachers, whose competencies and commitment are key determinants of effective schooling, must be centrally involved in the shaping of education reforms. In cooperation with site administrators, teachers are increasingly the planners of educational change, rather than the objects of externally imposed change. Their experience in organizing as a bargaining unit and acquiring the self-assurance and sophistication to negotiate effectively with school management has been a maturing process for the profession, enabling teachers to participate more effectively in the kinds of collaborative leadership and decision making demanded by school-based reform.

3. *Integration of Research and Practice*: The historic gap between what researchers *study* and what teachers *do* has been narrowed by growing collaboration between colleges and K-12 schools, as well as by technology. Increased use of dialogic telecommunications networking has linked research to practice, while at the same time allowing teachers around the country to share practical ideas for improving their craft. As we have experimented with the computerized School Renewal Network that links our innovative sites with a nationwide electronic network, which will soon be available to the more than two million NEA members, and with cable TV as a medium for teachers across the country to share information on new instructional strategies, we have learned that the interaction of learning theory and teaching practice is synergistic: It contributes to the improvement of instruction and enlivens the work of the theorists with a bracing infusion of classroom reality.

4. *Building School/Home Connections*: The difficulties that complicate the education of some students are inextricably meshed into the fabric of family life; efforts to assist these children are apt to fail unless planners recognize parental circumstances. Teachers are persuaded that the first step in improving educational achievement is for parents to become actively committed to the schooling of their children. Guided by the individual family situation of each student, teachers increasingly are reaching out to involve parents in various ways, through systematic school-home communications (newsletters, telephone contacts, home visits) and through dropout prevention programs and parental gover-

nance or advisory committees. Teachers are enlisting parents as volunteers or paid aides in schools and classrooms, as well as showing them ways to help their own children at home.

What's Needed: An Extended Family of Learning

Children are the poorest Americans. The National Commission on Children reported in 1992 that more than 12 million American children, or about one in five, live in poverty, an increase of more than 2.2 million since 1989. In a 1992 Carnegie Foundation survey, kindergarten teachers reported that one-third of their students come to school not well prepared to learn because of poor health, inadequate nurturing, and language deprivation.

We must start reforming our education system at the ground floor. Education reform must begin before kindergarten if it is ever to achieve its goals. The public schools should be a primary provider of early childhood services because of the professionalism of the public school employee and the accountability and universality of the public school experience. Such services should address the needs of both parents and children and should integrate both day care and education components. Parents should be actively involved in a partnership with teachers in the design, delivery, and evaluation of all childhood services.

Until our nation begins to invest fully and adequately in prenatal care for pregnant women and in health care, day care, and education for the youngest and most vulnerable members of our society, we will never begin to achieve the first and most important of our six National Education Goals: to ensure that all children come to school ready to learn.

We also must recognize that school reform — or even effective traditional schooling — is not something that the schools can do alone. A 1992 Carnegie Foundation report speaks of the social problems that prevent many schools from carrying out their educational purposes:

> The evidence is overwhelming that the crises in education relate not just to school governance but to pathologies that surround the schools. The harsh truth is that, in many communities, the family is a far more imperiled institution than the school, and teachers are being asked to do what parents have not been able to accomplish. Today, the nation's public schools are being called upon to stop drugs, reduce teenage pregnancy, feed students, improve health and eliminate gang violence, while still meeting academic standards. And if they fail anywhere along the line, we condemn them for not meeting our high-minded expectations.[2]

The most important thing that public agencies can do to improve the lives of poor children and their families is to get together for this essential purpose: to establish institutional linkages among schools, families, and social service providers. The school is the logical place in which to center the myriad family and child services that will help make it possible for children to learn.

Our New Jersey Education Association has introduced a bold new agenda for accomplishing just such coordination of school and family services. The association's vision for the future bears excerpting here:

> Our vision of excellence is the community learning center, a program in which children, staff, family, and community members are involved in lifelong learning opportunities.
>
> We believe it's time to redefine the focus of our educational system and provide a comprehensive approach to learning that involves the whole child, the community, and society in general.
>
> Imagine a public school that opens its doors at six in the morning and doesn't close until late in the evening.
>
> Imagine this as a safe haven where working parents can bring their children before leaving for work and know that they will be cared for by professionals.
>
> Imagine a place where children can receive not only the best education, but health care, social services, and counseling opportunities.
>
> Imagine a classroom where parents and children sit side by side *learning how to use computers*. For the adult, this can open doors to new employment. For the child, it can open new horizons for learning and provide the tools for the workplace of the next century.
>
> Imagine a place where children can receive unlimited remedial as well as enrichment programs; a place where they can attend scout meetings, space camps, and dance classes.
>
> Imagine, in this same community learning center, programs for senior citizens, parenting classes, GED, and continuing education programs. . . .[3]

The association's planning is in harmony with programs already under way in New Jersey. The New Jersey School-Based Youth Services Program (SBYSP) is the first statewide effort to place comprehensive social services in or near high schools. At 30 sites throughout the state, SBYSP offers teenagers a comprehensive set of services on a "one-stop-shopping" basis. Each site offers health care, mental health and family counseling, job and employment training, and substance abuse counseling. At many sites, staff and facilities are available for teen parenting education, transportation, day care, tutoring, family planning, and hotlines. The programs operate before, during, and after school, and also during the summer; some operate on weekends.

The New Jersey program also has expanded into seven elementary and middle schools in the state and has been replicated in Iowa and Kentucky.

Among other centers of coordinated school/community services is Longfellow Elementary, a Riverside, California, school and a member of the NEA Mastery in Learning Consortium. Longfellow is located in a neighborhood of high crime, drug, and gang activity. Ninety-five percent of the students qualify for free or reduced-price lunches. Longfellow's Project SMART (Service Management through Action, Responsibility, and Teamwork), working with other community agencies, has centered a broad array of social services at the school. At Longfellow, parents can register for public assistance; they can talk to a bilingual social worker, who is on campus four days a week. The social worker might drive a family member to a job-training session or recommend attendance at a parenting class held at the school site. There are other classes for referral on shopping, money management, and nutritional cooking. Longfellow's early intervention services include Head Start, all-day kindergarten programs, and a 1-to-15 teacher/student ratio in first-grade language arts classes. The school is headquarters for a full-time youth services center counselor, two public health nurses, and a mental health counselor. Through Project SMART, Longfellow encourages families to be part of the school and to come to the school site for all the services they need related to health, safety, security, and nutrition.

Comprehensive school/community partnerships such as these significantly increase the chances of educational productivity for schools — and life achievement for children and their families.

Future Promise

The 1983 Report of the National Commission on Excellence in Education may have misdiagnosed some of the ills of education, and its prescriptions for cure were certainly flawed. Nevertheless, the title of that report still rings with truth: America remains in many ways a nation at risk. The truth that seems to have escaped the commission was the interrelatedness of all the institutions that make up America's communities and influence children's lives.

Surely the true test of our democracy — and of our public schools — is the way in which we respond to the crying need of the children who live in the nation's poorest neighborhoods, wherever they are. This is not to say that only poor children have problems that need special attention from the schools. Young people of every social and economic class suffer from the stresses of contemporary life. It is the responsibility of our schools to be sensitive and responsive to the particular needs of all children — rich, poor, and in-between. We simply must act on the principle that all children are valuable, that all children can learn.

The task before our schools is to prepare every child in America for the challenging world of the 21st century. That world will demand problem-solving skills, the ability to work with other people, and the capacity to continue learning throughout life.

That world demands educational excellence for all. With the election of a President who gives every evidence of caring about children and families, and with the commitment and talent of all members of our education community, we have reason now to believe that we may finally begin to achieve this goal.

Footnotes

1. Harold Howe, "Remarks on Equity and Excellence," *Harvard Educational Review* (May 1987): 199-202.
2. Carnegie Foundation for the Advancement of Teaching, *School Choice: A Special Report* (Princeton, N.J., 1992), p. 76.
3. Keynote speech by New Jersey Education Association President Betty Kraemer to the NJEA Convention, Atlantic City, 5 November 1992.

THE TASK BEFORE US

Albert Shanker

Besides the advantages flowing from national standards and nationally coordinated curricula and assessment, Mr. Shanker, the AFT president who has become a persuasive spokesman for all of public education, sees much to learn from other industrialized countries in such realms as governance, student incentives, accountability, and public policies supporting schools, families, and children.

It often surprises those of us who are familiar with the failings of the American education system that people from other countries find much to admire in it. They are right. In a country of immigrants, education has always been the path to becoming an American. We still educate the great floods of immigrants who come to the United States seeking opportunity. And in our schools, children of various races, ethnic backgrounds, and classes mix as in no other school system. Nowhere else in the world can a student who fails get a second, third, or fourth chance to finish high school and go to college and even graduate school. Nowhere else is such an enormous amount of inquisitiveness and creativity expended on education. This sometimes leads to trendiness and a susceptibility to fads; but it also leads to the accomplishments of a Deborah Meier or a Theodore Sizer and to the inspired teamwork that has created the National Board for Professional Teaching Standards. These are things that the traditional and stable education systems of other countries cannot match.

Nevertheless, our education system has been and continues to be in a state of crisis, which affects our democratic system of government, our values, and our way of life. As the crisis persists, we see the gap between the ideals we profess and what we really are accomplishing — a gap that continues to widen. A generation is growing up unprepared for citizenship, work, and family life.

Some people call for a return to the Golden Age of American education from which we have declined. This is a mistake. If a Golden Age

---

Albert Shanker is president of the American Federation of Teachers.

ever existed, it was for only a small number of people. In fact, our schools are performing, in most respects, better than ever. They are graduating more students — and students who have greater personal problems — than at any time in the past. Unfortunately, we will not succeed merely by doing better than we did in 1920 or 1940. The problem is that our schools are not doing as well as they must do *now* to prepare citizens who can sustain a democratic society and workers who can help our nation compete in a world economy.

Many think that our problems are only with inner-city, poor, and minority youngsters; but we have problems throughout our education system — at all levels and with all students. At one end of the scale, a huge number of students leave school, either as dropouts or as graduates, with such low levels of achievement that they are unprepared for any but undemanding and low-paying jobs. Many are still handicapped by the problems they faced when they entered first grade, and they are almost certain to remain so. At the other end of the scale, the percentage of our graduates who achieve at high levels is the smallest in the industrialized world.[1] Average students, too, compare poorly with their counterparts in other industrialized nations. An enormous number of our youngsters are being shortchanged by our current educational system — and so is our country.

It is true, as some apologists for our education system maintain, that comparisons with other countries are difficult to make and are often imperfect. For example, some international examinations have unfairly compared large and broadly representative groups of U.S. students with smaller and more select groups of students from other countries. Nevertheless, the many careful comparisons that have been made show other countries doing much better with all groups of students — those in the top, middle, and lowest achievement groups. What are they doing and what can we learn from them?

Pulling All One Way

It would be a mistake to think that the education systems in other industrialized countries are all the same. Most of them are doing a good job, but each does it differently. However, there is a common element: They have national standards and national or nationally coordinated curricula and assessments, and their educational systems are directed toward making sure students meet these standards.

National standards are based on a clear and agreed-upon picture of what youngsters leaving secondary school should know and be able to

89

do. In countries with national standards, educators work backward, deciding first what students need to learn and when they need to learn it. They also decide what constitutes excellent, adequate, and failing levels of performance. Youngsters and their parents comprehend these standards. So do teachers. And with the help of parents, they pressure their students to meet them. Textbooks and other materials are tightly focused on giving students the content they need. Also, high stakes are involved in meeting or failing to meet the standards.

Exams go hand in hand with these standards; and unlike our standardized tests, they are based on the curricula that students have been taught. Students are carefully prepared for these exams and study hard to pass them. When they pass, they have a credential that certifies to all concerned – parents, institutions of higher education, future employers – what they know and can do. This contrasts sharply with most of our high school diplomas, which certify primarily that recipients have spent the required amount of time in school and have passed a state minimum competency exam where such exams exist.

Countries with national education standards and examinations also benefit from having a better-prepared teaching force. Once you achieve consensus on standards and examinations for students, you have gone a long way toward answering the question of how you educate and assess teachers: Teachers have to be able to teach curricula that reflect the national standards, and they have to be competent in the various techniques and strategies for teaching these curricula. Our silly and destructive debate about whether it is more important for teachers to know content or pedagogy does not exist in these school systems. Teachers must have a command of subject matter and of how to teach it to youngsters.

Our Chaotic Non-System

In the United States, there is no consensus about what students should know and be able to do except in the most general terms. We generally agree, for example, that students in high school should study English, math, and science. But even for most college-bound students, there is no agreement about what those courses should include or what a student who has taken them should know and be able to do. The answer to these questions will vary according to where you ask them, because our 15,000 school districts and 50 states all have rights and responsibilities in the area of curriculum. Answers could vary even within a

90

school, because when there are no external standards, standards often are set by individual teachers.

This absence of clear and agreed-upon standards leads to a crazy non-system of curricula and requirements and tests. A few commercial textbook series form the basis for the curriculum in many districts. This might be no problem if the texts were excellent, but they are not. Publishers want to sell as many copies as possible, so they try to reflect the varying wishes of state curriculum guidelines, which are usually broad recommendations rather than specific curricula. As a result, the texts are massive, unfocused, and boring.

Standardized tests, which are supposed to be curriculum-neutral (so they can be used in school systems with differing curricula), exercise a powerful and negative influence on the practice of teaching. Because test scores influence public support for schools and teachers, teachers are often under pressure to prepare kids for the tests. As a result, teaching emphasizes test-taking techniques and recognition of lots of meaningless bits of information the tests are deemed likely to require.

In the absence of a specific curriculum, there is enormous variation in what is taught. Even within a school, teachers can never be sure what kids entering their class in September have already been taught. And, of course, a child entering a new school, or even a new class, could spend the rest of the year just trying to figure out what is going on.

If any standards do exist, they are likely to be ad hoc and adjusted upward or downward in a given classroom. Teachers sometimes ask less of certain students than of others because of their socioeconomic or racial or ethnic background. So they offer a watered-down curriculum and shortchange youngsters who could do real work if, as happens in an education system with external standards, they were given the required material and helped to do so.

Sometimes when teachers demand higher standards of their students, the students and their parents complain and put pressure on the teacher to let up. They say the teacher is not being fair because other teachers or schools do not expect that kind of work. However, where there are external standards, the situation is very different. Kids and their parents know what standard a youngster has to meet in order to succeed. And the teacher is seen as a coach — someone who is helping kids — rather than as a nasty person making arbitrary demands. The parents, too, bolstered by the external standards, support teachers in their demands for the hard work needed to meet the standards.

How have we rationalized a system that is so obviously irrational — especially when we can look at the examples of other countries whose students perform so much better than ours? We have told ourselves that education in those countries is under the control of central governments, whereas we value our tradition of local control; that those countries are homogeneous and ours is diverse; and that their education systems are elitist, determining the future lives of kids by testing and tracking, whereas ours is a mass system dedicated to equity.

This formulation is very flattering to us, but it ignores some obvious facts about our education system and the systems of our competitors. The local control we like to talk about has been drastically curtailed in recent years. Most states now pay more of the bill for public education than local districts, so they have taken back a lot of the power and responsibility they originally handed over to localities.

We have seen state takeovers of local systems suffering from "educational bankruptcy," state reform initiatives that imposed wide-ranging new rules and regulations on schools, and, in the case of Kentucky, the court-mandated reorganization of an entire system. Some local school boards themselves seem ready to throw in the sponge: In Chelsea, Massachusetts, the school board handed over control of all of its schools to Boston University. A private company, Education Alternatives, has been hired by local boards to manage a school in Dade County, Florida, and a number of schools in Baltimore, Maryland; and it was asked by the school board in Duluth, Minnesota, to manage its entire school system on an interim basis.

We also have failed to notice that some of our competitor nations are no longer as homogeneous as they once were and that diversity has not kept them from insisting on what students should know and be able to do or lessened popular support for standards. Indeed, French students rioted last year because they feared standards were being relaxed, thus devaluing their hard-earned credentials. Nor are these systems elitist in the way we like to think. Japan, France, Germany, and Korea, for example, are as committed to mass education as we are. These countries have managed to raise both the floor and the ceiling of student achievement, in many cases producing a much larger group of top performers than we do while getting the performance of their poorest students to the level of our average performers.

There has been a massive attack, largely justified, against tracking as it is practiced in the United States. However, it is true that all of the industrialized countries that are doing better than we are also track their students. So the question is not whether to track, but how to do it. Tracking in the United States leads to failure. In other countries, there is tracking for success.

What are the differences? Though we give lip service to egalitarian ideas, we often begin separating children into reading groups as early as the first grade. Few other industrialized countries track or otherwise label children in the early grades. Germany, which starts tracking earlier than most other countries, does not begin until the fifth grade. All these countries track students in high school; but so do we, though we may try to conceal our tracking under the fig leaf of student "choice."

The big difference is that students in most systems with national standards are challenged and stretched no matter what track they are in, so every student gets an education that offers something of value. We generally fail to give youngsters in nonacademic tracks a worthwhile education. For many of these kids — especially the ones in general tracks — school is nothing more than a holding tank. And because of our lack of standards, we are not doing well with kids in the academic tracks, either. Our failures may not be due to the fact that we track but because we do not have high standards and high stakes for all tracks.

"Does It Count?"

Students often ask this question when they are given a homework assignment or an in-class essay to write. It is one we need to take seriously when thinking about our education system and comparing it with the standards-driven systems of other industrialized countries. In these countries, meeting the standards not only counts in school but also is closely linked to what students are able to do when they get out of school. Our students have little incentive to work hard in high school because, as they see it, nothing rides on high achievement. High school graduates have no trouble finding a college that will accept them, even if they have learned little. The only exceptions are youngsters who want to go to elite colleges; they have to work very hard indeed. And students who go to work after graduation find that employers are interested only in whether the kids have diplomas. They seldom ask for a high school transcript and do not care what courses their prospective employees took or the grades they made. In the absence of common standards, this makes sense from the employer's point of view. Grading is often very loose. Furthermore, what an A or B means is likely to vary a great deal from school to school and teacher to teacher; so it is nearly impossible for an employer to interpret what a student's record means.

It is different in other industrialized countries. There, students in the academic tracks work hard to meet the standards because, unless they meet these standards, no college will admit them.[2] But this is not just something for kids who plan to go to college. Hard work brings rewards in nonacademic tracks as well, because there are clear employment standards related to a youngster's achievement of the education standards; how well you do in school counts for what job you get. These systems push all their students in the direction of achievement from the time they begin school until they graduate.

A New Direction

Until recently, we ignored the experiences of other industrialized nations despite what they show about the power of a standards- and stakes-driven education system. However, the National Education Goals that came out of the Education Summit in 1989 have started to change the direction of our discussions about school reform. The goals put student achievement and giving students and schools the capacity to achieve front and center:

> American students will leave grades 4, 8, and 12 having demonstrated competency in challenging subject matter, including English, mathematics, science, history, and geography. . . . (National Education Goal 3)

Admittedly, the goals need further definition. What is "challenging" subject matter and what constitutes a "competent" performance in mathematics for a fourth-, eighth-, or twelfth-grader? We don't have the answers to such questions yet, but at least the goals have prompted us to ask them. And for the first time we are moving in the right direction — toward a standards-driven education system. Also, some observers have raised the question of whether, with all our diversity, we will be able to reach consensus on standards as a nation. While this may be difficult in some subjects, there is no doubt that we can reach national consensus on the ability to read and write well and be able to understand mathematics and solve math problems.

Creating a Different Kind of School

Some people argue that national or state standards and assessments will stifle creativity, force schools to march in lock step, and set back the movement to restructure our schools. (Our failure to have standards until now has certainly not fostered creativity.) Of course this could happen, but it does not have to. To the contrary, new standards and assessments and high stakes could lead to a search for radically different school structures that would be more effective in helping students meet the standards.

American schools that require children to sit still most of the day and to learn mainly by listening do not succeed with most of our students, and they never have. This model of schooling, which has remained relatively unchanged for more than a century, is a leftover from the days when most children were not expected to go beyond eighth grade. We need new kinds of schools that resemble modern workplaces, just as the traditional schools resembled the factories of their time. And we need schools that incorporate recent knowledge about the way children learn and that are designed to educate every child, not just those who fit into the current school model. Such schools will take into account the multiple intelligences that psychologists such as Robert Sternberg and Howard Gardner have described and that schools, as they currently are organized, largely ignore.

Unfortunately, in spite of enthusiastic support in many places, radical change is difficult and slow. Many of the schools and school districts that have been working to restructure themselves have proceeded on the assumption that, if the command structure in school districts were remade so people in individual schools had the power to decide how learning should be organized, enormous improvements in student achievement would automatically follow. This has not happened. We undoubtedly were expecting too much too soon. It may also be that, in the absence of accepted goals, some restructuring teams have spent much of their time debating what their goals ought to be or have adopted too many goals to be effective in achieving them. With agreement about what students should know and be able to do, schools could become centers of inquiry about how best to meet the goals.

Support for restructuring will mean giving the people involved a freedom and flexibility that is difficult to attain under current school rules. Many of these rules came about because the administration and the teacher union did not trust each other. But whatever their original purpose, school rules can be a terrible roadblock to experimentation; and (with the exception of regulations dealing with civil rights, health, and safety) they must be relaxed if restructuring, or even significant change in our traditional schools, is to take place.

Support for restructuring also means giving staff substantial time and resources to plan and make changes. There is no chance that a school staff and administration will be able to carry out a restructuring effort with committees pulled together in free periods or in committee members' spare time. They will need time to read widely, to think and talk together, as well as opportunities to observe or learn about current and past experiments with restructuring, such as we see in Montessori schools, schools in the Coalition of Essential Schools, and the German Holweide school.

Restructuring will not succeed unless there is a commitment to on-going staff development. It is pathetic that an enterprise devoted to education places so little value on educating its employees. Workers in the Saturn plant, where General Motors and the United Autoworkers have developed a new process for manufacturing an automobile, spend 5% of their time (or at least 92 hours a year) in training; 5% of their pay depends on their completing this training.[3] The Saturn management team understands that you cannot restructure a manufacturing process or the way employees have always worked without giving people extensive and continuing training. This is no less true for schools. Some companies provide positive incentives as well as the time in which to upgrade skills by offering pay-for-knowledge. If we expect teachers in restructured schools to expand their teaching repertoires and become familiar with the many alternatives to whole-class teaching, such as team teaching, cooperative learning, peer tutoring and seminars, and the use of computer technology, we will have to devote resources similar to those that successful businesses devote to retraining their employees.

Restructuring lags behind what we hoped for, but we knew that the process would be neither quick nor easy. One thing has become clear, however: Restructuring in the absence of specific goals, that is, something more concrete than the agreeable "improving student achievement," is like a meeting without an agenda — an unnecessarily slow, difficult, and frustrating experience in which goodwill often becomes cynicism. Rather than derailing restructuring, national or state standards can provide the substance and focus that often has been missing.

Saturn and the Cadillac

It is unrealistic to think that all, or even most, schools will try to re-structure themselves. These efforts will take place in a relatively small number of schools. In many others there is no interest in this kind of reform. The people involved — teachers, parents, and other communi-ty members — prefer traditional schools. And if we concentrate all our energies on creating new models in a few schools, what happens to youngsters who still go to these traditional schools? Isn't it criminal to expect the vast majority of our students simply to mark time while we experiment with various ways of restructuring a comparatively small number of schools? There is a much better alternative. Most schools in other industrialized countries are performing much better than ours, and generally they are what we would consider traditional schools. This means that those who work in traditional schools should not wait for the development of restructured schools; they should start work immediately to create more successful traditional schools. Indeed, we need to work on both kinds of schools, substantially improving the schools we have while at the same time working to create new models.

General Motors and the United Auto Workers are doing something like this. One of the first steps they took in developing the Saturn automobile was to throw away the old manufacturing process. This was a big risk; they might have created an Edsel. In fact, they have produced a car that, while not revolutionary, is a big success. And they are continuing to work on it. But no matter how good the Saturn is, many GM buyers will never want one. They will continue to prefer a traditional model, such as the Cadillac. GM knows this, so it has continued working to change and improve these traditional cars and the traditional manufacturing process that builds them. We must do this with our schools, too.

Improving Traditional Schools

Successful school systems in other industrialized countries are all different, but they share certain characteristics. They are all made up of a number of elements that are interconnected and push in the same direction. Here are some common elements that should be incorporated into our new traditional schools to give them this kind of coherence.

1. *Standards, curriculum frameworks, and assessments.* Though we do not yet have national standards or curriculum frameworks and assessments to support them — and may not for some time — this is not an excuse for waiting until they are in place to start raising standards in our traditional schools. States and districts can begin by adopting the best of the new curricula and curriculum frameworks currently available and helping and pushing everyone in the system to work within them. The National Council of Teachers of Mathematics has developed such a curriculum framework, and California has developed outstanding curriculum frameworks in history and language arts.

We also should use the best kinds of assessments currently available, ones that test students' grasp of a body of material rather than how well they do in relation to other students. The assessments based on

97

California's curriculum frameworks are one example. And there are older models that should be used while assessments that relate to the new curriculum frameworks are being developed. They include the Advanced Placement and International Baccalaureate exams and the older New York State Regents examinations.

2. *Teachers.* Since students are unlikely to meet high standards if their teachers are not adequately prepared, we will need to raise the knowledge and skill levels of many teachers when we raise student standards.

The observation about the poverty of staff development made in connection with restructuring holds for traditional schools as well. We should consider a pay-for-knowledge strategy that some businesses use as an incentive to get their employees to learn needed skills. Pay-for-knowledge, which is based on proving that you have mastered the material in question rather than on simply taking courses, could be used as an incentive to get teachers to qualify in areas of shortage as well as to upgrade their knowledge and skills in line with the new standards. It also could be used to encourage teachers to seek certification from the National Board for Professional Teaching Standards, which is developing standards and performance-based assessments designed to identify highly accomplished teachers.

3. *Student grouping.* Part of the reason for the hot ideological debate about student grouping in this country may be that we have not been very successful with either heterogeneous or homogeneous grouping. When we group students homogeneously, only students in the top track get challenging material that will teach them anything worth knowing. When we group students heterogeneously, we tend to teach to the middle group, with the result that the bottom third is lost and the top third is bored. There are, however, successful examples of both heterogeneous and homogeneous systems. We must determine the conditions under which homogeneous and heterogeneous grouping are successful in maximizing student achievement and the conditions under which they fail.

There are techniques for successfully using whole-class, direct teaching with a heterogeneous group. Harold Stevenson and James Stigler give a striking example of this practice in Asian elementary schools in their book, *The Learning Gap*.[4] But generally speaking, heterogeneous grouping is most likely to be successful if there is relatively little teacher talk and if the school is organized around individual student work or the work of subgroups within the class. For example, it would have been foolish for a teacher in a one-room schoolhouse to try to teach

98

the whole class together, because students could range from first through eighth or twelfth grades. So students worked individually or in small groups under the supervision of the teacher. However, if teachers are going to talk a great deal and cover lots of ground, classes must be grouped homogeneously so that students can follow together.

Where there is homogeneous grouping, we should follow the practices of other countries. Students there are grouped on the basis of achievement (a combination of effort, ability, and level of development) and *not* on the basis of someone's judgment about their innate ability. For the most part, students are not grouped in elementary school, even within classes; they all are given the same work and are pressed and helped to do it. At the point where students are grouped, youngsters in every group are given work that is very challenging to them and is designed to encourage them to learn to the maximum of their abilities. As in boxing, there may be lightweights, middleweights and heavyweights, but they all are boxers and all have to work hard to stay in the game.

There must be chances for students to move to other groups, depending on how well or how poorly they do — which is not common practice in other countries. And we should encourage the practice of grouping students differently for different subjects to reflect different strengths and weaknesses.

4. *Student incentives.* Some people think that if we nurture students' love of learning, we will not need any external incentives. That's a nice idea, but it doesn't work for adults and it won't for students. Suppose Congress passed a law tomorrow saying that we could all get our pay and benefits without coming to work. A few people would still show up, but most would not. That is what we do when we give kids what they want without their having to do anything to earn it. And then we wonder why they don't work hard at learning.

Students in other countries work hard because they know they cannot get what they want without working. They will be tested on what they have been taught, and how well they achieve will determine whether they get into college or what kind of job they get. Assessments without stakes do not mean much — or as the kids say, "They don't count."

High stakes do not make sense in elementary school, where students are unlikely to understand or be motivated by distant consequences. But by the time they are in high school, most youngsters have an idea about what they hope to do after they graduate: They have long-term goals. High-stakes assessments will motivate them, and these assess-

99

ments should be the major factor in qualifying for college and for better jobs at better wages.

Our low college-entry standards should be raised gradually over a period of 12 to 15 years — the time it takes for a kindergarten class to reach college — until they correspond with standards in other industrialized countries. The college graduation rates of other industrialized countries lead us to believe that we would not reduce the number of college graduates if we introduced high standards. Students who do not meet four-year-college standards should have community college, technical school, and other continuing education opportunities.

Students who do not meet entrance requirements for college when they graduate from high school must have an opportunity to meet them later on. It is important that we continue to offer multiple chances for success.

5. *The other half.* Our system devotes enormous resources to college-bound students, but we neglect high school graduates who go immediately to work. These young people need and deserve at least the same investment of resources as college-bound students get. We must establish school-to-work links for them as well as other opportunities for ongoing education in community colleges, technical schools, on-the-job training, and the like.

Employers also will have to do more for young workers than they are now doing. Most of the relatively small investment our businesses make in training goes to courses for executives. Businesses say they do not want to spend money on their other employees because many will move on to other jobs. And unless every business offers training, the ones that do are at a competitive disadvantage. Other industrialized countries have solved this problem by requiring all businesses to invest a certain percentage of their payroll in training *all* of their employees. Thus, if they lose employees they have trained, these people will be replaced by employees trained elsewhere. We should pass similar legislation.

6. *A note on accountability.* The accountability system in other industrialized countries is limited to high stakes for students. In the United States there has been little call for stakes for students but many proposals for rewards and punishments for adults. Fortunately, simple-minded notions of merit pay are no longer under consideration. They have been replaced by public-private school choice and competition. Such competition clearly will not raise academic achievement. In the absence of standards and high stakes for students, few people will choose schools

that get their kids to work the hardest. Convenience, friendship, athletics, popularity, good marks for little work, and safety are the reasons that dominate. The ability of schools to attract students has little to do with their ability to educate them.

Far more likely to bring positive results than choice and voucher systems are incentives for adults that would provide rewards to entire schools that substantially raise student achievement from the level where it started. Give help to schools that do not improve student achievement and, ultimately, close down the lowest-achieving schools and start them over again. Here, professionals would be rewarded for improving student achievement rather than for luring students.

Outside Problems

Creating our own version of a standards- and stakes-driven system is a way of mobilizing all the resources we put into education toward the goal we seek: raising student achievement to acceptable levels. A standards-driven system is particularly attractive because it is consistent with efforts both to seek new models for our schools and to improve traditional schools. In fact, answering the most basic question in education — What do we want our students to know and be able to do? — would probably strengthen these efforts.

Unfortunately, our schools face some extremely serious problems that have nothing to do with teaching or standards or curricula. These problems, pertaining to school governance, public policy relating to school finance, children and families, and school discipline, are not going to disappear because we adopt national standards. They are also likely to stand in the way of any big changes we try to bring about in our schools, either by creating new models or improving our traditional schools. Here again, the practice and conditions in other countries offer a stark contrast to ours. Unfortunately, they do not offer a lot of guidance in dealing with these problems.

1. *School governance*. Schools in other industrialized nations are managed by professionals, and that is what is supposed to happen here. However, school boards often interfere in the running of their school district. This tendency to micromanage is a major impediment to improving U.S. schools.

School board members do not spend their time looking over the superintendent's shoulder because they are bad or unworthy people. It is just that they want to get re-elected, and the way they can stay in the public eye is by commenting on how the schools are being run and pointing out any mistakes the superintendent makes. As a result, superintendents who want to keep their jobs are likely to manage their school districts defensively. Mishaps are more likely to occur when someone is trying something new than when maintaining routines. So superintendents are unlikely to be risk takers and are unlikely to encourage risk-taking in their subordinates.

John Chubb and Terry Moe, voucher supporters and authors of *Politics, Markets and America's Schools* (Brookings Institution, 1990), blame school failure on the democratic control of schools. But is it only the democratic control practiced in the United States that has this effect? If other countries can have democratic control and high achievement, so can we. We need to experiment with school governance that maintains democratic control but that allows professionals to operate the schools. If school boards like Chelsea and Baltimore can contract with outside institutions to run their schools and offer them the freedom to do so, why can't other school boards contract with professionals from within their systems and give them the same freedom?

2. *Public policies supporting schools, families, and children.* We are often told that the United States has the highest level of spending on elementary and secondary education in the world. This is not the case. Other industrialized countries spend about the same percentage of their GNP on education (kindergarten through postsecondary); but since we spend more on higher education than they do, we spend less proportionally on elementary and secondary education. This relative neglect of elementary and secondary education guarantees that many students going into college will be unprepared and will require extensive remediation. Thus it is one reason for the lowering of standards in our colleges and universities.

However, the amount we spend on elementary and secondary education is not the only issue; there is also the way we divide it. Most of these other systems are national or state systems, so they spend about the same amount of money per child whether the child lives in a wealthy suburb or a miserable slum. And they provide either the same resources for all schools or additional resources for schools that have many children in need. In the United States the expenditure depends on local real estate values, the wealth of the community, and the politics behind school funding formulas. Children in poverty often go to miserable schools that do not meet even minimum standards of decency.

The frequently disgusting conditions in the schools attended by children of the poor have been well documented, but no one has described them as vividly as Jonathan Kozol in his book, *Savage Inequalities*. In New York City, he visited a school where the staircase became a waterfall when it rained and where blackboards were so badly damaged that teachers feared youngsters would cut their hands if they did board-work.[5] Many schools did not even have enough books. A history teacher with 110 students had 26 textbooks, some of which were missing the first 100 pages.[6] And close by all these schools were districts where computers in abundance, well-stocked libraries, Olympic-size swimming pools, and other luxuries were taken for granted.

It may not be politically possible in our system to reach absolute equality in school spending, but we should have a set of high minimum standards that would guarantee that no schools operate under the horrible conditions described in *Savage Inequalities*.

Whatever we do in schools will not be enough. Other countries recognize this and help children become better students by offering them assistance outside school as well. Our first National Education Goal, "All children will start school ready to learn," shows that we understand this need; but unlike other industrialized nations, we have social policies that do little to help children or support families.

In France, for example, there is a national health plan that covers everyone, generous family-leave legislation, and a public child-care and preschool system. French public policy in this area is based on the belief that society owes "a welcome to every child." We know how different things are in our country, how our youngest and poorest citizens are unlikely to get the kind of medical and child-care services they need. Indeed, they are all too likely to start school already so far behind their more privileged peers in mental, physical, and psychological development that they are at serious risk of never catching up.

Government alone cannot solve these problems. There are things that only families can do for their children. Nevertheless, there are concrete steps that government can and should take — for example, providing family and medical leave, making sure that health care is available for all children, offering inoculations, improving the quality of and expanding access to Head Start and other preschool programs, ensuring follow-up in the schools, and expanding intergenerational literacy and parent-education programs.

3. *School discipline.* Some of our schools experience horrible violence: a child shot on his way into school, a devoted principal killed while looking for a child he believed to be in trouble. But even schools where nothing like that has happened are often places where there is

103

constant disruption. All you need in a class is one kid who torments other kids or upsets the class by shouting obscenities at the teacher to make sure no work gets done. This is why many parents send their children to private or parochial schools. It's not necessarily that they think private or parochial schools are academically superior, but that they know these schools do not accept disruptive children and expel any child who gives them too much trouble.

Schools in other industrialized countries are relatively safe and free from the disruptions that are a daily occurrence in too many of our schools. Instead of supporting an often mistaken view of students' rights — by which is meant the right of a few disruptive students to make it all but impossible for teachers to teach and students to learn — the legal systems in these countries support school regulations that are needed to maintain a proper educational atmosphere.

Why don't we do that? Is it because taking legal steps to expel such youngsters is too time-consuming and expensive? Or because of political pressures? Or because of a belief that there is no such thing as a bad boy (only bad adults — bad teachers and bad principals)? Of course, there are kids who misbehave because they are going through a rough time; their problems are short term. I am not talking about them but about the ones who consistently make life a misery and a danger for teachers and other pupils, the ones whose behavior is way beyond anything schools can deal with. What is it that keeps schools from moving quickly to get these kids out?

It is time to deal with what has made many of our schools the most disorderly and the least safe in the industrialized world. If we don't, vouchers will come. Some worry that we will not help disruptive youngsters or their communities if we simply throw them out onto the street, and that is true. We need to provide special facilities for these youngsters. Some also worry that African-American and other minority children will suffer disproportionately if current rulings about school expulsion and related matters are set aside. Great care should be taken that minority children are not discriminated against in such proceedings. But just as crime in our society disproportionately affects minorities, so we must remember that minority children suffer disproportionately in classrooms where disorder and even violence make it impossible for learning to go on.

The problems relating to public policy and school discipline affect our poorest children most severely. This often means that students in poor circumstances, who have the greatest need of a good education, are least likely to get it. If there were easy answers to these problems, perhaps we would already have found them. If we do not find them, we risk consigning a whole group of youngsters to the trash heap.

The Common School

There has recently been an enormous and frightening surge of nationalism and religious and ethnic strife throughout the world. Groups that have lived together in relative peace now call themselves enemies and attack each other. At the same time, our own increasingly diverse society has become more divided. There is greater insistence on what divides people than on what draws them together. But continuing the agenda of the common school, the idea that children of all races, religions, classes, and national backgrounds should get a common education and learn to live together in a diverse, democratic society, is as important as ever. This means an emphasis on learning history, civics, and the principles and practices of democracy. It means learning about the contributions of all peoples to our multicultural society. It means teaching history accurately, with pride in our national achievements but also awareness of our past sins and present shortcomings. It also means opposition to those curricula and programs that pit groups against each other and stress *pluribus* more than the *unum*.

It is also an era of incredible commercial specialization. Products to satisfy every conceivable taste, are marketed. General magazines are disappearing, replaced by magazines for particular groups: hang-glider enthusiasts, vegetarians, semi-automatic gun owners. There is talk of a 500-channel cable TV system. What we see in the works is a society in which nobody will ever need to come in contact with anyone who has different ideas or interests from his own.

Voucher supporters say we need schools that fit in with this era of specialization and heightened ethnicity and nationalism. They talk about "niche schools" created to give a particular group of parents exactly what they want for their children. They talk about schools for "like-minded" individuals. This is a dangerous direction in which to go. Our society and our civic culture were built on the meeting and clashing and compromising of people with very different ideas and values. To the degree that we are strong, it is because we have learned to learn from each other. As technology and increased nationalism move people toward greater diversity, it is important to support public education as an institution that will pull them together. There are many examples in the world today to show us what the alternative looks like.

105

Footnotes

1. The number of 17-year-olds who score in the highest categories of the National Assessment of Educational Progress (NAEP) exams is always less than 10%, even though these exams are not very demanding. For example, to reach the highest category in math, a student has to be able to solve multistep problems and handle beginning algebra. In 1988, less than 6% of U.S students reached this level. To reach the highest level in writing, a student has to produce written material that goes "beyond the essential." Only 4% of U.S. students reached this level in 1990 when asked to handle an assignment like this: "After reading a paragraph on the food eaten by pioneers, write an essay discussing the reasons for the differences" (Educational Testing Service, *Performance at the Top: From Elementary Through Graduate School*, Princeton, N.J., 1991, pp. 17, 19).

   Comparisons with other industrialized countries cannot be exact because the assessments in these countries are not the same as ours and because students work harder and take more demanding courses. However, their exam results give us a pretty good indication of how many of their students would be able to reach NAEP's top categories. French students taking the *baccalaureat* exam write long essays in subjects such as history, geography, French, and philosophy. The German *Abitur* consists of written and oral exams in four subjects covering three broad categories. Would students who can pass these exams reach the top categories in NAEP? Undoubtedly. How many do so? In Germany, 30% of all 19-year-olds pass the *Abitur*. In France, 67% of all 15- to 16-year-olds were enrolled in college-track secondary schools in 1990; 50% of the total number of 15- to 16-year-olds took the *baccalaureat* and 38.5% passed (Max A. Eckstein and Harold J. Noah, "How Hard Are the Examinations? International Comparisons," paper presented at the September 1990 conference of the Office of Educational Research and Improvement in Washington, D.C.; and National Endowment for the Humanities, *National Tests: What Other Countries Expect Their Students to Know* (Washington, D.C., 1991), pp. 9, 10. Figures were compiled before German reunification and refer to West Germany only).

2. *National Tests* gives some specimen questions from school-leaving exams in other industrialized countries that are useful in indicating the standards of achievement in these countries. For example, one of the questions in a recent history/geography *bac* asked French students to spend two hours discussing "The Evolution of Domestic Policy in the Soviet Union from 1953 to Today." Or they could have chosen to write about the development of the American presidency since 1945 or European resistance to the Nazis between 1939 and 1945 (*Tests*, pp. 11, 12, 14). A question on general history in the 1989 *Abitur* asked German students to discuss "The Weimar Republic and National Socialism" by describing "the political conflicts that

106

took place at the national level between the proclamation of the republic and the opening of the constitutional assembly" and determining "political convictions" from the excerpt of a speech (*Tests*, p. 31). U.S. students taking the SAT were faced with such questions as:

> Choose the word or phrase that is most nearly opposite in meaning to the word in capital letters . . .
>
> PROPENSITY: (A) punctuality (B) aversion (C) ability to guess (D) lack of courage (E) grace in movement

(The College Entrance Examination Board, *10 SATS, Plus Advice on How to Prepare for Them*, New York, 1990, p. 73).

3. Beverly Geber, "Saturn's Grand Experiment," *Training* (June 1992): 29.
4. Harold W. Stevenson and James Stigler, *The Learning Gap: Why Our Schools Are Failing and What We Can Learn from Japanese and Chinese Education* (New York: Summit, 1992), pp. 174-91.
5. Jonathan Kozol, *Savage Inequalities: Children in America's Schools* (New York: Harper Perennial, 1992), p. 37.
6. Ibid., p. 37.

QUICKENING THE PACE: THE NEED FOR FASTER IMPROVEMENT IN PUBLIC EDUCATION

Ted Sanders

A state superintendent of schools summarizes the progress U.S. schools have made since A Nation at Risk, *specifies what remains to be done, and lists five requirements for success in doing it.*

Ten years ago, the National Commission on Excellence in Education stunned the American public with its solemn declaration that the United States was "a nation at risk." Its report spoke of fading American competitiveness in the world marketplace, an eroded culture, and a betrayal of the promise to give all of the nation's people "a fair chance and the tools for developing their individual powers of mind and spirit to the utmost."[1]

Almost everywhere the commission looked, it found some weakness or failure in education to decry. Low SAT scores, widespread functional illiteracy, underqualified teachers, inadequate curricula, insufficient time-on-task, and poor performances by U.S. students on international comparisons of student achievement were all cited as evidence that the risk was real. The commission said its recommendations for change promised "lasting reform" and would require "time and unwavering commitment" from people outside as well as inside the school community.[2]

Five years later, *Newsweek* magazine, in an article titled "A Nation Still at Risk," examined what had been done nationwide in response to the national commission's report. It found that all 50 states had attempted in some way to improve their education systems. Most of those state efforts, such as increases in high school graduation requirements and mandated competency tests for new teachers, had not required dramatic changes in their manner of doing business. *Newsweek* ac-

---

Ted Sanders is superintendent of public instruction, State of Ohio, Columbus.

knowledged that there were some signs of "significant progress" to report, most notably a 16-point recovery in SAT scores since 1980. But it also lamented continued shortcomings, particularly in math and science achievement, and pointed out that students at the bottom of the heap had been largely untouched by the reforms.[3]

In a recent *Phi Delta Kappan* (October 1991) article, Gerald Bracey argues that "American schools have never achieved more than they currently achieve," and in some respects are "performing better than ever." Bracey takes aim at many of the findings that originally moved the national commission to make its dire assessment. He notes, for example, that when GED completers are taken into account, the proportion of Americans who hold a high school diploma or its equivalent jumps from about 75% up to the 85% to 90% range. Similarly, Bracey finds that test scores among American students are not all that bad. Standardized norm-referenced test scores have risen steadily since the mid-1970s, he asserts, while scores on tests administered by the National Assessment of Educational Progress (NAEP) have done no worse that remain stable. As for the SAT, Bracey explains that changes in the characteristics of test-takers, rather than poor schooling, have kept scores from reaching the heights they once did.[4]

The arguments put forth by the National Commission on Excellence in Education, by *Newsweek*, and by Gerald Bracey serve to amplify a basic fact: At any given time, it is possible to identify a great number of things that are right or wrong with America's public schools. Public education is, after all, a vast multibillion-dollar enterprise than encompasses some 41 million students in classes taught by almost 2.4 million teachers and supported by about two million staff workers in 84,538 schools operating in 15,358 districts.[5] Not only is it a huge enterprise, it is also very diverse. It reaches into the inner city as well as remote rural communities, and it touches people from every ethnic group and socioeconomic level. Students – just by themselves – contribute to this diversity in no small measure with their different abilities, interests, learning styles, and degrees of motivation. Given these characteristics of our public education system, it is not surprising that almost any assessment of that system gives us a mixed picture.

But missed as it may be, the condition of public education in America over the last few years does lead me to draw a conclusion that has broad implications: Public education in America is improving, but the improvement is not systemic enough nor fast enough to meet the needs of a dynamic and increasingly global society.

Key Areas of Concern

Consider the following four key areas of concern:

1. *Literacy.* NAEP figures show that over the last 20 years, average reading proficiency has held steady for 9- and 13-year-olds and increased somewhat for 17-year-olds. At the same time, ETS figures reveal that young adults (21-25 years old) have achieved a 97% basic literacy rate, meaning that they can understand and use information contained in texts such as newspapers and pamphlets. No one would seriously dispute that these are positive developments.[6]

However, despite positive reports from the NAEP and others in the testing industry that we are holding our own in reading and adult literacy, future prospects are bleak. That is because just holding our own may not be enough to give us the highly skilled work force that America needs in order to compete successfully in the world marketplace. A growing number of jobs require an ability to interrelate ideas and make generalizations or to summarize and explain facts drawn from specialized reading materials. Such abilities call for literacy beyond the basic level.

2. *SAT Scores.* Since 1975 every subpopulation taking the SAT has shown improvement. White and Asian students continue to outperform other students, but the gap is narrowing. According to the Sandia National Laboratories, the fact that SAT scores have declined about 5% over this period results from the fact that "a more diverse, lower-performing group of test takers is being added to the traditional pool of test takers."[7]

However, even if Sandia is correct and lower SAT scores do not reveal a decline in the effectiveness of public education, they are still a source of concern. Given the pressing need within the emerging global society for higher-order thinking skills, communication skills, and technological know-how, today's college-bound students must be better prepared for higher education than ever; they are likely to suffer if the present generation of college students can do no better than match the performance levels of previous generations.

3. *Mathematics Proficiency.* Between 1973 and 1990, average mathematics proficiency improved slightly for 9- and 13-year-olds and held steady for 17-year-olds. During this period, black and Hispanic youth narrowed the gap in mathematics proficiency with their white peers. Meanwhile, during the last 11 years, the total number of Advanced Placement calculus examinations taken has increased fourfold.[8]

However, at age 13, American students' knowledge of mathematics and science is well behind that of students from both Europe and Asia.

In fact, fewer than one out of every five American students in grades 4, 8, and 12 has reached the national education goal of demonstrating competency in mathematics. And despite the relevance of mathematics to economic competitiveness, technological advancement, and lifelong learning, many schools still are not treating it as an instructional priority.[9]

4. *Delivery of Educational Services*. Schools are doing a better job of meeting the special needs of students than they have in the past. Students with disabilities are having more doors opened for them, and at-risk youngsters are being reached through an ever-growing number of initiatives. In Ohio, for example, state funding for the federal Head Start program has enabled us to make preschool available to an additional 6,700 eligible young children.[10] Another Ohio program — Graduation, Reality, and Dual-Role Skills — is helping pregnant students and young parents complete high school and learn important child-rearing skills.

However, even with these expanded services, many students still "fall through the cracks." Preschool opportunities for disadvantaged children may be increasing, but we still have a long way to go before 100% participation is achieved. Large numbers of gifted students also are not being identified and properly served. And then there are the students described by Arthur G. Powell, Eleanor Farrar, and David K. Cohen as "unspecial"; that is, "average 'nice' kids with low motivation." In their book, *The Shopping Mall High School*, these three educators note that unspecial students, lacking forceful advocates or special opportunities, often drift aimlessly through school, unaware of the guidance and other resources that could be made available to them. As one counselor put it, unspecial students "are the ones who with the right pushing can take off and fly, but without it simply fall back and get nothing done."[11]

What can be done to increase the pace of school improvement? The problem is not so much one of quality as it is one of design. Our education system, despite a decade of reform, is still structured essentially the same as it was at the beginning of the century. For example:

- Learning is still largely an individual function confined to a classroom where all students automatically are given the same amount of time to learn new material, even though some students need more (or less) time to achieve mastery.
- Teachers still serve primarily as dispensers of knowledge to students who advance toward graduation through a lockstep system of grade levels.

- Clear curriculum goals have yet to be set; leadership still largely comes down from the top and seldom involves the creativity and spirit of local schools.
- The duration of school days and school years has yet to change.
- Most schools continue to operate in a system that does not demand accountability for results.

Moving from the Traditional Model

Clearly, we need to move away from the traditional school model. We need to do this not because the traditional school has failed, but rather because it has now done its job. Public education has played an indispensable role in making the United States the world leader it is today. The richness of our culture, the industrial might that sustained us during World War II and the Cold War, and the inventive genius that gave us mass-produced automobiles, microwave ovens, photocopying machines, and trips to the moon all had their origin in the children prepared by our public schools.

These schools were magnificently geared to the needs of a society that operated according to the routines of the farm and the factory, a society where change occurred slowly and where a basic knowledge of the Three R's was enough to guarantee success in the job market. Now we find ourselves living in a global society characterized by rapid change, high technology, collaborative action, and a vastly expanding volume of information. We need a new type of school tailored to the demands of the modern world, one that prepares students to survive and thrive within its complexity.

Key features of the new school might include the following:

1. Artificial age and ability groupings are eliminated; students become part of a supportive learning community that includes children of many ages and ability levels, as well as many adults. In this environment, learners often work independently or in groups of various sizes, focusing on the accomplishment of real-life objectives. Learners are no longer expected to master academic content according to some predetermined timetable that makes no allowance for individual differences. Instead, they move from basic to advanced skill levels at their own speed, bolstered by instruction that is directed to their individual learning style.

2. An individual plan of instruction guides the learning of each student. Students are largely responsible for pursuing their own learning. Promotion is based on performance assessed through multiple means, in-

cluding written tests, oral presentations, skill demonstrations, and portfolios.

3. Teachers, though still occasionally dispensing knowledge, more commonly serve as facilitators of learning who are continuously involved with assisting performance. Often working in teams, they promote the investigation of ideas, identify resources, make connections between new knowledge and previous knowledge, and provide timely feedback on learner performance.

4. The boundaries between traditional academic subjects are less rigid and are replaced by transdisciplinary themes. Student work ties in to a simplified core curriculum that covers less ground than the traditional curriculum but at greater depth. Much of what learners do addresses authentic projects, problems, and issues of concern to the community.

5. Computers and other innovative technologies are used to enhance both administration and instruction. Report cards are replaced with detailed, computerized records of each learner's progress and achievement. In classrooms, computers are used to design projects, solve problems, and create entire information systems.

6. Schooling takes place outside of the school building more often, and the larger community has a sustained presence in the school. Students have access to individual multimedia workstations, laboratories, libraries, conference facilities, and nature preserves. Schools themselves stay open more hours each day, seven days a week, 12 months a year.

7. School governance is characterized by a decentralization of decision making within a framework of clear goals, accountability for results, and fewer state and federal regulations. The school and community together are accountable for educational achievement.

Four Essentials for Transformation

Changing our schools in these ways will give us an education system that is in closer harmony with the work and cultural patterns of our society. The transformation will carry a high price in time, energy, and money. Resistance from many well-meaning people should be expected. We can dispel some of their misgivings about radical change by going about the process in a deliberative manner.

First, everyone must know that we are not tampering with a well-oiled machine that is working effectively in the interests of our children. On the contrary, we are dealing with an institution that, in its present form, cannot deliver what this and future generations of students require. People also must know that we are beyond the point where some minor adjustments in the status quo will be enough to turn things around.

Second, we must be firm and clear about our commitment to the values that underlie schooling in a democratic society and make sure that these values are reflected in policies and practices. Among these values are that the best schools serve all children equally well; and schools that serve all children will recognize that, although different, all children 1) are capable of learning, 2) must be offered rich opportunities, 3) must be held to rigorous intellectual standards, and 4) must be expected to succeed.

Third, we must constantly seek to develop a range of strategies that give us the power to address underlying problems. In formulating these strategies, educators should draw on solid theory, research, and professional experience. At the same time, however, they should feel free to ignore conventional wisdom and take risks. The strategies that emerge should be analyzed and debated, and those that withstand scrutiny should be tested in the field. If found to be valid, they should be shared throughout the education community.

Fourth, we must be patient. As Michael Fullan and Suzanne Stiegelbauer point out, "educational change is technically simple and socially complex."[12] It involves a number of variables that cannot be fully controlled, even with careful planning. We also should remember that because it is so complex, education change usually emerges in small increments and can be experienced unevenly at different levels of the education community. It may be possible, for example, to engineer a sweeping overhaul in the infrastructure and organization of our schools, yet have trouble changing the assumptions and beliefs that, in the long run, determine their effectiveness. Similarly, school and classroom rhythms and routines may be changed, while power relationships among members of the school community remain essentially intact. It will be challenging, to say the least, to keep the unfolding of change on an even keel and to ensure that change in one part of the education community does not generate frustration or unrealistic expectations in another part.

Conclusion

Americans who are born and raised in the next century should live in a society that is better than the one we are living in now. And the only way to ensure that is to give the current generation an education that is geared to the opportunities and realities of the world in which they live. We should not overestimate the risk we take in moving away from the familiar pattern of schooling toward one that is yet to be clearly defined. Instead, we should remind ourselves constantly that we risk *even more* in lost human potential and lost economic vigor by staying where we are. As Seymour Sarason has shrewdly observed, "the biggest risk in education is not taking one."[13] It is also worth bearing in mind that while children are only 25% of our population, they are 100% of our future.

Footnotes

1. The National Commission on Excellence in Education, *A Nation at Risk* (Washington, D.C.: U.S. Department of Education, 1983), p. 8.
2. Ibid., pp. 23, 36.
3. "A Nation Still at Risk," *Newsweek*, 2 May 1988, pp. 54-55.
4. Gerald W. Bracey, "Why Can't They Be Like We Were?" *Phi Delta Kappan* 73 (October 1991): 104-17.
5. See Tables 40, 80, 84, and B5 in *Digest of Education Statistics 1992* (Washington, D.C.: National Center for Education Statistics, 1992).
6. *The Condition of Education 1992* (Washington, D.C.: National Center for Education Statistics, 1992), p. 42; and *The National Education Goals Report: Building a Nation of Learners* (Washington, D.C.: National Education Goals Panel, 1992), p. 42.
7. *Perspectives on Education in America* (Albuquerque, N.M.: Sandia National Laboratories, 1991), pp. 38-46.
8. *The Condition of Education 1992*, p. 46; and *The National Education Goals Report*, pp. 27, 36.
9. *The National Education Goals Report*, pp. 27, 36.
10. "Early Education and Care Projections," fact sheet prepared by the Division of Early Childhood Education, Ohio Department of Education, 1992.
11. Arthur G. Powell, Eleanor Farrar, and David K. Cohen, *The Shopping Mall High School* (Boston: Houghton Mifflin, 1985), pp. 172-232.
12. Michael G. Fullan and Suzanne Stiegelbauer, *The New Meaning of Educational Change* (New York: Teachers College Press, 1991), p. 65.
13. Seymour B. Sarason, *The Predictable Failure of Educational Reform* (San Francisco: Jossey-Bass, 1990), p. 176.

PERFECT POLICIES AND IMPERFECT PEOPLE: WHAT HAPPENS WHEN THEY COLLIDE?

Kati Haycock

Ms. Haycock urges educators who see coordinated services for children as a panacea to concentrate instead on their core mission: providing high-quality instruction to all.

Two years ago, when I was executive vice president of the Children's Defense Fund, we sponsored a rather grand dinner to honor six Southern California young people who had "beaten the odds." Each of these youngsters had overcome very difficult personal circumstances, some in this country and others overseas, and had gone on to succeed in school.

As I sat down yesterday with my assigned task of writing about what is "right" and "wrong" with American public education, my thoughts turned immediately to these six young people. Why? Because they and millions of youngsters like them — youngsters who have lived in deplorable circumstances, stared down unimaginable horrors, yet somehow emerged unbowed — are what is right with American education. Our *response* to them is what is wrong.

Take Tamika, for example. Tamika's early years were full of pain. Her mother was dependent on alcohol and cocaine, exchanging her body regularly for drugs. Before the age of 8, Tamika was sexually abused by a number of men in her mother's life. She was shipped from relative to relative, foster home to foster home, first in Florida and then in California.

If you asked most educators what Tamika needed, they would make up a very long list: "counselor, health care, social worker, mentor."

Kati Haycock is director of the Education Roundtable, American Association for Higher Education.

But if you asked Tamika, as we did, the answer was very different. "Teach me," she said. "Teach me everything they teach the rich white kids in the suburbs, and more. I want to *be* somebody."

High Expectations/High Content

That, fortunately, is what Tamika's high school did. The staff put her in the toughest classes, held her to the highest standards, and did not give in — or allow her to give in — when the going got rough.

How often, though, do we do this for the Tamikas in our schools — for the increasing number of students who come to us not from comfortable, two-parent homes, but from high-rise tenements, or cardboard shanties, or far-away war-torn countries? Sadly, not often enough. The patterns of our response to such students are clear: As they enter our schools in increasing numbers, we lower our standards further and further, reducing both what we expect of *them* and what we expect of *ourselves*. We reduce, too, the quality of educational "inputs" we provide, from the preparation of teachers to the quality of curricular materials. And in so doing — in changing the things we should never have changed — we have contributed mightily to the cycle of despair and low achievement that keeps families and whole communities from fulfilling their potential.

We educators have done these things ourselves. But when we are asked what must be done to improve achievement among disadvantaged students, we only rarely talk about the fundamentally important things that we must do, such as revitalizing curriculum and instruction or raising standards for student performance. Instead, our answers tend to focus on what others must do — social workers, health care providers, mental health counselors, and even parents. Indeed, educators like me, with "impeccable" child advocacy credentials, are *expected* to push in this direction. "Would you come talk to our teachers about coordinated social services?" they ask. "We do hope you will write about the need to integrate health and social services into the school," urged the sponsors of *this* symposium.

Coordinating Social Services

I am not so heretical as to deny the need for integrating and/or coordinating the delivery of educational, health, and social services. Many children and families are simply too fragile to wend their ways through the various systems to get the help they need. Many students are falling between the cracks; their unmet needs do get in the way of high achievement, and we must work together across systems to meet those needs.

However, I do wish to question the *priority* currently attached to coordinated social services and the *order* in which we take on the twin tasks of improving schools and reducing nonschool barriers to student achievement.

My worries about our current tendency to see service coordination as the first priority stem from years of experience with the lowest performing schools in California. During the earliest of those years, my staff and I used to talk with school-level professionals about both of the key factors in the achievement gap — problems inside the school and problems outside. Over time, however, we began to de-emphasize discussions of external problems because of a very troubling tendency among the teachers and administrators to want to fix everything outside of the schools — especially parents — before getting around to fixing their schools.

This is problematic for a variety of reasons. For starters, school people are generally way over their heads on the family/community side of things. Most educators can make considerably more progress by focusing on that which they have at least some preparation to do: improving the school itself.

Perhaps more important, though, this external focus diverts educators from realizing that *they hold in their own hands* the levers to make changes more important than any other. Only schools can both help youngsters to dream big dreams for their futures *and* equip them with the knowledge and skills to make those dreams a reality. Simply by expecting more and challenging more, educators can make a big difference — no matter how poor the child or how distressed his family.

Delivering First on Our Core Mission

One of the most important lessons from efforts to coordinate social services is that such efforts usually will not succeed unless participating institutions are performing their core missions well. Cooperation and collaboration and coordination are, in short, no substitute for good schools, good job-training programs, good child care, or good family resource centers. Yet this lesson is being ignored in the rush toward coordinated services as a panacea for all that ails us.

It is vitally important that we educators remember our core mission: providing high-quality instruction to all. Helping all kids to think, analyze, stretch their minds. If we don't do that well, all of the collaboration in the world will not make a difference.

Fortunately, over the last three years a consensus has begun to emerge among national education policy leaders about key dimensions of a policy framework to support the improvement of our core mission. That framework includes:

- clear standards for what students should know and be able to do;
- rich new assessments to measure whether students meet the standards;
- considerable discretion at the school level in deciding how to get students to the standards;
- professional development for teachers and administrators to support them as they seek to get their students to the standards;
- clear communication with parents on how their children are progressing toward the standards and on what they can do to help; and,
- an accountability system that rewards schools making progress in getting increasing numbers of students to the standards and penalizes those that do not.

In effect, each piece of the policy framework is lined up, and *standards* are the unifying focus.

A Standards-Driven Approach for Tamika?

Many argue, though, that a standards-driven approach to reform is not appropriate in schools that serve poor or minority students – or students like Tamika. I strongly disagree. Based on my experiences with teachers and administrators in low-performing schools, I concluded long ago that their improvement efforts are seriously handicapped by the fuzzy information we provide them on how their students are doing and by their lack of clarity on what students ought to know at a particular age. At best, staffs in schools serving poor children know that their students are "a year or two behind grade level" or that they have "a way to go to reach national norms"; more often, they know only that their students are doing "about the same as similar students elsewhere." These are hardly goals around which people can be rallied.

I was reminded powerfully of the need for much greater clarity on what we want students to know on a recent visit to an inner-city junior high in the Midwest. Early in this visit, the principal told our group that the school had four goals: "Our Four A's," he called them.

"The first A is attitude," he explained to us, then elaborated on why attitude was important in his school and what the school was doing to

119

cultivate more positive attitudes among students. "The second A is attendance," he said, explaining that the current attendance rate hovered around 80% and that they were trying mightily to increase it. The principal then offered a long description of what the staff was doing to improve attendance and the many barriers they faced in the community.

Next, the principal volunteered that "the third A is atmosphere." He proceeded to explain why atmosphere was important and how the staff worked to build it.

By this point, of course, the visitors were in agony: Would the fourth A be achievement? To our immense relief, it was. But the relief was short-lived, for the principal had neither specific goals for student achievement nor a strategy to reach them. Under questioning, he expressed some desire that the students would someday "meet national norms," but indicated his own sense that his students were "about where inner-city kids are these days."

Clear Goals for Student Performance

Experiences like these — where even bright and well-meaning educators are terribly fuzzy about their goals and strategies for getting there — have convinced me that the policy wonks are on the right track. We *do* need to agree on very clear expectations for what we want all of our students to know and align all aspects of the system with those goals.

But we also must *commit* ourselves — and prepare ourselves — to help each of our students to meet the goals. I worry, however, that this human dimension of reform is getting only a fraction of the attention that the policy framework gets. In meeting after meeting, able and committed reform strategists gather to perfect the policy framework. We debate whether the framework has eight key elements or nine. We wrestle through definitions of terms like "content standards," "performance standards," and "delivery standards." We agonize over whether consequences for students should be attached only *after* delivery standards prove they had adequate opportunity to learn, or whether they should be attached earlier.

While these may indeed be important matters, they pale in significance to a much more important question: What happens when this ever-more-perfect policy framework bumps up against the not-so-perfect *people* who staff our schools — people who typically have imperfect training and inadequate content and pedagogical knowledge, and who often do not believe that all students can learn?

Certainly, we know what will happen unless we take this dimension of reform more seriously than past reformers: The new policies may get implemented in name but never in spirit. Educators will duck this way and that and change the words around to make it seem as though schools are different. But in the end, schools will go on as usual for children.

The Human Dimension of Reform

It's time to turn our attention to this human dimension of reform, to build a bottom-up strategy as carefully as we are building the top-down policy structure. But where do we start? We start, I think, with the most obvious problem areas as we seek to implement a bottom-up reform strategy. What are these areas?

1. *New Standards and Current Teachers*. In Kentucky and in other states that are pressing ahead with new standards and assessments, it is becoming increasingly clear that many teachers do not meet the standards we want their students to meet. In all too many cases, teacher knowledge of subject matter is not deep or current enough for them to be able to present the critical core ideas of their disciplines clearly, cogently, and in the myriad ways that may be necessary to engage all learners effectively. If not addressed, this Achilles heel of the movement toward high standards will cause that movement to implode.

2. *Collaborative, Site-Based Decision Making and Current Managers*. The reform policy framework calls for state-imposed or nationally imposed standards for what all students should know and be able to do, with considerable building-level discretion about curriculum and instructional strategies that will enable students to meet the standards. Experience to date suggests that the principal's attitudes and skills are the single most important variable in whether collaborative approaches work. Yet most principals were not trained for this task, and there is little support as they struggle with this new approach. Their missteps are causing the collapse of site-based collaborative efforts, even as the reformers call for still more site-level shared decision making.

3. *Race, Poverty, and Low Expectations*. The words "all kids can learn" are virtually everywhere these days — everywhere, that is, except in the hearts of teachers and administrators in schools serving minority and poor children. Certainly these educators mouth the words, as they stand beside the governors, business leaders, and others who are crafting the policy rhetoric and framework of reform. In the teacher lunchroom, though, the comments are quite different. Racism is ram-

121

pant; but even teachers who are themselves black or Latino typically hold lower expectations for black, Latino, and poor white children. Those expectations are communicated in thousands of ways every day, undermining the promise of standards-driven reform.

4. *Collaborating with Other Child-Serving Professionals.* Almost everybody talks about serving the "whole child." And, as noted earlier, coordination of services is considered a tonic to cure all that ails us. But coordination is much easier said than done. Child-serving experts have been pushing for greater collaboration since 1930 — and just see how far we've come. If we are to move further faster, educators must have an opportunity to learn the language of the other child-serving fields. They must have time and support if they are to understand how they fit into the broader picture and how they can build ties with other providers.

When confronted with these obvious problems, those who are crafting the reform policy framework respond rather glibly by saying they have provided funds for professional development. But the amounts are universally pathetic.

Even if the dollars were adequate, however, from whom should this assistance be purchased? The current providers of staff development? District or state administrators miraculously transformed from overseers to helpers? Anyone familiar with what passes for staff development in this country can only shudder at the possibilities.

If the current reform effort is to succeed, we must invest heavily in professional development. We also must build a support structure capable of supporting all teachers and administrators as they seek to enable their students to reach high standards. This is especially important for staff members in our nation's lowest performing schools, where standards have slipped the furthest and where management typically reels from crisis to crisis. But it is important, too, in suburban schools, which — if standards are set high enough — will no longer be able to coast on the coattails of affluence.

Building a Professional Development Infrastructure: Categories of Need

In thinking through ways to assemble an infrastructure for professional development, it seems useful, first, to think about the most critical needs. In my experience, at least, the needs of schools engaged in transforming themselves tend to fall in three basic categories:

1. *Improving schoolwide organization*, including help in establishing a clear vision, in analyzing where the school is in relation to that vision, and in improving the overall organization and functioning of the school to realize its vision.
2. *Improving curriculum and instruction*, including help in improving curriculum, teaching, and learning within and across the key academic disciplines.
3. *Tackling specific problem areas*, including tasks such as overhauling counseling and guidance services, eliminating tracking, engaging parents, and coordinating with social service providers.

To my knowledge, there is no single model that provides education professionals with carefully crafted models for all three categories. However, there are wonderful models in each category that point the way to how we might assemble an adequate infrastructure.

In the matter of helping schools to build a clear vision and reorganize around that vision, Ted Sizer's Coalition of Essential Schools, Henry Levin's Accelerated Schools Network, California's Achievement Council, and the Philadelphia Schools Collaborative all have developed powerful techniques to reshape attitudes and organizations.

In the various academic disciplines, teachers and university professors have worked side by side to develop new opportunities for teachers to wallow in the subjects they teach, deepening their own knowledge of their subjects and improving their abilities to communicate and assess understanding of critical concepts through observation, trial, and feedback. The Yale/New Haven Teacher Center and California's Subject Matter Projects are particularly powerful examples; so, too, are many "academic alliances" and "teacher collaboratives."

A variety of individuals and organizations are developing expertise in helping school staffs with particular tasks. Experts from the Massachusetts Advocacy Center, for example, help with untracking, while those from the College Board help with improving guidance and college prep mathematics instruction. In general, these helpers share lessons from other sites that are further along in tackling particular problems; arrange for site visits so staff members can see for themselves; and assist the school staffs in planning, implementing, and monitoring change.

Building a Professional Development Infrastructure: Organization

Beyond thinking about categories of need, it is also important to think through what we have learned about the organization and delivery of effective professional development — and to match our approaches to the demands of the reform strategies we have chosen. Judith Warren Little offers six principles for professional development aligned with the current reform strategy:

1. Professional development should offer meaningful intellectual, social, and emotional engagement with ideas, with materials, and with colleagues both in and out of teaching.

2. Professional development should incorporate an explicit historical and contextual sensitivity: a means of locating new ideas in relation to individual and institutional histories, practices, and circumstances.

3. Professional development should offer support for principled and informed dissent.

4. Professional development should be grounded in a "big picture" perspective on the purposes and practices of schooling and should provide a means of seeing and acting upon the connections among students' experiences, teachers' classroom practice, and schoolwide structures and cultures.

5. Professional development should prepare teachers to employ the techniques and perspectives of inquiry.

6. The governance of professional development should ensure bureaucratic restraint and a balance between the interests of individuals and the interests of institutions.[1]

These principles stand in stark contrast to most of the staff development we currently provide to teachers and administrators, which seeks to "train" teachers to make technical improvements in their practice rather than to produce thinking citizens of the larger educational enterprise. But today's reform strategies require teachers and administrators to become thoughtful activists, to be able to take broad concepts and make them real at the building level, and to invent as they go, rather than simply copy approaches used elsewhere. Clearly, our professional support structures must be designed with this bolder vision in mind.

Moving Ahead to Create Necessary Support Structures

Creating support structures that meet the three categories of need I have outlined, and that do so according to the tenets of effective professional development, will be a monumental undertaking.

Some states and communities already have a good deal on which they can build. Their primary task will be to grow their high-quality programs quickly, fill in the gaps, and knit the various initiatives together in a way that provides more comprehensive assistance to the lowest-performing schools. Other states and communities will have to build from scratch. They will have to make sure that their work is informed by the lessons learned elsewhere.

Unfortunately, despite the clear necessity of moving quickly to build such support structures, work is not yet under way on anywhere near the necessary scale for at least two reasons: lack of money and apathy within higher education.

Funds for Change

Private-sector leadership seems to understand that change costs money. Especially in corporations committed to pushing decision making down the hierarchy, leaders are investing heavily in training and team building. In these organizations, professional development has become a routine part of the work day and work week. Employees have considerable say about the types of training they need and are given regular feedback as they attempt new approaches.

Though the changes we seek from today's teachers and administrators are at least as dramatic as those being pursued in private enterprise, we have not been willing to pay for similar support or to reorganize the school day and school week so that professional development is a regular part of the work schedule. We also seldom consult educators at the building level to see what kind of help they need as they struggle to improve their results. Instead, somebody in the central office tends to decide what the teachers and administrators need. And they get it, herded into a large room after school for a series of 90-minute doses, each unrelated to the one before it.

This has to change. What are some possible strategies to secure the needed support? The usual route, of course, would be to seek increased investments at the state or local level. However, while some states — notably Kentucky and Vermont — are plowing increased dollars into professional development, policy makers in other states are shying away from such uses for their increasingly tight revenues. While we should not be deterred from pressing this matter on state and local governments, perhaps using business investments in human development as a model, two other avenues may be more productive in the short run. These include increased investments at the federal level, through the creation of professional development set-asides in large programs like Chapter 1 and Chapter 2; and rearranging the school day to free teachers for collaboration and professional development, much like the Asian schools described by Stigler and Stevenson.[2]

Remote? I hope not, for the success of the current reform effort depends on it. And work is already under way. In December, a 28-member commission put forward a proposal for shifts in the federal Chapter 1 program. If the commission is successful, at least $1.8 billion per year will be redirected toward professional and school development in schools serving poor children. In tandem with an effort to think more creatively about the school day, this amount should be sufficient to get work on the necessary support structure well under way.

Apathy Within Higher Education

There remains, however, the vexing matter of apathy within higher education, which, for better or worse, is a necessary partner in building a professional support structure.

Much to the annoyance of governors and other reform leaders, higher education has been sitting on the sidelines in the current reform effort. While individual professors here and there have become involved with local schools, higher education as a sector has played little or no role in reform policy discussions. Even on issues where colleges and universities have a clear stake and much to add — such as the content of new national standards — higher education has not found a voice.

This inattention is especially troublesome because higher education has a monopoly on many of the resources needed to build the professional support structure and to otherwise help in the reform effort. This includes physicists to help with the physics curriculum, geographers to help prepare teachers to teach geography, researchers who can help weigh alternative instructional approaches, and public health experts to help schools gain access to Medicaid. But when schools turn to higher education for assistance, they find either researchers who do not even understand their questions or a series of small, unconnected "helping" programs, offered hit and miss, which are not easily accessible — especially to professionals in the most troubled schools.

If we are to assemble a professional support structure of high quality, higher education must be a fully engaged partner. This is especially true of infrastructures in the various academic disciplines but applies to other areas as well. Higher education simply must step out of its pet-project mode and into a more strategic role in fostering systemwide improvements.

126

Needed Reforms in Higher Education

But it is not merely a question of Little Brother K-12 needing help from Big Brother Higher Education. As the nation gets further into the K-12 reform effort, it is becoming increasingly apparent to those who are looking ahead of the reform curve that all of their efforts will not make much of a difference without certain reforms in the way higher education goes about its own business.

Many believe, for example, that the new national standards and assessments will not make a bit of difference unless colleges and universities use the results in the admissions process — and stop making offers to any 18-year-old with a pulse. Others maintain that the curricular reforms into which we have all poured such energy will implode without teachers being much better prepared than the ones we are producing today. And that will require reforms not only in education and human services departments but in the regular arts and sciences courses where future teachers learn to teach through an "apprenticeship of observation."

Clearly, then, higher education must come to the table; changes in one system simply are not possible without changes in the other.

Moving Forward

Changes of the sort described here — changes within systems and across systems — are a lot of work. I am confident, however, that with strong leadership, a lot of energy, and a little bit of luck, we can actually pull this off in virtually every region of the country.

My optimism stems from recent experience with 10 American cities where leaders from K-12 education, higher education, and the broader community are working hard to set clear goals for student achievement and reorganize their systems to work together toward achieving those goals.

In El Paso, Texas, for example, the Collaborative for Educational Excellence, governed by two college presidents, three school superintendents, and numerous community leaders, is hard at work turning around historically low performance patterns in this mostly Latino city. Together, these leaders hammered out an approach that pairs clear citywide expectations for higher student achievement with a bottom-up approach to school improvement.

Last summer, 10-member teams of teachers and administrators from more than 50 schools attended three-day planning institutes on the University of Texas-El Paso campus. There they had an opportunity to analyze their data, hear from leaders in school improvement efforts elsewhere, and plan how to improve achievement in their own schools.

Back at their sites, each team had support from the central office and the university in beginning an overhaul process. Particular players on these teams — principals, counselors, and the like — receive regular assistance in improving their knowledge and skills. Today professors in the two colleges are working with the teachers to launch a standards-setting process — informed by but not limited to the national process. As they work, they also will design a professional-development support structure to ensure that all teachers have the wherewithal to teach students to meet the new standards. Over time, graduation requirements and college admissions requirements will be brought into line. And work is already under way to overhaul teacher preparation, since the University of Texas-El Paso provides nearly 90% of the teachers for the three districts.

While some foundation money has been secured for various pieces of this initiative, existing resources pay for the bulk of the effort. This money is redirected from programmatic initiatives to systemic change. To provide clearer signals on what they want, system leaders are shifting the focus of their accountability systems from programmatic inputs to student outcomes.

A similar effort is going on in Pueblo, Colorado, where public school educators, college professors, and business leaders have teamed up to improve student achievement in this city of about 100,000. Board members of School District 60 voted to merge their district with the University of Southern Colorado, and the district superintendent has become a vice president of the university. Thus a single planning effort — K through graduate school — has been launched, and joint facilities and purchasing offices have been created. The district's curriculum consultants are now housed in a new Center on Teaching and Learning at the university, and it works to improve teaching at *both* levels. Continuous quality-improvement techniques guide this new system's efforts to improve results.

Neither these nor the other eight communities in this Pew-initiated project are far enough along to show achievement results. They do show, however, how powerful a joint effort can be in both the energy it creates and in the consistency of signals it sends to teachers, students, and the broader community. They also show the power in simultaneous top-down and bottom-up education reform strategies. Will these communities tackle the health and social service coordination problems I was supposed to write about? You bet they will. But they will do so within the *context of a more comprehensive reform effort*. And when improvements in the core mission of schools have taken root or other structural arrangements have been made, then tackling this additional challenge will not bring the entire school-change effort to a screeching halt.

Footnotes

1. Judith Warren Little, "Teachers' Professional Development in a Climate of Educational Reform," University of California, Berkeley, September 1992.
2. James W. Stigler and Harold W. Stevenson, "How Asian Teachers Polish Each Lesson to Perfection," *American Educator* (Spring 1991).

KEEPING OUR PROMISE TO AMERICA'S CHILDREN: A STANDARDS-BASED VISION FOR SCHOOL REFORM

Pascal D. Forgione, Jr.

The state of Delaware is establishing detailed standards of achievement in the basic subjects — math, science, English/language arts, and social studies — for the state's public schools. Every student is expected to meet these standards, so time becomes the variable. State Superintendent Forgione describes the thorough planning and preparations already undertaken to ensure success for this very promising project.

What is best about our public schools is their uniquely American mission of offering a high-quality education to every young person. But this mission goes largely unfulfilled, with too few children receiving the excellent education they need. Our task must be to deliver on our promise and provide educational excellence and equity for all.

The idea of the common school, a unifying experience shared by all members of our society, has long been America's educational ideal. It is a concept that enjoys broad public support, with Americans overwhelmingly agreeing with Horace Mann's description of education as "the great equalizer of the conditions of men" and "the balance-wheel of the social machinery."

We have never achieved this ideal, of course. Although public education has enabled large numbers of Americans, new and old, to realize the American dream, reformers have long argued that our results, whether viewed in terms of excellence or of equity, are not good enough.

Pascal D. Forgione, Jr. is superintendent of public instruction for the state of Delaware. The opinions presented in this article are those of the author and do not necessarily reflect the views of the Delaware State Board of Education.

The realities of today's world clearly require us to do better. Demographic trends and trends in the work force are combining to impel us to deliver on our democratic ideals. We must reach new and higher standards of performance. We must produce both excellence and equity on a scale well beyond our past level of accomplishment.

The case for change is all too familiar. Most U.S. students don't work long or hard enough, aren't sufficiently challenged, and produce disappointing results in comparison with the performance of their counterparts in other countries. In many schools there exists a double standard, with those students not headed for college too often abandoned as not worth the effort. Moreover, those schools with substantial low-income and minority populations generally are not nearly as good as those in higher-income areas.

Fortunately, the current wave of education reform is more promising than similar frenzies of the past, which lacked staying power and focused more on educational fads than on underlying change. We finally have begun to address fundamental issues, and the business community and other essential constituencies give evidence of staying with us for the long run. The public, too, is beginning to awaken to the fact we have a problem; and political leaders are responding to that wake-up call as well.

One result of that awakening was the creation of the six National Education Goals and associated state and local goals. Together, such goals give us valuable targets and broad standards against which to measure progress. Some criticize these goals for being too broad and, in some instances, too challenging. As one who was involved in the design of the national goals, I believe that they are appropriate and useful for our country. Like many states, my home state of Delaware is developing statewide profile reports to track our progress toward state and national goals for elementary, middle, and high schools.

But such goals are only a beginning. If we are to succeed, we must pursue these goals with a vision that is shared widely among educators and the public. In this article I outline such a vision, briefly describing some of the needs that we must address and some of the strengths on which we can build. I argue strongly for the classroom fundamentals; for while I don't believe they are our only needs, I believe they are the key to dramatic and sustained progress.

Standards and Assessments

One of the things that is seriously wrong with America's public education system is that our standards have been largely unstated — and clearly not rigorous enough. Meanwhile, our assessments have compared students to one another, rather than measured their performance against objective criteria. Fortunately, at both the national and local levels, we are starting to acknowledge this problem.

In formulating a vision of what we want our schools to be, we must answer three questions that seem simple but are actually complex and interconnected. (One measure of the complexity of these questions is that few schools have adequately addressed them.) The questions are: 1) What is it that all students must know and be able to do? 2) How will we know when students have accomplished the task? 3) What are the best ways to enhance student learning?

Our ultimate criterion of success or failure must be student outcomes. The one real example of placing the cart before the horse in American education is that student outcomes have become the variable. What is fixed is time – 180 days for most students. We have it all backward. Time should become the variable; we must not compromise on outcomes.

Thus we must not waiver and hedge on answers to such questions as "What are the destinations in mathematics that a third-grader should reach? What kind of enabling skills should that child have? And what level of performance does he or she need to demonstrate success?" It may be that to reach the goals set for eighth grade, one student might need four years and another might need two; but at some point both students must reach specified destinations.

Our tendency has been to water down or trivialize outcomes and to undervalue the demonstration of excellence. We've tended to alter the expectations for our children, assuming that some can "make it" and others cannot, which is unfair to all of them and a failing strategy for our nation. In large measure that is because we have not had agreed-upon standards of performance.

Thus, developing and implementing standards – along with developing and learning how to use meaningful tools to assess the performance of students, teachers, and schools against those standards – becomes the logical starting point for solid and sustained progress.

The Delaware Experiment

In Delaware we've launched an all-out effort to create world-class standards and assessments, which we call New Directions for Education in Delaware. We believe that the way to ensure that students have a meaningful, engaging, and substantive experience is to build high expectations. Those expectations will be created by establishing specific and rigorous content and performance standards that define a common core of learning for all students in kindergarten through grade 10. Students in grades 11 and 12 will prepare for college or a technical career or pursue a workplace apprenticeship. This system spells the end of today's "general track," a path that leads neither to college nor to a job.

Last summer four commissions made up of Delaware teachers, other content experts, and community representatives began the difficult job of establishing curriculum frameworks that will determine what students should know and be able to do at various grade levels in four core subject areas: mathematics, science, English/language arts, and social studies. These curriculum frameworks will provide a blueprint from which will come student and teacher standards, as well as dramatically increased staff-development initiatives.

These commissions, which are co-chaired by a classroom teacher and a state content expert, meet monthly in public session and will produce the curriculum framework for mathematics in the spring of next year. Science follows in the fall of 1994, English/language arts in the winter of 1995, and social studies in the spring of that year.

At the same time, the commission members are interacting with members of other framework commissions to ensure that our curriculum is fully integrated. Similar work in physical education/health, foreign languages, visual/performing arts, and vocational/technical education will be initiated in the future.

Even as we work on standards, however, we are preparing to replace assessments that focus on average or group performance (norm-referenced tests) with those that focus on the performance of individual students as measured against the new standards. Beginning this spring, we will administer new, interim, statewide assessments in English/language arts and mathematics to all public school students in grades 3, 5, 8, and 10.

These new assessments will provide students, parents, and teachers with feedback on student performance that is designed to complement the evolving curriculum frameworks, student-performance standards, and performance-assessment measures. During the next four years, we will phase in at all grade levels new comprehensive, statewide, performance-based assessments that will be integral to classroom instruction and will grow out of the work of the four curriculum framework commissions. This program will be tested and benchmark data will be collected during the 1995-97 period, with full implementation of these performance-based assessments scheduled to begin in the 1997-98 school year.

Design work for New Directions is the responsibility of our state education department. Development is taking place under the leadership of a privately funded Delaware Educational Research and Development (R&D) Center at the University of Delaware and Delaware State College. The independent university setting allows us to attract specialized talent to our project.

Members of the curriculum framework commissions and staff members of the Research and Development Center will build on work done by groups such as the National Council of Teachers of Mathematics, the National Academy of Sciences, and the New Standards Project. Delaware's State Systemic (reform) Initiative, funded by the National Science Foundation, will work closely with the curriculum framework process, helping to develop exemplary lessons that embody the standards and at the same time helping to educate teachers on how to implement them.

In addition, we are assembling a team of outstanding national experts to oversee our work. These national experts will review our progress twice each year and report to the state board of education, to the business community, and to other interested parties.

We are confident that New Directions will establish a foundation for excellence. But what about the third fundamental question we asked earlier? What are the best ways to enhance student learning? How will we translate these rich, world-class standards and assessments into better-educated students? Equally important, how will we ensure that all young people have an equal opportunity to succeed? I will discuss the implementation issue first, briefly covering professional development, parent and community involvement, school governance, consequences, and resources.

Professional Development

One thing that is right about our schools is the presence of many dedicated teachers, administrators, and support staff. While I occasionally hear comments about lazy, uncaring teachers and overpaid bureaucrats, I rarely hear such comments from people who have spent time in our schools and administrative offices. Those familiar with what goes on overwhelmingly describe capable, caring people who work under difficult circumstances.

It is true that we have failed to give our educators adequate tools to do their jobs. Such tools range from decent working conditions to moral support. Perhaps foremost among the tools educators need is a thoughtful system of professional development. In other fields — for example, industry or the military — it is accepted that employees will grow and perform to their full potential only with regular training that is closely related to the organization's goals and objectives.

For educators, professional development too often consists of several inservice days, consumed largely by a series of workshops that deal with peripheral or disjointed topics bearing scant relation to improved student learning. We need something much richer and more useful.

For New Directions to succeed, we must restructure and upgrade our education delivery system and expand, through continuous educational opportunities, the capacities of Delaware teachers and administrators. Our state schools of education will play an important role as educators demonstrate continuous improvement in their efforts to help students meet the new student performance standards. One of the reasons we are involving classroom teachers so deeply in the New Directions project is that this work provides a wonderful development experience and helps train a cadre of educators who are well versed in this new approach.

One of our first steps must be to apply the concept of high standards to our teaching force. It is just as important to understand what constitutes good teaching in, say, sixth-grade math as it is to determine what a student should know and be able to do, since one will strongly influence the other. We plan to build on what groups such as the National Board for Professional Teaching Standards are doing to develop standards for the teaching profession. We also are working to upgrade the process by which teachers are licensed to make it consistent with our broader objectives.

Most administrators started as teachers, but the skills required of a teacher are quite different from those required of a principal. Training can facilitate the transition from teacher to administrator. I believe that administrators can learn a lot from industry; and in areas such as leadership training, schools can borrow industry programs.

Parent and Community Involvement

Increased parent involvement and strengthened community support will be crucial to our efforts to implement new standards and assessments. I see these two as overlapping needs, because in both cases we must strive to improve ties between our schools and our communities.

Many of us remember the high level of support for public schools that existed in this country during the 1950s and 1960s and into the 1970s. Even tax referenda enjoyed strong public support. But many things have changed since then, including the disintegration of traditional American families in many areas. Moreover, parents whose own experiences with school were negative often feel uncomfortable about coming to their children's schools. We must reach out to make parents feel welcome.

At least for a time, we might have to *over*communicate with our stakeholders — parents, government, business, and taxpayers in general. We need to explain to them what we are doing and why, and we need to invite their participation and assistance. We need to help them understand, for example, that a failing public school system negatively affects every member of society, while effective schools will build a stable society and a growing economy that will pay for the expense of schooling many times over.

Having seen how the lack of broad support can derail even the best reform proposal, we have created four groups of partners for New Directions. These partnership arrangements are designed to help ensure that state-level educators keep in close touch with local educators and with the public.

In addition to the 180 members of the various curriculum-framework commissions, all 19 school districts have signed on as partners with New Directions. There are also "school partners" — representatives of each discipline in each of the state's schools, as well as representatives of the parent/teacher organization and of groups of Chapter 1 and special education parents. "Development partners" include classroom teachers and others from around the state who work in tandem with the curriculum-framework commissions to develop exemplary lessons and performance tasks that incorporate or reflect the content standards. Finally, there are hundreds of citizens identified as "community partners."

Our aim is to communicate regularly with these partners and, through them, to reach all interested citizens and organizations in the state. My impression is that the concept of broad participation in school reform has generally been more a slogan than a real activity. We are determined to provide substantive, authentic involvement in New Directions for a wide variety of constituencies.

School Governance

We also need a more intelligent system of school governance. It is probably true that our current system worked pretty well at one time, as did the same kind of hierarchical system of management in American industry. Both follow the military model, in which decisions are made at headquarters and are referred down the chain of command to subordinates who carry out orders.

We are finding that this system can be destructive in many settings. It is often demeaning, wastes human talent, stifles creativity, and results in poor decisions based on incomplete or inaccurate information. Changing from such a top-down system to one in which the people closest to the action — for example, classroom teachers and building principals — make most of the decisions is difficult but necessary.

When we consider school governance, we also must consider the highly controversial issue of school choice, a concept that is positive in the abstract but that many people believe to be harmful to our pursuit of equity. The concept of school choice has implications that transcend education, and I believe that each community must sort out its position on the matter — but only *after* adequate standards and assessments are in place. Once we have agreed on the educational results we are seeking and on how to tell if we have achieved them, we can decide, district by district, how best to reach those standards and whether choice should be part of that formula.

A System of Consequences

The use of so-called consequences — stakes and incentives — is another controversial aspect of education reform that we must address. Traditionally, consequences in education have applied only to children. If a school or teacher did a poor job, the children suffered, but little happened to the teacher or school. Given our lack of clear standards and effective measurement tools, perhaps that was just as well.

But the kind of standards-based performance that I have described and the accompanying process of embedded assessment will require educators to change and to grow. Incentives can be effective ways to engender such change. It seems irresponsible not to apply such a powerful tool to this situation.

Granted, there are important issues to resolve. A system of positive and negative consequences could be extremely unfair, although it needn't be. Still, I believe that we can and must design a system that is fair and will benefit not only our students, but a majority of our educators as well. Such a system might include a vision of shared stakes in which groups of teachers feel responsible for the success of individual students.

137

Resources

The final item on this list of ways to ensure that a standards-based system really works is resources. While a well-functioning system based on standards and assessments should not cost significantly more than we are spending today, some initial investment is required to develop such a system.

In Delaware we estimate that it will cost approximately $12 million in new funding over the next five years to design, develop, and administer our New Directions plan. We are seeking to pay for this effort with a combination of funds from state, local, and private sources.

Moreover, we also must face the issue of finding resources for more general reforms. Where will we get the money for enhanced professional development? For the technology we need to begin integrating into our curricula? I believe honesty compels us to say that, over the years, society has funded public education fairly well. Many states certainly saw large spending increases during the 1980s. And in Delaware and some other states, the unit-funding formula has guaranteed general financial stability. What has been wrong, I think, is that the system has continued to drive funds into various units without providing any incentive to change or to produce identifiable results.

We all recognize that there are no simple answers to the financial problems many schools face today. However, if we can convince the public that our standards are appropriate and that our children have to meet them to succeed in life, the public will be as forthcoming with its future support as it has been in the past.

Any discussion of resources will ultimately lead to a consideration of questions of equity. In fact, the way states fund education has become the chief battleground for issues of educational equity as plaintiffs allege that many state funding formulas favor affluent children.

There have been commendable efforts to address this problem — for example, Delaware's equalization formulas — but the need is far from being met. And again, the current system offers little incentive to eradicate the inequities. If our system of public education is to be "the great equalizer" or "the balance-wheel" of which Horace Mann spoke, if it is to provide alternative approaches for children with differing needs and offer second and third chances to those who are not successful the first time, and if it is to develop the raw material for tomorrow's globally competitive work force, then we must do things differently.

But how do we ensure that all young people have an equal opportunity to succeed? One answer requires changing attitudes and behavior, which again suggests a central role for a thoughtful system of stakes and incentives. We must shed our preconceptions, biases, and lingering doubts and behave as though we truly believe that all children can learn at substantially higher levels and that every child needs an advocate. New staffing patterns, in which the student does the work and the teacher coaches, can free up time to make the idealistic statements above a reality. But such changes also require corresponding behavioral change.

Here again, a standards-based approach is crucial. If we raise expectations for all students and require that these expectations be met — although not necessarily on a single timetable — we will have gone a long way toward ensuring greater equality. And that does not mean we can't and shouldn't provide extra help for a child who needs it; it just means that we should not be satisfied until that child has realized his or her full potential.

Some argue that this view is unrealistic, that many children just can't cut it, and that it is cruel to expect them to do so. But the experience of such educators as Jaime Escalante prove otherwise. Setting high expectations for all is not cruel. Cruel is what we are being today by expecting little and demanding less.

A third way to promote equity is to address the fundamental unfairness related to differing backgrounds and environments. That means finding ways to better prepare children for school, especially in their early years. Head Start is one of the things we have been doing right, but we need much more of it. We also need to link schools with deliverers of social services. We need more and better prenatal care. And the list could go on.

Another kind of preparation is needed at the other end of public schooling in the form of school-to-work transition programs. America is the only industrialized country without such a formal program to ease the path from school to work. Today, there are two classes of high school students: those who are headed for college and those who are not. The latter often receive treatment that is at best second-class.

For reasons of idealism and self-interest, we cannot permit this discrimination to continue. Either by adapting the apprenticeship programs that have been so successful in Europe or by inventing something new, we need to close this gap.

I have given great weight in my analysis to a standards-based approach. While I don't mean to suggest that such an approach will cure everything but the common cold, I am convinced that it can lead us to real, lasting education reform.

What appeals to me most about this approach is that it is truly about education. It focuses on the learning process. Generally in life, we get what we expect, or we make changes so that we can get what we expect the next time. The problem with America's public schools is that we have not defined what we want. Thus we never know whether we are getting it or not.

Events here and abroad have made it clear that whatever we are getting is not what we need. It is time to do the hard work to determine, in detail, what our destination is. Then we can ask the American people to help us get there. This may not be our last opportunity for meaningful reform, but it is one of our best.

A CASE STUDY IN SYSTEMIC RECONSTRUCTION: THE STRUGGLE TO TRANSFORM THE SCHOOLS IN SPRINGFIELD, MASSACHUSETTS

Peter J. Negroni

Superintendent Negroni offers his system as a model for school reform in progress. Among its special features: a high level of community involvement, the early introduction of site-based management, a massive information program involving all of the media, and long-term relationships with outside institutions with special resources.

The challenge of public education before all of us in this country is clear. We must work toward full educational access and equity for all children. We began this work in Springfield, Massachusetts, in September 1989 by bringing together all the constituencies in the development and support of the school improvement process. Our work is offered as a model for school reform.

Our premise in Springfield was different from that of most of the reform efforts in the country. We began with the understanding that institutions do not reform themselves; for significant reform to take place, we needed the system to feel pressure from the *outside*. This pressure had to be such that it did not upset the *inside* so much that it would respond negatively and become immobile. This is, indeed, a delicate balancing act.

While the Springfield reform effort of the last three years has not been without tension between the inside and outside constituencies, it

Peter Negroni is superintendent, Springfield School Department, Springfield, Massachusetts.

has been reasonable enough that it continues to have broad support from all the constituencies. In our estimation, it is impossible to sustain any reform effort that does not recognize the full interdependence of the school and the community. In addition, the reform process must bring all of the constituencies together, understanding and recognizing each of their self-interests in the development and implementation of a common purpose.

Basic to our work in Springfield and the struggle of transforming America's public schools into places that educate all children effectively, we must embrace the belief that all children can and will learn. This belief must be accompanied by a recognition that the student body of the past — mostly white and middle class — is not the student body of today or of our future. Children will continue to come to school in the next decade as they do today; but increasingly they will be brown and black, certainly poorer, and more than likely not ready for school. These are the children all of us will be responsible for educating effectively and appropriately. These are the children we must prepare for an increasingly complex 21st century.

The job before us is a difficult one. Poor children are indeed more difficult to educate than middle-class children. However, when a community decides to transform its schools into effective ones that work for all children, they *can* be educated. The proof is in the success of hundreds of schools in America. This is the new *challenge*: to teach children to the best of *our* potential, and not merely to the best of *their* potential, as has been the goal in America's public schools previously.

In order to get different results, schools must change what they are doing. Educators and schools must make the difference. However, the need for change cannot be viewed as personal failure. Rather, change is merely a response to new conditions and information. The fact that change is necessary cannot be interpreted as a failure on the part of educators or parents — and certainly not of children. Parents send the schools the very best children they have; they do not keep the good ones at home. So these are the only children we depend on to make this great democracy flourish.

A major reason for the condition of public schools today lies in the history of the independence of schools. They were set up on the hill separate and apart from the community, often totally isolated. It was the job of the educator, the "expert," to teach the children; and we would do it by ourselves, independent of everyone else. After all, we were the experts and we needed no one's help. Today, we see the results of that way of thinking.

Most Americans have not made the connection between the quality of life in a community and the quality of public schooling in a community. We have not recognized the complete and total interdependence of community, schooling, and democracy. We are virtually alone and unsupported by the public. We cannot be successful until the workers in the public schools and the total community understand this interdependence. Of course, the problem is now complicated by the fact that 75% of American adults do not have children in the public schools. The seniors and the childless families all ask, "What's in school reform for me?" Underlying much opposition to public school support is this question, "Why should we pay to educate these children who don't even look like us?" Educators must help these groups to understand the interrelationship of effective schools and effective, productive communities. Everyone has a stake in the success or failure of the public schools.

Three compelling reasons for school change must be addressed:

1. Society is changing.
2. The expectations of results are changing.
3. The client group (our students) is changing.

These reasons for change are at the very core of the reform effort in Springfield, a community that is truly a microcosm of America. What has been true in Springfield, a school community that is two-thirds minority and one-half in poverty, is true or will be true of most communities in America by the year 2000.

The Springfield Reforms

Our work in Springfield initially sought to bring the needs of the schools to the attention of the total community. We sought involvement at all levels and from all the constituencies. Springfield accepted this challenge and opportunity. The city got involved in a process that sought all the necessary transformations simultaneously and established the major beliefs to set the direction of the school system:

- Systemic change is essential to be responsive to all of the needs.
- Every child can and will learn.
- All the constituencies must be involved in the schools.
- Teaching for learning prepares students for a changing and complex world.
- Student performance determines success or failure and guides the direction of reform.

These beliefs were first articulated in *Blueprint for Excellence*, a document prepared by administrators with input from various constituencies to set the direction of the school system in the improvement process. This framework outlined the system's mission and vision and established guidelines for the implementation of school-based management teams and for greater involvement by all the constituencies.

School-based management teams were introduced and implemented in all 40 schools during the first year of the reform effort. Composed of the principal, teachers, parents, a community person, a business person, a central office administrator, and students at the secondary level, these teams set to work on establishing their school's vision, with mission and goals based on this vision. Three years after this introduction, the school-centered decision-making process was defined and incorporated in the teachers' contract.

The model of involvement of all the constituencies was replicated outside the individual schools. The reform plan, Phase I: The Policy of Inclusion, included establishing task forces in major areas of concern: School Organization, Central Office Organization, Effective Schools, and Curriculum for the 21st Century. The recommendations of the task forces directed these organizational changes in the next year:

- reorganization of grades to create K-5 and K-8 elementary schools, middle schools with grades 6-8, and four-year high schools with grades 9-12;
- reorganization of the central office administration through consolidation of services, implementation of a computer information system for comprehensive student data, scheduling, student assignment and transportation, and other support services;
- activities and alternative teaching strategies to affect the school environment;
- additional alternative programs to meet student needs, including the Education Alternative Program (EAP), an Assessment Center, the Middle College Program, Anti-Violence Initiatives, Mediation and Conflict Resolution programs, and an alternative program for older students (16+) at the Massachusetts Career Development Institute;
- curriculum revision to include multicultural infusion, a repertoire of teaching strategies, and use of technology as an instructional tool.

To reach out and bring the total community into the schools, new initiatives were introduced and existing initiatives were expanded. Accessibility to the superintendent was a major goal. The superintendent was the spokesperson for the vision of the system. An open-door policy was established, encouraging access beyond hierarchic lines. The superintendent accepted speaking engagements and other opportunities to deliver the system's message that all children can and will learn, given appropriate resources and instruction. On Sunday afternoons the Superintendent's Roundtable brought together 15 to 30 people to discuss school issues in two-hour sessions that were open to anyone in the school community as well as interested Springfield citizens. On a more personal level, parents, students, teachers, and community members could expect a telephone call from the superintendent or could visit in his office. No concern was considered inappropriate. The superintendent's personal involvement legitimized the belief that each individual has a stake in the public schools and that the schools must be responsive to each individual.

With access comes greater involvement. Organized groups were encouraged to form and establish their common goal with the school system to better the education of Springfield's children. In this first year of school improvement, formal partnerships were established with the business community, with parents, and with social service agencies and organizations. Each of the 40 schools developed a relationship with a business partner who provided mentors, attendance incentives, and other support services. With the assistance of the superintendent, the Springfield Parent Advisory Network, composed of PTO presidents and representatives from all schools, established by-laws and became officially recognized by the Springfield School Committee (school board) as the representative of parents. A new subcommittee of the School Committee was created for parent concerns. This recognition in the formal organization of the school system established the role of parents in the education process. All of the subcommittees of the School Committee became more involved, since more issues were sent to the subcommittees for recommendations on action to be taken. This type of involvement allowed School Committee members to investigate all issues and to take ownership of the ultimate recommendations from the superintendent.

During the next reform phases, the policy of inclusion expanded to frame formal partnerships with the religious community. An "education summit" on 28 May 1992 brought together more than 750 individuals from all constituencies in the community to examine, discuss, and develop a community action plan for involvement and to share concerns about the schools. A Parent Information Center has been developed and expanded over the past two years to provide school registration services as well as information on schools, programs, and services. All the changes that have occurred in Springfield have been possible as a result of the support of the School Committee, the parents, the teachers and administrators, the business community, and the various support organizations.

To maximize the opportunity to deliver the message of the school system, the superintendent was visible through the media, both in school-produced programs and the commercial media. "Focus on Springfield Schools," a 30-minute cable television weekly program on the school system, features the superintendent as host with two or three guests discussing school issues, programs, or activities. Public service announcements for radio and television presented important issues and school activities; radio and television talk shows often featured the superintendent discussing school changes in Springfield; public hearings on acquisition of land for a new school were televised, with the capability for questions to be telephoned in; newsletters on the *Blueprint for Excellence* and the many initiatives were produced regularly for the schools.

The media community believes that the schools belong to the community and that the involvement of each is essential. The local major newspaper has had a long commitment to covering education issues and for years has assigned one reporter to cover the School Department. New columns devoted to school information have been introduced; and a new series on Mondays focuses on special events, schools, or individuals in the system. A Marketing Committee, composed of media executives and School Department personnel, was formed in the second year of the reform and led to greater involvement of and support from the various media. A local television station has assisted in preparing public service announcements, including an animated cartoon character who is seen as a champion for education. In addition, the station has invited our high school television-production class to produce a monthly 30-minute show to be broadcast on its channel. Other television stations and radio stations have assisted in communicating our message by broadcasting public service announcements and special programs. Billboard space donated by local companies in Springfield carry an education message directed to parents. "If you love learning, so will your children" is seen throughout the city and was featured on the sides of a school bus in the Springfield Thanksgiving Day balloon parade. Graphic designs for the billboards and for school system publications are donated by a graphics company. The Annual Report, a new initiative, which began after the first year of the reform efforts, has been published by area businesses at no cost to the school system.

The most significant change to ensure parental involvement and school reform to be implemented in Springfield was a Schools of Choice Plan. This intradistrict plan complies with the state court-ordered desegregation plan and allows parents to select a school in Springfield within an education zone or from citywide or zone magnet schools. Applying controlled choice to the student assignments, the system is able to control class size at individual schools and grade levels and can maintain a racially balanced system. This plan was presented to the community in public hearings and neighborhood meetings prior to unanimous adoption by the School Committee and approval by the Massachusetts Board of Education in December of 1991. The first School Fair, which launched the school application period, brought 10,000 people to view the displays of each school and speak with staff members. The School Fair continues to be an integral part of the school choice process.

When we began our reform efforts, we believed that four transformations had to take place: 1) organizational transformation, 2) pedagogical transformation, 3) social and attitudinal transformation, and 4) political transformation. We also believed that these four transformations had to take place simultaneously and be part of a systemic effort that involved all of the constituencies. Thus all of the phases of change were carefully crafted around these transformations. What follows is a brief description of each of the four basic transformations, which we view as necessary for America's schools to work in a globally competitive marketplace.

Organizational Transformation

In reforming our schools, we must challenge what we believe about teaching and learning and what we have been doing for more than 200 years in our schools. We must ask, "Is the present organizational model used in public schooling an effective one?" The following are some elements in current school organizations that require reconsideration:

- the 180-day calendar;
- the six-hour school day;
- age-grade grouping;
- subject concentration in secondary schools;
- restrictive scheduling practices that facilitate tracking;
- 45-minute periods;
- no built-in time for staff interaction, staff development, or school improvement discussions;
- no built-in time for working with parents and/or other agencies;

- Carnegie unit completion rather than performance as the basis for measuring success;
- retention as a solution for failure;
- lecture as the main delivery strategy;
- one teacher for 20 to 30 students in an individual classroom;
- teachers working independently of each other;
- top-down governance structure, that is, command and control as an organizational strategy;
- instruction organized around the principle of remediation;
- children in rows and in lines one behind the other;
- little school or program choice on the part of teacher, student, or parent;
- acceleration as the exception;
- tracking as an organizational strategy;
- schools organized around covering the content rather than having children learn the content.

These organizational structures can no longer be supported. To expect a change in student outcomes, we must begin immediately the organizational transformation of our schools. Each one of these organizational structures was justified when initially established, but none of them is effective to meet the needs of the 21st century. We, as educators, have found it very difficult to discard that which is no longer relevant and necessary. We cling to the old because it is comfortable; however, we can no longer continue to insist that we can make a structure work for our schools when it is outdated and outmoded. If the Berlin Wall could come tumbling down as quickly as it did, there is hope that the present organizational structure of schools can undergo dramatic change.

Our schools currently are organized around an industrial model rather than an informational model. Schools persist in aiming to produce young people who are capable of working in isolation and taking direction, to produce young people who can relate to machines and not to other people. Schools rooted in the past attempt to extinguish the natural desire of people to gather, to be inquisitive, and to interact. Learning can no longer be viewed as a private matter. The new world requires a total transformation of the organizational structure of schools.

Collective bargaining contracts with our teachers and administrators must reflect the new organizational structure. The school day can no longer be limited to six hours, nor can the school year end after 180 days. If time is needed to plan, to confer with students and parents, to attend professional development programs, that time must not come at the expense of instructional time, which is already at a minimum. The Springfield teachers' contract ratified in December 1992 adds 15 minutes each day for instruction, as well as 75 minutes once a week for planning, professional development, and parent conferences. It also adds seven days without students for professional development. Educators cannot do more in the same amount of time, nor should we expect them to. Learning for both the adult and child requires time — time for exploration, for understanding, for discovery, for mastery.

Schools must become places where the organizational structure and the pedagogical models stress the importance of producing students who have a repertoire of skills for the new world. Such skills include:

- higher-order thinking skills;
- ability to frame new ideas and solve problems;
- ability to access information;
- creative thinking;
- ability to conceptualize;
- adaptability to change;
- human relations skills;
- ability to work in a team atmosphere;
- ability to re-learn;
- oral communication skills;
- negotiation skills, that is, the ability to reach consensus and re-solve conflicts;
- goal setting, motivation, know-how to get things done;
- self-assurance and task commitment;
- leadership, that is, the ability to assume responsibility and moti-vate co-workers.

To achieve these skills, we must transform the organizational norm to one that recognizes and supports people who are able to work to-gether and collaborate on problem identification, analysis and inquiry, and solutions. Since the needs of the students must become the focus of the organizational structure, the following need examination and adjustment:

- present use of time in the structure;
- present practices of grade levels;
- scheduling;
- time devoted to specific subject areas;
- relationship between subject areas;
- content coverage;

- length of school day and school year;
- available course offerings.

Pedagogical Transformation

Pedagogy and organizational structure are interwoven and are treated separately here only to emphasize that both must take place. One cannot simply rearrange the chairs in a classroom into a circle and proclaim that this will help instruction. In America's public schools, we historically have asked children to sit one behind the other and told them to be still, to be quiet and never talk to each other. If all we do is put them in a circle and tell them to be still, we have done little to change the results.

A growing body of evidence indicates that current instructional delivery models cannot survive if we are to meet the needs of a 21st century. The required changes are not faddish changes in methods and approaches. The changes are based on physiological evidence that recognizes the very complex functioning of the human brain. Research and experience have established that different people learn in different ways and that educators, as the engineers of learning, are capable of adapting teaching styles to the learning styles of children. Only one-tenth of what we already know is currently being used, and the research continues to explode before us. The new knowledge will require us to adjust our pedagogy. *The new paradigm is that individuals learn in different ways and that success can be measured in a variety of ways.*

Pedagogical transformation is a revolution, not an evolution. It is not a new method or approach. It shatters the very essence of what we have believed for years. And it will not come about as a result of legislation from the federal or state government that imposes new regulations or higher standards. It also will be stymied if we try to remediate to undo what has been done. Pedagogical transformation will require the liberation of the American educator from the past and from the security that comes from doing the known and comfortable.

Pedagogical transformation can happen only in conjunction with organizational transformation. Children will require more time in school, but not more time doing the same thing. If children are not to be doing the same thing, teachers also will have to act differently. This pedagogical transformation will not come easily and will require enormous effort on the part of teachers. Teachers and principals will have to work longer days and longer years, with ample time to interact, plan, and learn. The changes in working conditions require that teachers be compensated appropriately. Educational leaders must provide support as teachers apply what they know about the learning process. If all constituencies understand that the social, attitudinal, and political transformations must take place at the same time, unions will not be an impediment.

Pedagogical transformation must address what we teach, how we teach, and how we measure what the students have learned. Since the expectation for results has dramatically changed in the last 10 years, the American public schools will be expected to be successful with all children. This is the first time in the history of public education that we are expected to educate all children equally. Heretofore, the role of the American public school was chiefly to sort and select, to decide who would go to college and who would enter the world of work. Today, the new requirement of the school is to provide an effective and appropriate education for all children, no matter how they come to school. Our new vision that all children be successful has caught the public schools of America by surprise. *This shift of responsibility to the school requires a critical shift in perspective.* It means that public school educators cannot point to children and say that some children come with so many problems that we cannot educate them; it means that we have to recognize the problems and issues confronting children and plan ways to solve those problems so that everyone can be educated effectively and appropriately.

If we accept this new requirement for schools, we must recognize that the current pedagogical models are not acceptable. Any student dropout is an indicator of a failed system. When the dropout rate over four high school years, as in Springfield, reaches 40%, or even 60% among Hispanics, it screams at us that the practices of the past are not successful today. We must combine what we are learning about teaching and learning with changes in organizational structure to meet this new requirement of teaching all children.

To teach all children implies that administrators and teachers undergo enormous changes in the skills and knowledge they possess today. A new discussion is essential concerning the responsibility of teachers and administrators to acquire new knowledge and skills. Both management and teachers have a responsibility to change. Teachers must recognize that the skills and information they brought to teaching are no longer adequate. They must participate in staff-development programs to expand their repertoire of instructional strategies necessary to be successful with all children. Training and support for teachers to acquire these new skills are critical to pedagogical transformation.

151

Institutional Collaboration

In addition to *conventional* components in professional and curriculum development programs, the Springfield Public Schools have entered into long-term relationships with several major institutions to work on the issues of educators' belief systems about learning, appropriate teaching strategies, more authentic and performance-based assessment, and learning outcomes as evidence of the quality of the education endeavor.

All teachers and administrators are participating in professional development workshops conducted by the Efficacy Institute of Lexington, Massachusetts. The basic premise of this work is that intelligence is developmental and not given at birth. *In the new paradigm, effort and development, not innate ability, lead to success.* This developmental approach supports the belief that all students can master a high-quality curriculum. Moreover, all children have the right to study high levels of mathematics, science, foreign language, and English.

This belief system has lead us to a second collaboration with Research for Better Teaching in Carlisle, Massachusetts. Our teachers and administrators are involved in workshops that focus on understanding the teaching repertoires that all teachers need to know and use. Teachers and administrators are learning more about teaching and administering schools as instructional specialists engaged in a collegial endeavor. This collaboration will help teachers and administrators work together in a systemic way to improve instruction.

A changed belief system and a new approach to instruction lead naturally to a discussion about more innovative assessment practices. We now are engaged in a long-term effort with the Educational Testing Service to develop "big idea" learning outcomes, for which we are developing authentic, performance-based, curriculum-assessment activities for the spring of 1993. Foreign language teachers will administer oral interviews to a sample of Level 1 French, Spanish, and Chinese language students to gather data about student ability to perform identified speaking tasks. English teachers will administer a writing sample and a literature-based assessment to measure the achievement of curricular goals. Mathematics and science teachers will pilot some specific interdisciplinary and subject area tasks at identified grades between K and 12. These are but a sampling of assessment projects in progress.

All of these previous efforts are contingent on the identification of agreed-on K-12 learning outcomes for the system. The individual grade level and subject area outcomes must be developed to help students reach the agreed-on end point. We now are working to establish such outcomes and building consensus about how to reach them.

Another major component of the pedagogical transformation is the integration of technology in our teaching and learning process. In Springfield we are using technology to support our ongoing reform effort, which reflects a philosophy of access to equity and academic excellence for all students. Springfield will use technology in three major areas:

- as a tool in the delivery of a high-quality core curriculum,
- as a tool in the management of school information, and
- as a subject area in the curriculum.

Technology includes computers and computer networks, VCRs and videos, large-screen projection devices, hand-held video cameras and studio video production, and satellite links. Students must be able to access information and analyze data in meaningful ways. Technology provides new techniques for access and new power for analysis. Students can access courses through distance learning, use worldwide library resources, and share information through international computer networks. Students can connect to the educational setting from their homes, from libraries, and other support locations. Students can participate in educational programs in nontraditional settings and in nontraditional time frames.

As a new and developing tool, technology also must be learned and mastered by educators. In Springfield, we currently are experimenting with a variety of technologies. We have taught technology in business and vocational settings. We have computer-assisted learning stations for academic reinforcement, microcomputer labs using languages such as LOGO, and computer simulations and commercial software to support academic instruction. Middle schools have computer labs that are used in the writing process and that provide instructional support in other subject areas. High school computer labs are used to teach computer applications, computer languages, word processing, and computer-aided design. Television production is available in mini-lessons at various schools and in a sequential program of studies at the high school level with access to a broadcast studio. The goal is to have these technologies available to all students at all schools.

Thus the reform movement can be supported by enlisting the help of technology. This inclusion can best be accomplished by working with community resources, such as the area library and museums and business partners. Springfield is currently involved in a partnership with the MITRE Corporation, a nonprofit company devoted to study of the uses of technology and the design of information systems. Focusing on education, MITRE and the Springfield Public Schools have joined to explore the use of technology in K-12 education and to support instruction that incorporates technology. In addition, they are helping to create a computer-based curriculum management and assessment tool. Together, we can strengthen our educational system to truly prepare our students for the information age.

Recognizing the pedagogical needs in Springfield, professional development — even at a time when financial resources are rapidly diminishing — becomes of paramount importance. Available funds were devoted to providing teachers with a repertoire of instructional strategies. Since after-school workshops required additional payment, and since all staff members needed to embrace the same vision and information, six half-days were petitioned for and granted by the Massachusetts Department of Education to hold professional development programs during released time. Federal and state grants were aggressively sought. When any additional grant funds were available, they were used for professional development. Teachers were encouraged to visit other classrooms, both within their school buildings and at other schools. All this support would lead to learning varied strategies and, equally as important, to open communication and exchange of ideas among teachers, who often work in isolation. This process must continue, for all educators must be continually open to new developments in education and, above all, must be open to trying something new in search of the best method for each child. A climate must be established that supports educators in taking risks.

Social and Attitudinal Transformation

The social and attitudinal transformation requires everyone in the community to understand fully the interdependence of school and community. *One cannot have an effective quality of life in any community without effective public schools.* Each school district must form broad alliances with the following constituencies: parents, business members, religious leaders, human service providers, community agencies, and senior citizens. As a nation, we have not believed that schools should work as part of a larger and interdependent society. In fact, we have attempted to keep these groups in the community separate. We now have recognized the need to work with the entire community if we are to educate all children successfully.

As America moves from an industrial to an information society, major changes in social attitudes are required. During the industrial period, America had a well-defined set of expectations for the distribution of results. Society, then, was controlled by a few at the top — usually white males — with most people in the middle working and taking direction. Society took care of a small group at the bottom, a group that was viewed as throw-away people. As we moved into the information society, we recognized that every individual must be a successful contributor to the economy.

Equity is the single most critical issue in education today. Does every child born in America have equal access to an effective and appropriate education? Our present system is such that children who are born poor will more than likely receive an inferior education. The research is clear in support of the implementation of early childhood programs that provide a firm foundation for continued development and academic achievement. The changes in society and the workplace indicate that the worker of tomorrow must be capable in many skill areas and must have higher-order thinking ability. By beginning earlier and providing a continuum of educational opportunities, we will address these new challenges.

Present conditions are moving us from a moral imperative to educate all to an economic imperative to educate all. American business is facing a most critical challenge in the coming century. The work demands of the future underscore the need for rapid systemic change in American education.

American industry will develop 16 million new jobs by the early 21st century; however, there will be only 14 million people to fill these jobs. Of these 14 million new entrants into the workplace, a majority will be female and/or minority, a group that historically has been underprepared. A country that already will have a shortage of two million workers cannot also cope with workers who are unprepared for the job market. In addition, a majority of these 16 million new jobs will require skills far beyond those we expect of entrants into the work force today. It is estimated that 50% of these new jobs will require a college degree; 75% will require at least two years of college.

Although American industry today is spending between $30 billion and $40 billion on training efforts for their employees, this investment is not enough. The schools must produce a new kind of worker for the 21st century, a worker with a new literacy and ability to relearn and be adaptable. Today's first-graders will probably change jobs from six to nine times during their lifetime. Up to 51 million may need retraining in the next 15 years — 21 million new job entrants plus 30 million current workers.

America needs every citizen to be a productive and contributing member of society. People who were traditionally not expected to succeed must now succeed if our economy is to survive. This requires a complete social and attitudinal transformation on the part of our society, and more especially on the part of our teachers. *Again, the challenge has now become not teaching students to the best of their potential, but teaching students to the best of our potential.* It is what we do in schools with children who come to school that will make the difference. This transformation is possibly the most challenging and the most difficult for the American public school to make. It means that teachers, administrators, parents, and even students must totally change their perspective. They must discard the notion of school as we understand it today and create new institutions with new visions. This is, indeed, difficult for all of us.

This challenge is compounded by the fact that schools are expected to teach more to more children. The task is made more difficult because ours is a heterogeneous and pluralistic society unlike any other in the world. Our country is made up of different races and cultures and language groups with different values and perspectives on life. And yet this difference, the diversity of our people, may be our greatest asset.

Our country and our schools have struggled with our multicultural and diverse nature and have attempted to view our differences as part of our strength. As of yet, we have not been fully successful in using the diversity of our nation as the asset it can be. In education, we have developed multicultural and diversity units of instruction as a solution. However, we have had limited success, in great part because the approach has been fragmented.

Inclusion, a new approach, is being implemented in Springfield as well as in other school systems. Through inclusion models, teachers work cooperatively with all children. Current research indicates that students learn a great deal from each other and that differences in children, when handled appropriately by the teacher, are assets in improving the teaching and learning process.

In the past, the trend in American education was to create as homogeneous a learning environment as possible. This led to the separation of children who were different and created a very fragmented and exclusive instructional process. Current research, however, has led to a new examination of exclusionary practices in our schools. This new inclusion model for instruction has taken hold and is being piloted all across the country. Springfield has become one of five pilot districts in Massachusetts to implement inclusionary models and has dozens of programs that are inclusionary. Inclusion also has led us to implement two-way bilingual programs that allow English-speaking students to learn a new language, Spanish or Russian; and Hispanic or Russian students to learn English. This approach has great promise and is predicated, in part, on the four transformations.

Political Transformation

This area of transformation has several components and includes political change within the school structure as well as in government and society in general. First, it is important that we recognize that we live in a society that has had a strong middle class as its underpinning. National birth rate data indicate that the middle class is having about 1.5 children per marriage, hence the natural replenishment of the middle class is not taking place. By comparison, the birth rate for poor people is exploding.

The political questions here are: Does the country have the will to educate those who traditionally have been ignored? Will American society understand the political and economic repercussions and implications of not educating its poor? Will American society support public education in urban centers when the people being educated do not resemble both in class and color the people controlling the economy of those urban centers?

The additional fundamental issue of equity and excellence also must be addressed within the political context. At present, where a child is born will determine to a great extent the quality of the child's education. There are communities in this country that spend $1,200 per child for education, while others spend as high as $14,000 per child. While the issue is not money alone, an inherent inequality in funding is clear. The federal government must play a more intensive role in the funding of American public education. The link between our economic survival as a nation and education has been clearly defined. We are at the crossroads of choosing to pay adequately for the education of all children regardless of where they live, the color of their skin, or the language they speak, or of choosing not to pay and losing our democracy.

Appropriate and sufficient funding is crucial to any educational reform. In Springfield, at the end of the first year of the school improvement process in 1990, a campaign was launched to override the tax-limiting Proposition 2½ in Massachusetts. Successful override brought an additional $3,400,000 to the city for the School Department budget. The success of this campaign — the only one in the state to support education — indicated the high level of public support for the public schools. During 1991-1992, the Massachusetts legislature formed committees that included several public school educators, including this author, to develop school reform legislation. Efforts still continue for the total reform package; but the state legislature did add funds for education, which resulted in an additional $20,000,000 in the Equal Education Opportunity Grant for Springfield for 1992-1993.

Massachusetts adopted a school choice plan that allows communities to decide if they wish to participate, with the intent that creating competition among schools will result in improvement. The participating communities establish the number of students they will accept from other communities. The sending community pays the tuition for each child. Unfortunately, this legislation depletes the resources of the urban centers. Since all children from a sending community are eligible, the sending community is responsible for the tuition of even those students who previously were in a private or parochial school but who elect to attend a public school in another participating community. To offset this inequity, the state has reimbursed sending communities a minimum of 50% of the tuition costs. But this program does not offset the inequity for individuals, since there is no transportation allowance. Of the 150 students exercising the school choice option from Springfield, 94% attending schools in neighboring communities are white and 54% are students who did not attend the public schools previously. The aim of this state choice plan will not be realized, since its basic assumption is flawed. Moreover, parents and students do not necessarily select a school because of an excellent education program. Other issues govern the selection, including proximity to a school, previous attendance at a school, and race relations.

The final political transformation requires American public education and its governance to remain at the local level. All attempts to nationalize education are filled with danger. Local issues and local values contribute to the effective delivery of educational opportunity in the individual classroom.

The federal government, however, does have a role to play in setting broad standards concerning expectations of learning outcomes. We are the only industrialized country in the world that does not have national standards or expectations. Another role the government must play is in providing the broad research necessary to link instruction and assessment through the use of technology. Although there are thousands of school systems across the country duplicating efforts in the area, none of these districts have the resources to implement this needed transformation effectively. The federal government could complete such a project in conjunction with some of the major corporations in less than two years.

The four transformations can take place in America if we understand and accept the following precepts:

- Money is not a panacea; but without money, we cannot accomplish our goals.
- Children do not come to school the same way; however, it is our response to how they come that makes the difference.
- Some children cost more to educate than others. It is in our best interest to educate them all.
- The current system of funding public education is inequitable and must be changed.
- The classroom and school is the unit of change; and for that reason, local governance must be promoted, encouraged, and maintained.
- The current model of education must be adjusted so that for the first time quality, not remediation, becomes the norm.
- The relationship between the school, the home, and the community must be understood and internalized. Schools need to work with families and the community, and the community needs the schools. They cannot exist independent of each other.
- Our curriculum must reflect our goals. What must be learned and how it is assessed are basic questions that must be posed.
- Technology must be viewed as the key to the future. We are not using even one-tenth of the power of technology. We must move from the chalkboard to the electronic board.
- The principle of organized abandonment must be learned. Abandon what has not worked for a long time.
- Our schools must be transformed from places where people are told what to do to places where students, parents, teachers, and administrators identify the issues and provide the solutions.
- Interdistrict choice as a school reform device must be used with great care lest we create new inequities for a segment of our population and a divider of the haves and have-nots.
- Ongoing staff-development programs and support at the school level are needed.
- Additional time in the school day where teachers can plan together around the issues that confront them is essential. Schools must

become the units of change where teachers see the interdependence of what they teach and how they work and support each other.

- Everyone in America must understand the interdependence of the quality of life in our community and the quality of our schools.

Conclusion

American public education has an awesome task, giving educators what is possibly the greatest opportunity any one group of people has ever had. America is poised for its greatest failure or its greatest success. America can become a nation of haves and will-haves. The great American experiment called democracy cannot and will not survive without an educated populace. For educators, this is a great opportunity to realize equity through education. For our children, this is the only opportunity for realization of the American Dream in a thriving world economy.

We in Springfield believe we have begun the process for realizing the full transformation of our public schools. We are hardly done, but we have a strong beginning. We have had an impact on every constituency in our community. Although we still have many bridges to cross and issues to resolve, there is a new spirit that sees realization of our vision as possible. We may not merit distinction at this moment, but we certainly do merit watching.

THE BUTTERFLY EFFECT — SMALL CHANGES WITH BIG CONSEQUENCES: CHALLENGES FOR PUBLIC EDUCATION

Sally B. Kilgore

A Hudson Institute senior fellow analyzes the choices, good and bad, made in America's school reform movement to date and draws attention to problems for which remedies must be found.

Are public schools doing a good job? Yes, of course, if we are concerned about achievement and compare current student performance with that of the early 1980s. No, not at all, if we compare current achievement to the mid-Sixties or to standards considered competitive with other countries.

Our current high school graduation rates are high. Students are enrolling in Advanced Placement Courses in record numbers. High school graduates enter postsecondary institutions at a higher rate than at any other time in history. We may be, in fact, a world leader.

Looking beneath the surface, though, we know best by hindsight that the early 1980s constituted an achievement trough — preceded, as it was, by a long decline and followed by a steady upward trend that has yet to match the levels of achievement of the 1960s. During the 1980s achievement in most grades and subjects improved for low-achieving students, whether measured by the National Assessment for Educational Progress or Scholastic Aptitude Tests. For the top 10% of students, however, the achievement levels have remained stable and never really returned to the levels of the Sixties.

Barbara (Sally) Kilgore is senior fellow and director of education policy studies, the Hudson Institute, Indianapolis, Indiana.

While we have world-class attendance rates to postsecondary institutions, we also have a world-class remedial course enrollment in that sector: at least 20% of our students enrolled in four-year colleges are enrolled in one or more remedial courses. Most countries do not even have such courses available. Should we praise our system for keeping channels of opportunity open? Should we condemn it for creating inefficiencies when youth aspire to go to college but are not ready for its demands? How should we evaluate our college attendance rate when only 50% of those who enter our four-year colleges and universities actually complete a degree? In economic returns, the added return for a few years of college is, at best, marginal. But in other terms, the experience could be quite worthwhile.

These dilemmas represent only a sampling of the problems one encounters in trying to evaluate the performance of public schools relative to their past performance in this country or to the performance of schools in other nations. Certainly, further debates are possible. The comparison groups constitute different populations of students – in terms of racial composition, family structures, and experiences with poverty, crime, and homelessness. They are different in ways that likely disadvantage youth in the Nineties. But to say that our schools are doing a good job, given what they have to work with, misses the point. Even Lester Maddox had that problem figured out when he said that the only problem with prisons was the population of inmates they had to manage.

Teachers are right to insist that things are different now: different students, different constraints. Travesties occur, though, in how we choose to address the differences across cohorts. In the Seventies and Eighties, many teachers (and professors) coped with differences by adjusting the standards. In essence, when students could not achieve the standards we announced by the methods we used, standards were changed, not the methods. More recently, some observers have chosen to argue that the old standards are unworthy of student effort or irrelevant to new populations of students. That is yet another mistake.

I will not try to solve the dilemmas that these statistics pose, because such resolution necessarily involves some choices about what we want in an education system – some presuppositions about what is good and desirable for individuals as well as the society. Instead, I will try to disentangle the choices we have made up until this point and draw attention to problems for which remedies must be found quite independent of one's content or discontent with the current condition of education.

The Larger Context of Change in Education

For the last 25 years, public schooling has functioned in a remarkably turbulent environment. The ground rules that governed how teachers taught and what students did have shifted considerably. By turbulent environment, I refer not simply to increasing crime, homelessness, and broken families but also, and perhaps more fundamentally, I refer to new ground rules that courts and legislatures have established regarding the conduct of schooling. While public schools may be relatively unique as institutions in terms of the level of turbulence they have experienced, they are not unique in their poor adaptation to it. Actually, adaptive organizations are relatively rare. But the importance of creating schools that are more adaptive is of great consequence. Let me establish the case.

New Ground Rules

In the past 25 years the ground rules for dealing with teacher assignment, student discipline, and curriculum content — to name a few significant areas — have shifted notably. While all the shifts I discuss here are the result of legal precedents, the critical responses often occurred outside the schoolhouse. In each case, though, simplistic or faulty responses undermined the viability of schools as places of learning.

When court litigation led to new constraints and processes in disciplining students, teachers and principals often found it easier to *not* see misbehavior than to wade through what appeared to be confusing constraints on their action. Both as a result of those court rulings and more recent litigation on child abuse, state officials generally advise teachers: Whatever you do, don't touch the students.

Judicial decisions limiting the promotion of religion in public schools led teachers and administrators, as well as textbook publishers, to eliminate all references to religion, thereby altering the intent of the original decision. Texts and teachers simply became silent about the existence of religious groups. When, in our school texts, "pilgrims" became people who take long journeys, should we be surprised that history makes little sense to children? How can one even make sense of the present world in the midst of such silence?

Educators have not been alone in ignoring, simplifying, or misconstruing new ground rules. For example, when judicial decisions and legislative actions constrained the way employers can use information about high school performance when evaluating the relative merits of applicants, prospective employers chose to ignore everything about high school performance rather than face the prospect of having to defend themselves in court. Thus doing well in high school becomes irrelevant to the futures of easily half of the students enrolled there, a fact that inevitably affects what students do in the classrooms and corridors of our schools.

One of the changes in ground rules that had profound consequences for the educational welfare of youth relates to curriculum. In this instance, the critical actors may well have been public colleges and universities, not elementary and secondary schools. During the early Seventies, as institutions of higher education sought to address issues of equity, open admissions became a common policy for our public universities and colleges. High school prerequisites were thrown out the window in the name of equity. Secondary schools followed the lead of these institutions and eliminated many course requirements for high school graduation, as well as for completion of the precollege curriculum. By 1982, 40% of public secondary schools required only one year of mathematics for graduation; 50% had no science course requirements. Evidence is fairly persuasive that this shift had a deleterious effect on the average student in high school, at least in two respects, one predicting the other. First, without the requirements, students quit taking the courses. Second, without the coursework, student achievement scores declined. Remedial courses grew concomitantly in institutions of higher education. Yet, all we hear about these circumstances are off-stage mutterings.

If the practices that result from changing ground rules had only trivial consequences, there would be no cause for alarm. I argue that the consequences are not trivial. Moreover, if faulty or simplistic translations of new ground rules were endemic among all social institutions, then one might be forced to conclude that while the consequences were undesirable, it is an inevitable process that we cannot surmount in the educational sector. Rather, it would require some shift in human nature or the structure of society itself. But I will argue that the consequences were neither trivial nor inevitable as a fact of "human nature."

Non-Trivial Consequences

In 1975, the *Goss* v. *Lopez* U.S. Supreme Court decision required due process for all students facing disciplinary action in public schools. No longer could a teacher simply say, "You will be in detention hall this afternoon," and count on institutional support for the demand. Teachers' claims regarding misbehaving students now required witnesses, evidence, and hearings. A teacher's word was no longer sufficient to back a reprimand or other disciplinary action.

Unaccustomed to the new and certainly more complex procedures, many principals and teachers found it easier to pretend that they did not see students engaged in a fist fight, did not notice a crib sheet on the floor during the course of an exam, or did not hear a taunt to a colleague in the hallway. The simple way to deal with the new ground rules for disciplining students was to wipe out any official existence of misbehavior. Many observers have noted the consequences of this and other changes. Student behavior has deteriorated. High numbers of students regularly taunt or verbally assault teachers in the classroom. Twenty-nine percent of teachers surveyed in 1990 reported verbal abuse of teachers as a serious or moderately serious problem.[1]

Recently, authorities in one school district, after a long stretch of ignoring their own discipline code, created an even greater threat to institutional legitimacy when they returned to strict enforcement of it. Twenty percent of the first-graders were sent home as a disciplinary action when the teacher reported that they had used foul language. During the same year, more than 40% of the secondary students were subjected to disciplinary action. Public reaction was predictable: When too many deviants are created, citizens and students begin to question the rules, not the deviants.

Clearly, for many schools the fact that misbehaving students disrupt the learning opportunities of other students is secondary to the anticipated costs of controlling the disruption. In some circumstances, that calculus may be reasonable — for example, when the interruption is minor and potential time lost in correction great. However, over time such responses can only increase the incidence of disruptions to the point that learning cannot occur.

Choosing to ignore disruption had non-trivial consequences in at least some cases. In a limited 1988 survey of U.S. eighth-graders, 40% reported that their learning was affected by misbehaving students in their classroom.[2] From the institutional point of view, this consequence must be small relative to the costs of finding ways to reduce the incidence of misbehavior, whether through discipline or the reorganization of the classroom. Yet we know that disruptions do affect the achievement of students. So the consequence is non-trivial.

Not touching children has become an accepted strategy for avoiding the accusation of child abuse. Protecting teachers in this way is important. But what about the welfare of the children? Do six-year-old children need touching? We know that it is essential for young children as part of the process of bonding with parents. We know that adults lower their blood pressure by giving or receiving shoulder hugs. Was the no-touching rule made in the interest of children? No, it was made to protect teachers and administrators when insurance policies fail to cover the costs of child-abuse accusations. Actually, we do not really know what the best interests of children are in these circumstances.

The irony, I argue, of college and university efforts to achieve greater equity by reducing or eliminating prerequisites is that they have actually generated greater inequity in at least two respects. First, parents who knew little about colleges thought nothing of it if their sons and daughters were not enrolled in mathematics and science courses in high school. College-educated parents, on the other hand, knew the significance of such courses; and many of them probably pushed their children to enroll even in the absence of such requirements. Thus social-class inequities likely increased in the absence of course requirements. Second, women and minorities were more likely to opt out of mathematics and science courses when given the choice. Gender and racial inequities have probably persisted, in part, because of differential enrollment rates in these academic courses.

Cognitive psychologists tell us that people learn best when they are pursuing a subject, or more particularly a question, that interests them. No one would doubt that conclusion. But to infer from that conclusion that it is better to remain ignorant of a subject than to pursue knowledge of it simply because one lacks interest is false. Certainly, most women over age 40, and possibly many men as well, can identify a course they were forced against their interests to take. Many of them found, as I did, that what they thought was a dreadful subject turned out to be fascinating.

The relative importance of immaturity, sexual stereotyping, and native ability in initial subject matter preferences is not clear. What is a fact, though, is that preconceived notions of interesting topics are not perfect predictors of what indeed turns out to be interesting. Moreover, it is better to know a little about science and mathematics, regardless of pre-existing interests, than to know nothing. Whether we follow the evidence of Clifford Adelman on the positive effects of mathematics coursework on earned income or the plethora of evidence on the effects of high school course enrollment on achievement and college entrance scores, we should conclude that this freedom to choose did not serve minorities and women well.

Alternatives to Compromising Solutions

The cost of losing learning opportunities, incremental as they are, do not show up on the spread sheet in the same way that lawsuits do. The cost of depriving young children of hugs is invisible in comparison to the price teachers may pay if false accusations arise. Somehow businesses find it more cost effective to use special proficiency tests than to identify what aspects of high school performance are relevant to a job. In general, the loss to individual students is so diffuse in comparison with potential losses in a lawsuit that pressure to seek alternatives may be absent.

Can we envision alternative responses to legal rulings that would not have compromised the educational mission of our public schools? In most instances, the answer is yes.

Several good strategies for reconstructing student discipline do exist. Parents, and in some instances students, can be involved in reformulating the code of conduct to create a much broader base of support for its enforcement. For younger children, especially, the structure of the school day can be reframed to allow for more movement and conversation, thereby accommodating more active students. School choice is also effective in reducing discipline problems throughout entire districts, perhaps in part through the support garnered by parents for the school their child attends.

Similarly, alternatives to "don't touch" exist. Limiting touches to public places, rather than prohibiting them entirely, allows for numerous witnesses. Youth organizations have instituted the practice that one adult is never alone with one or more children. School practices may be more or less amenable to a two-adult rule, especially for young children, where the practice is likely most deleterious; and teacher aides are increasingly common in classrooms.

State reform efforts in the Eighties sought to improve the level of academic preparation of high school graduates, and the amount of academic coursework completed by high school students has increased in the past decade. In fact, that shift upward in course enrollment may be the single most important factor in the rise of achievement scores among high school students during the Eighties.

Challenging institutions of higher education to raise their standards, as Al Shanker recently did at President-elect Bill Clinton's economic summit, is certainly one way to redress the loss of inducements to learn in our secondary schools. But given shortfalls in enrollment, few colleges and universities may be willing to take the lead. Clearly, the

167

greatest lever for change exists within state legislatures, where open access policies often originated. A close analysis of costs incurred for remedial programs is an appropriate eye-opener for state legislators.

Renewing the link between school and work after high school — compromised by employers' disregard for high school performance — could take several forms. New collaborations with schools and corporations could, somewhat like the German model, integrate apprenticeships with schooling and make those apprenticeships conditional on student performance in school. Some districts, as in Fort Worth, Texas, seek to integrate the world of work into the curriculum in terms of both the context in which students learn about various subjects and in the ways in which they learn. Even enhancing the intrinsic satisfaction of learning is within the scope of alternatives applicable to most students; learning mathematics and science while designing a new park, for instance, can provide new and powerful motivations for learning.

Conclusion

Because of both compromises in existing practices and failure to respond to new ground rules governing how teachers teach and what students do, the quality of education is not what it could be. No walls will crumble, no mass exodus will occur. But unless we reconstruct meaningful inducements for students to learn, as well as sensible places for youth to be, we will have children ill-prepared for the 21st century.

Footnotes

1. *The Condition of Education, 1992* (Washington, D.C., National Center for Education Statistics, 1992).
2. *National Education Longitudinal Study* (Washington, D.C., National Center for Education Statistics).

RECLAIMING AMERICAN INDIAN EDUCATION

Norbert S. Hill, Jr.

For Native Americans to retain the integrity of their culture and gain control of their future, the ideal of educational equity must be interpreted in new ways. Fortunately, says Mr. Hill, there are recently developed models of strong, autonomous leadership from which to learn.

The American Indian population before the Indian holocaust totaled 10 million to 12 million people by conservative estimate. One hundred years ago there were only 195,000 survivors. Today there are approximately two million Native Americans in the United States, still far fewer than in 1492. We (I write as an advocate for my people) have survived despite the disease, warfare and genocide, removal and relocations, and destruction of our way of life that are the legacy of European domination of the Americas.

American Indians have been subjected continually to inadequate and unfair educational practices. Since the 1790s, the U.S. government's goal has been to assimilate Indians into the dominant culture. The government's focus has been to educate us in the ways of the white people by using teacher-directed methods that render obsolete the American Indian tradition of interactive learning. Conformity to the practices of the dominant culture has been a measure of one's worth. This orientation still permeates schools both on and off Indian reservations. Thus our own educational heritage has been weakened and in some cases destroyed.

While including no Indian members in its ranks, the National Commission on Excellence in Education, in their 1983 report, *A Nation at Risk*, succinctly and eloquently supported the principles of equality and excellence: "Part of what is at risk is the promise first made on this continent: All, regardless of race or class or economic status, are entitled to a fair chance and to the tools for developing their powers and

---

Norbert S. Hill, Jr. is executive director, American Indian Science and Engineering Society, Boulder, Colorado.

mind and spirit to the utmost." Unfortunately, the committee went on to treat "equal opportunity" almost exclusively in economic terms. National policy still seeks to help minorities overcome "deficits" and thus become more like the privileged few who formulate and benefit from the dominant model. That model does not recognize the unique characteristics and potential of Native American children.

Some educational institutions mistakenly believe that equality is dependent primarily on the right to participate in academic governance. While participation in all forms of policy making is critical, it is the means to participate in the deepest *personal* sense that enables Indian people to assert their influence effectively. Our means of control are our identity and dignity. They sustain us as a people within the vast array of experiences and economic interactions that characterize American life. When we accept compliant, obedient roles, we are robbed of our ability to draw strength from our own deeply rooted traditions.

Our challenge is to recapture our legacy and reclaim our educational process for our own people, using our own ways of teaching and knowing. For American Indians, education is significant beyond personal achievement and opportunity. Education that integrates Indian values holds the key to our survival as sovereign nations with distinct cultures and perspectives. Such education instills confidence and competence in people and is the key to self-determination, the right to determine and direct our own affairs. It helps us navigate through the complexity and ambiguity of the world inside of and surrounding American Indian communities. It helps us become better prepared to clearly define and defend our goals. Clarity of direction and informed decisions are basic to our control over the one-third of our nation's energy resources that lie beneath Indian lands. We need the ability to express our viewpoints and engage in problem-solving approaches consistent with our unique cultural traditions and perspectives.

In high school and college we cannot give back to young adults what has been effectively destroyed in childhood. We must guide children from a young age in learning how to determine when and how to merge Indian and non-Indian value systems. In order to do this, children must be able to identify and discriminate between traditional Indian values and the values of the dominant culture. By the time our students get to college, many of them have lost the ability to clearly state their unique needs and purposes as American Indians. If our students suffer from cultural amnesia because of inadequate exposure to their heritage, they will lack the necessary framework for making reasonable decisions related to personal, cultural, social, professional, and spiritual growth throughout their experiences in formal education and beyond.

Contemporary pedagogy may be politically convenient and comfortably familiar to the dominant culture. However, homogeneous expectations related to content and procedure have produced tremendously unequal and expensive outcomes for Indian people. For example, although the Cherokee Republic had a higher percentage of well-educated people in the late 19th century than the white settlers of Texas and Arkansas,[1] American Indians now "out-disadvantage" all groups. Of every 100 minority children attending kindergarten today, 45 will drop out of high school before graduation. The dropout rate for American Indian high school students stands at the disproportionately high rate of 65%. The post-secondary dropout rate is estimated at 75% to 93%.[2]

Apathy and anomie, the primary reasons that Indian children drop out of school, are largely the result of a pedagogy that isolates them from opportunities to develop their potential. Hundreds of Indian students drop out of school, in effect, even without physically missing a day. Our schools have become lands of the walking dead. Our students currently associate education with the subjugation of their needs and interests to an irrelevant academic agenda with a narrow curricular focus. The current system insists that all children learn the same thing in the same way at the same time. Our educational institutions routinely inhibit instinct, emotion, and innate intelligence. Students too often are deprived of the opportunity to develop the skills and gain the confidence they need to manage their lives effectively. Many students drop out of school to take a job, for doing so holds the promise, often illusory, of an opportunity to demonstrate competence, a need that was never fulfilled in school.

It is senseless to employ a dysfunctional and alienating pedagogy as a means of preparing our children for a dysfunctional and alienating society. What, then, are our alternatives? How can we enable more of our students to become active, critical thinkers in school systems that implicitly, if not explicitly, promote docility and obedience? How can we re-conceive learning to maintain the necessary balance of knowledge and well-being? How can we offer opportunities for our students to acquire knowledge that is based on a respect for relationships and a commitment to a holistic, sustainable vision of a better world?

American Indian tradition itself provides some of the answers. The historical inseparability of education, personal growth, and traditional Indian values is well documented. Indians have traditionally empha-

171

sized an encompassing educational process rather than the narrow notion of "schooling" within four walls. According to the Indian way, "the universe is the university." The acquisition of life skills, including technical skills, was largely a by-product of life experiences, including observation and participation in the activities of adults. These experiences catalyzed methods of inquiry that were neither formulaic, sequential, nor dependent on the coercive methods of external authority. Assistance and guidance, rather than domination and control, were the way of our elders, our greatest teachers. Further, their reverence for wholeness and interdependence precluded the construction of reductionist models of learning employing fixed and static pieces of information. In their effort to understand the world, traditional Indian people were not content simply to analyze something to see how it worked and was used; of utmost important was its underlying meaning.[3]

The "drill and kill" approach of formal education is linear and based on artificial and isolated tasks. We must replace routinized, sequential, and alienating practices with opportunities relevant to evolving needs and interests. Traditional Indian learning is cyclical and integrates a variety of methods in a way that honors each individual as well as relationships and correspondences. Each student is implicitly empowered to believe in her or his own unique view of the world, including its cultural underpinnings. The result is engagement, rather than control, and the acquisition of dependable knowledge rooted in experience, rather than rote learning. Internal discipline replaces the external authority of teacher-directed "time on task."

We are not asking teachers to abdicate authority. We are asking that they become more effective role models by engaging children in opportunities to learn by posing questions, exploring relationships, and making real decisions. In a manner similar to the role our elders play, teachers must serve as advanced learners who support and guide children. They must develop opportunities for even our youngest children to learn to constructively resist and challenge habitual and compliant forms of expression, so that learning becomes personally relevant, purposeful, and satisfying.

We need real experiences — instead of contrived activities — both inside and outside the classroom, through which students can identify personal and cooperative interests, abilities, and talents. Imagine, for example, the study of birds. The methodology of lectures, visual aids, and work sheets pales in comparison to the real-life challenge of caring for a wounded bird. Students are encouraged to raise numerous questions and suggest approaches in order to uncover many varied yet complementary ways of knowing. Students are supported in expressing their spiritual, aesthetic, emotional, and moral perspectives. Instead of reinforcing the unnatural isolation of academic disciplines, students come to understand the interrelatedness of all aspects of inquiry.

In our example, an enlightened teacher would encourage students to engage their curiosity through co-generating and participating in a variety of activities related to the wounded bird, such as: the creation of a manual on traditional and Western healing practices, in-service learning at an animal clinic, a documentary about community members who practice healing, colorful posters on the anatomy of birds, an original book on the cultural significance of different kinds of birds, tape-recorded bird stories from community members and original tales from classmates, photographic displays, paintings with feathers, innovative bird feeders, and charts and graphs of birds sighted in the schoolyard or community. Students see themselves as powerful and creative decision makers as they help devise self-directed opportunities to enrich their talents and abilities and confirm or challenge their own beliefs and assumptions. School may end at three o'clock, but learning becomes a way of life.

Just as teachers ought not to "instruct," they ought not to "measure" students according to narrow standards of proficiency. The Indian way is to value a mistake as something that supports life. A mistake is sacred; like victory, it is associated with an opportunity to gain wisdom. In contrast to this viewpoint, evaluation in formal education, based on punishment for mistakes, has been a mechanism that commonly denigrates and demotes our children. Testing and tracking are tools of a coercive, assimilationist ideology that judges and stratifies people and destroys their ability to thrive.

Traditional Indian methods did not isolate and report on the measure of one's potential as if human beings could be broken into separate components. Education must abolish evaluation based on predetermined, uniform standards that measure performance related to tightly specified academic criteria. We do not need measures that depict our children as docile and disenchanted misfits in a system that defines "excellence" according to lifeless, authoritarian, and competitive values. "Excellence" is not a norm-referenced comparison of individuals. To use a cliché, it is the ability to be all that one can be.

If Indian students are to attain academic goals, evaluation must support them in achieving their unique power and potential. We must empower our children to confront their emotional, social, academic, and spiritual challenges creatively. We need to construct evaluation methods that broaden as well as reflect student awareness and potential. For example, growth might be charted through dialogue journals, both at home and school, filled with anecdotal descriptions; tape-recorded interviews; portfolios with periodic samples of work; displays depicting a range of abilities; photographic portfolios; and so forth.[4] These methods illustrate talent and achievement and simultaneously invite a broader respect for a child's evolution as a learner.

Vine Deloria, Jr. advocates that evaluation should become a community event. He cites the practice of the Five Civilized Tribes, who operated their own school system. In order to evaluate its effectiveness, they conducted several days of formal recitation of what students were learning in school. In this way, "the communities played an integral role in judging whether or not the school system was educating their children."[5] In our contemporary schools, we need to establish legitimate dialogue between schools, parents, and communities to ensure that all parties work together to sustain a productive, nurturing educational environment for students that promotes excellence.

It is meaningless to pose the question, "How ought we define excellence as it relates to our diverse student population, our diverse society, and our world community?" if our prospective teachers understand only one definition of learning. Like the rest of current education, teacher preparation in the United States implicitly inculcates students of all cultures with the values of the predominant Anglo culture. A respectful, cooperative, and responsible educational system can be created and sustained only by teachers who have not been forced to repress their own traditions and values in order to receive, memorize, and repeat someone else's past.[6] In order to understand how the pedagogy of domination has been used to destroy American Indian cultures and languages, Anglo and other prospective teachers must comprehend the implications of the training and cultural norms by which they themselves were shaped. They also must be given the opportunity to explore cultures different from their own so that they can in turn engender in their students an appreciation for diversity.

Effective teacher education programs can help to reconstruct the form and context of schooling. The primary challenge for such programs ought to be the rejection of models that create lists of discrete items for prospective teachers to master and their replacement with those models that embody the democratic and humanistic approach of involving prospective

174

teachers in designing their own pathways. In order to uncover and co-create pedagogy that will enable our children to become informed risk-takers, teachers must practice informed pedagogical risk-taking themselves. This strategy may be the only way to communicate the extraordinary power of self-direction and experience to those who will guide our youth.

Parents, as well as teachers, play an important role in education. Parental advice and guidance can make the school a true expression of a community's hopes and needs. It is necessary to examine and overturn the subtle mechanisms that inhibit meaningful parental participation in our schools. Although forced assimilationist policies are largely a thing of the past, Indian parents often are excluded from decision making in a variety of ways. Educational double-speak is confusing to parents. In off-reservation schools, there are often few or no school board members. Further, parents often do not feel welcome in their children's schools. As Deloria says,

> The psychological burden of even attending a meeting in a big, formal brick building is intimidating to many reservation parents. It calls back memories of their childhood and the summons to come to the agency, which always meant problems. . . . The presence of consolidated schools makes reform in this area a difficult proposition at this time. Wherever possible, local (reservation) communities should begin to take control of primary and part of secondary education. . . . Local control should emphasize control over curriculum with teaching about tribal history, tribal customs and traditions, and tribal language at the earliest possible age with a maximum use of traditional people. . . . This emphasis is in contrast to the present orientation, which is that the participants are Indian but the kinds of activities they are asked to support are basically non-Indian in origin.[7]

So that school is not just comprised of "white studies," we need an active commitment to multiculturalism. An educational environment that incorporates respect for all cultures encourages students to follow their natural desire to enrich and expand their views of the world. Our schools need to adopt an educational paradigm that embraces a deep understanding and appreciation of various cultural realities.

In regard to the education of American Indians, we must work together to create educational opportunities that recognize the nature of the American Indian cultural foundation as we embark upon conscious social reconstruction. We need more teachers grounded in traditional

Indian values and traditions — including more Indian educators at all school levels. We must support our emerging cadre of Indian educators and mentors.

All educators must convey to American Indian and all other students that Indian values are not wrong, although they may be different from those of the Anglo culture. Cultural norms must be honored. For example, Navajo medical students would find dissecting a cadaver contrary to cultural taboo. The Indian style of reflective thinking must be respected and not denigrated as being symptomatic of shyness or retardation. The Indian way of working to gain consensus and cooperation must be acknowledged as a valuable complement to the dominant culture's emphasis on aggressiveness, competition, and debate.

While diversity often receives lip service, we need to move beyond talk. Diversity must be woven into the very fabric of the curriculum. Isolated formulas and recipes lack sincerity, as well as efficacy, and ultimately reinforce the dominance of the monocultural design. Even well-meaning educators who advocate cultural pluralism simultaneously submit students to a monocultural pedagogy. A major challenge facing postsecondary institutions as they attempt to encourage and support diversity is to interact with American Indian communities in order to enrich one another's efforts and to forge a common vision. The emphasis must be on doing *with* rather than doing *for*. We must serve as advisors and counselors to one another.

History reveals that true advancement and productive interaction with European-Americans began only when Indians became participants in determining their own future. We would do well in 1993 to review a lesson learned in 1936, when Harvard University established a college-within-a-college for American Indian students. Then, as now, few Indians ever attended college; and many of those who entered did not stay. The college-within-a-college failed, because Indians did not participate in the formation and implementation of that format or any other educational agenda to which they were exposed.

We have many recent examples of strong, autonomous educational leadership from which to learn. Consider, for example, the success of the post-World War II Navajo Special Education Program in improving literacy and English language skills for young and old alike. Ultimately, the Navajo Tribe was awarded $24 million for education and health care to acknowledge and help undergird its strong commitment to education. This commitment led to the founding of the Navajo Community College in 1969, our first tribally controlled college. Today we have 27 tribally controlled community colleges that exemplify viable alternatives to postsecondary institutions, which often submerge American Indian students in a way of life that sharply contrasts with their personal belief systems and experiences. As we move toward educational self-determination, we must take leadership in putting forth curricular priorities at all educational levels that better enable us to overcome the destructive, paternalistic polices of the past.

The traditional Indian way is to view learning as a lifelong process. Young people are educated to become human beings with good values, instead of just narrowly defined professionals who have mastered content. This perspective enables students to sustain their responsibility as keepers of the future — a future that is much less predictable and certain than the authority-based assumptions of the American educational system might lead us to believe. There are special implications here for American Indian students of modern science and technology. They are entrusted with merging traditional values and the scientific framework in order to restore harmony to our planet.

The Ojibwa believe that dreams have magical qualities that make it possible to change or direct one's path in life. We can change the educational status quo by believing in our own creative vision of a more enlightened approach to the education of our children. While schools cannot avoid transmitting values, they can avoid reproducing failure. If we replicate the emotionally and spiritually hollow pedagogy of the past, we must be prepared to accept the perpetuation of epidemic dropout rates and power that is concentrated in the hands of a non-representative few. We must affirm that the purpose of education is the actualization of unique personal and cultural characteristics and potentialities. Educational experiences must be consistent with American Indian values, maximize students' potential, and nurture effective leadership in Indian country. The evolution of an educational process that is culturally grounded and forward-looking is critically important to American Indians if we are to retain our integrity as Indian people and gain control of our future.

Footnotes

1. Estelle Fuchs and Robert J. Havighurst, *To Live on This Earth* (Garden City, N.Y.: Doubleday, 1972).
2. Dennis R. Faulk and Larry P. Aitken, "Promoting Retention Among American Indian College Students," *Journal of American Indian Education* (January 1984): 24-31.

3. Vine Deloria, Jr., *American Indian Policy in the Twentieth Century* (Norman, Okla.: University of Oklahoma Press, 1985).
4. Elliot W. Eisner, *The Educational Imagination* (New York: Macmillan, 1985).
5. Vine Deloria, Jr., *Indian Education in America: Eight Essays* (Boulder, Colo.: American Indian Science and Engineering Society, 1991).
6. Paulo Freire, *Pedagogy of the Oppressed* (New York: Continuum Publishing, 1985).
7. Deloria, 1991.

REVITALIZING AMERICA'S PUBLIC SCHOOLS THROUGH SYSTEMIC CHANGE

Gene R. Carter

In a wide-ranging overview, Mr. Carter clarifies both the require-ments and the obstacles to systemic reform. He also offers a beguiling vision of benefits that a fundamental public school transformation can reap.

I am convinced that the public schools of today will shape the so-ciety of tomorrow. The fundamental challenge to us is to foresee change and shape it to our benefit. The belief that knowledge is power, and that it empowers people and nations, is the foundation on which we must build our commitment to public school education.

The strength of democratic America is an educated citizenry's per-sonal and civic morality, knowledge, and common agreement. John Adams said, "Liberty cannot be preserved without a general knowledge among the people." His friend and rival, Thomas Jefferson, said, "If a nation expects to be ignorant and free . . . it expects what never was and never will be." As the new Constitution was ratified in 1788, the Congress declared, "religion, morality, and knowledge being necessary to good government and the happiness of mankind, schools, and the means of education shall forever be encouraged."[1]

The innate rightness of certain basic concepts is the context for con-sidering what is right about public education in the United States. Edu-cation is essential for an enlightened, free society. The capacity to think independently and creatively is essential to avoid intellectual enslave-ment and forced subservience to the will of others. If we believe in the moral rightness of the Declaration of Independence, the Constitu-tion, the Emancipation Proclamation, and *Brown* v. *Board of Educa-tion*, equity in access to educational opportunity is a moral imperative. Americans have led the world in the quest for equity. We paid atten-

Gene R. Carter is executive director, Association for Supervision and Curric-ulum Development, Alexandria, Virginia.

tion to the issue of multiculturalism much earlier than did other nations. Our attention to the unique needs of children with disabilities is also noteworthy.

Public education has a large stock of talented, well-intentioned, generally motivated professionals. The successes cited in the Sandia report are largely attributable to this human resource, achieved in spite of many obstacles. Programs like the Coalition of Essential Schools, and others that attempt to reduce the size of the instructional unit and develop a lasting social relationship between students and educators over an extended period of time, seem to offer promise for reconstructing the school as a learning organization. Instructional technology is maturing. The power of learning technology is increasing and the cost is decreasing to the point where it can be a major benefit to public school educators. American schools have been willing to design practical curricula related to the life needs of a diverse student population.

However, it must be recognized that there have been no truly systemic changes in the last 70 years. The societal context has changed dramatically in almost every dimension: social, economic, technological, political, and philosophical. Seventy years ago the mission of education was primarily cultural transmission and preparation of (standard) units of production for an industrial society. The mission of education is much less clear now, and there are many conflicting expectations.

The time has come for a change in America's system of public education. James Baldwin once said that "in order to accomplish great things, we must not only act, but also dream; not only plan, but also believe. If we do not believe that we can make a difference in the lives of our children, then we will not. If we do not believe that we can experiment, make mistakes, and try again, then we will not. If we do not believe that we can effectively prepare our youth for success in the 21st century, then we will not."

The time has come for us to believe in ourselves and our children, for the future lies in the hands of the children today. It is our responsibility as educators, as leaders, as role models, and as mentors to ensure that our vision for excellence and equity becomes a reality.

Traditionally, our ideas regarding education have been rooted in the economic and societal need to maintain and improve an existing system. Today, we are propelled into the 21st century. The challenge can no longer be maintaining the status quo. The emergence of the Information Age requires a set of perspectives, skills, and behaviors that enable us to respond effectively to change.

There are about 110,000 public elementary and secondary schools in this country, distributed among approximately 16,000 school districts. There are good schools, effective teachers and principals, and great places where teaching and learning are occurring against great odds. The research base is much more accessible and useful. We know what to do, and we are fast figuring out how to do it. The biggest remaining question is whether we have the will to act. And without minimizing the difficulties involved, we are learning how to transform individual mediocre schools into effective centers of learning. But the fact is that we are not doing enough.

Over the past decade, a great deal of public attention has been focused on America's public schools. The success achieved earlier in this century in providing mass public education seems to diminish when we recognize the growing need of the economy for a highly literate work force. Much of the initial response to this need consisted of curriculum revision and tightening requirements for graduation from high school.

On closer examination, it became evident that uniform strategies to improve the achievement of individual students exacerbated the already large gaps between groups of students. In general, education reforms that ignored differences in access to education based on class, race, and gender only reinforced or enlarged already existing differences in student achievement.

This dilemma of education reform — the need to achieve both excellence and equity — is the basic challenge for education reformers today.

There are at least two constants in American public school education: 1) the demand for reform and 2) the perception that public schools are not as effective as they once were in educating students to realize their full potential.[2] The pervasive view is that our public schools must become more effective if the nation is to prosper and be competitive in the global environment. This perception has clearly influenced national and state policies concerning public education during the past decade.

Despite the press for systemic change, many of our public schools have been remarkably resistant to it. Innovations appear and disappear with regularity; few persist long enough to have a lasting effect on the educational system. Ralph Tyler has observed that it takes from five to seven years for most educational innovations to show results.[3] By this measure, most educational innovations do not last long enough for us to determine whether or not they are effective.

The need for a fundamental overhaul of American public schools continues to be discussed across the nation. Numerous restructuring proposals have been made, and many schools are beginning to take action. How far and wide will these changes spread? How many schools have adopted comprehensive restructuring as opposed to mere innovations?

Expanding the Focus on School Cultures

All societies use the schools to transmit their culture or heritage, and many use them to foster social mobility. But Seymour Sarason warned that schools have a distinctive culture that must be understood and involved if changes are to be more than cosmetic.[4] Another scholar says there are as many school cultures as there are schools, adding that:

> . . . within each school culture, subcultures proliferate − cultures of collaboration and cultures of change, cultures of teaching and cultures of resistance. These grammars created in the culture of the school must be listened to and understood if we are to interpret and improve schools. . . . In some of these cultures people work in isolation, and in other settings collegiality is evident.[5]

A major obstacle to reform appears to be a lack of the knowledge and skills needed to achieve lasting change in the culture of the public schools. Recently, educators have expanded their attention to include the concept of culture. What is being recognized is that leadership and culture are intimately connected. One thing is certain: If we want to improve public schools, we need a better understanding of school culture, educational leadership, and the ways in which they are related.

As schools restructure, guided by a shared vision of learning that is designed to help students be successful in a changing and competitive world, the definition of teachers' work is changing as well. Michael Fullan's concept of "teacher as learner" centers on four key aspects of the teacher's work: 1) increasing technical skills and teaching repertoire, 2) engaging in reflective practice, 3) conducting classroom research, and 4) participating in collaborative instructional problem solving.[6] The difference between "schools that are stuck and schools that are moving," Fullan said, is the role of cultural variables.

School culture is created through the experience and interplay of many people, a dialectic among all the key players in the school, of which the principal is one. How principals as leaders balance authority with a healthy respect for teachers' growing participation in key decisions is crucial.

Public school classrooms, for the most part, currently reflect a culture (in the organization of existing curriculum, instruction, and assessment) that emphasizes ability as the behavioral characteristic to be re-warded (that is, motivation to try hard and learning from errors are not rewarded or recognized as a practical part of the learning process). In this model, errors are viewed as an indication of failure and poten-tial to learn is overlooked. As Stevenson and Stigler remark, teachers must create an environment in which students learn from errors and effort is rewarded.[7]

We should not overestimate what we know about the culture of schools. The way schools are organized, the behavioral and program-matic regulations that characterize them, and the undergirding axioms that remain silent and go unchallenged are among the factors being con-fronted as we seek cultural change. Cultural change does not cause new ways of thinking, it is a consequence of those ways.

Education and leadership are the means to cultural transformations and economic growth.[8] These transformations must involve our schools, families, employers, and governments. The leadership com-mitment and skills of each individual are crucial to developing respon-sible school learning cultures. Such cultures must value individual development through lifelong learning and training. Changing school cultures to meet the needs of the community, staff, and students is the challenge of the decade.

Curriculum and Instruction

Curriculum and instruction must be tied to the cultural experiences/values of students; and assessment must facilitate the development of abilities and knowledge relevant to the lives of students and the needs of society.[9]

Curriculum development, instruction, assessment, and staff develop-ment need to be seen as four integrated, hence inseparable, elements at the core of school decision making. The specific strategies for each:

1. *Should be driven by a shared vision of what a school can be.* Peter Senge talks about the importance of shared vision in *The Fifth Dis-cipline.*[10] Without a shared vision, a "common caring" and movement toward a common goal are impossible. Public education lacks a widely shared vision. This lack is reflected in conflicting goals, bitter battles over resource allocations, and a confusion of purposes. For example, in some schools it appears that winning football games is more impor-tant than creating intellectual capital.

2. *Must be internally consistent within and between the core elements.* The assumptions that underline the decisions within each of the four

areas need to be questioned and examined carefully for congruency across all areas. It cannot be safely assumed that congruency exists *a priori*.

3. *Must be balanced with respect to time required.* According to Fenwick English, few curriculum development processes include estimates of the time required for instruction in each of the content areas. As a result, unreasonable demands often are placed on teachers and students, producing "curriculum of coverage" rather than substantive learning. While it is patently obvious outside of school that it is unfair to ask employees to complete tasks for which they have not been trained, this observation rarely seems to be acknowledged by teachers. Requiring poorly prepared teachers to deliver more content is counterproductive.

4. *Must result in the desired outcomes in terms of student learning.* Decision making without feedback or information on learning relative to realistic benchmarks is no better than gambling with unfavorable odds.

Educators must develop an expanded awareness and ability to value, understand, and engage culturally different students. Schools and classrooms must be organized to ensure the development of individual potential. Collaboration with community agencies and home environments must be ensured to promote student growth and learning.[11]

A New Kind of Teacher Required

As we attempt to build the capabilities of public schools to meet new demands, we need to develop a new kind of teacher, one who is responsive to the changing student and school environment.

Why is this task more critical today than it was yesterday? Haven't we always been concerned about this problem? Haven't we always wanted the best individuals in our teacher education programs and, subsequently, in our profession? The answer, of course, is "yes." But what is so different today is the "team" we have to "coach" as teachers. Also, the playing field on which we "practice" and "play" has changed.

Children in the 1990s are racially, ethnically, and linguistically more diverse than a decade ago; and this trend will continue in the future. A recent congressional report on demographics forecasts rapid growth of minority populations during the next two decades. Moreover, by the year 2000 a quarter of the nation's children are expected to be living in poverty, compared with about 20% in 1990. Clearly, students coming into schools are different; and we need new ideas to help them succeed.

Public schools traditionally have been called on to perform the most heroic of tasks: the shaping of the next generation of Americans. Concomitantly, teachers are being asked, as never before, to diagnose the needs of each student and provide appropriate learning activities to ensure success. Economic and demographic trends are converging so as to place public schools in an even more critical position in the future. If our public schools, particularly in the inner-city and rural communities, are allowed to deteriorate, many children will be deprived of their only means for successful assimilation into productive society.

Yes, the team members and the playing field have indeed changed; and we cannot expect to succeed using the same strategies and the same plays, nor with coaches who are discouraged easily. Continuous and continuing training and development of teachers is not built into the normal schedule. Many responsible authorities even regard professional development as irrelevant. This is a serious fault. Without weekly, if not daily, opportunities for discourse, formal and informal research, and information sharing, teachers cannot achieve their potential as educational leaders.

School restructuring shifts the focus of public school reform from *what teachers do* to *the results their actions produce*. In the process of defining the outcomes we want from teaching, we should be moving the focus of teaching and learning from a fact-based system to a problem-solving, interactive system more appropriate to the world of today and tomorrow.

Today, public school and university leaders must discuss the nature and need for an emerging agenda that focuses on effectiveness and productivity rather than on deficits and failure. This shift in focus is essential to promote more successful schooling for public school students.

Public expectations abound for change in public schools. But school reform cannot succeed unless teacher education reform succeeds. Leaders must articulate a vision of the kind of teachers needed in our public schools, and we must develop coherent programs that will produce such teachers. There is an emerging consensus that the kind of experiences we have provided in teacher education programs and staff development have not gone far enough in preparing teachers for the challenges and opportunities that exist in public schools today.

Clearly, no area of contemporary school life cries out for change more than teacher training, and no greater challenge exists for those in positions of influence than to see that it comes about. The fate of public schools will depend, in large part, on our ability to envision a totally new system of teacher preparation to address the complexities and challenges in our nation's public schools. The moral imperatives of teaching in a democratic society create a compelling framework to guide reform in teacher education.

As we approach the 21st century, the current population of teachers will play a major role in reshaping and improving our public schools. We must commit ourselves to providing the best education and training possible for prospective classroom teachers. The teacher education program must be based on the philosophy that the best teachers possess all of the basic skills of a well-educated person, have substantial knowledge of subject matter, and undergo state-of-the-art training in how to promote student learning. Colleges and universities must play a critical role in preparing teachers to reform schools. Universities and school linkages beginning to develop point toward a more meaningful role for higher education in preparing teachers.

Teachers in public schools must be prepared to look beyond the backdrop of societal and economic conditions and be encouraged to focus on what we know and can do to improve instruction. They must think strategically about learners — about their cultural differences and their differing needs, about the community context, and about ways to engage students with substantive ideas.

The future of the nation's public schools, and indeed its children, depends on the creativity, intellect, and drive of its teachers. The universities must teach prospective teachers the skills, methods, and scholarly and philosophical principles they will need to teach all children. Curricula at schools of education should reflect all the knowledge about teaching that we have today. Underneath it all rests a fundamental commitment to continuous, focused learning. In our world of complex change, the advantage and strength falls to those teachers who pursue the quest to be the best they can be at what they do.

Visions for the Future

Our nation's public schools are being challenged to accomplish far more in the 1990s than we ever expected of them in the past. In 1990, the Institute for Future Studies identified the top educational issues as: 1) children held in low esteem, 2) changing workforce demographics requiring a new vision of training and hiring objectives, 3) a corner-cutting ethic promoting mediocrity, 4) the development of ethnic "beachheads" that impede the assimilation of immigrants into American society, 5) leadership guided by public opinion polls, 6) the prevalence of

186

competitions and contests in schools, 7) reliance on "rubber" yardsticks in place of national education standards, 8) continued erosion of federal support accompanied by lack of financial equity in the schools, 9) preoccupied parents who spend little time with their children, and 10) a geometrically expanding information base requiring multimedia approaches transcending the printed word.[12] A great deal of cooperative energy will have to be expended to convert these challenges into opportunities for improvement in our public schools. Clearly, public schools must become very different than they are today if students are to possess the skills and attitudes necessary to function in an ever-changing national and global society.

The century ahead will be more complex, faster-paced, and turbulent than at any time in history. The information explosion, radical changes in technology, demographic changes, and the electronic immediacy of once-distant cultures are changing the ways we live and work. Tom Peters once said that "winners must learn to relish change with the same enthusiasm and energy that we have resisted it in the past." Others predict that tomorrow's workers will need to be retrained three or four times during their careers to remain competitive.

The emerging economic order needs workers with imagination, confidence, initiative, and independence, workers who can think clearly, solve problems, and exercise good judgment. Appropriate curricula for these workers must provide an amalgam of liberal and vocational education designed to prepare them for satisfying and stable employment, ongoing vocational training, and the continual cultivation of the life of the mind.

Educational needs of the future must be addressed, even though projecting into the 21st century is difficult. Educators need to envision a brighter future and believe that people can influence that future. They can do their job well only if they believe that the potential for continuous improvement is good. A coherent, congruent, shared vision or design for the future of public schools requires thinking about long-range possibilities rather than narrow specialties. The imagination needed to design an education for envisioning wider human fulfillment must come from educational leaders who are futurists themselves. Future educational aims should include learning to learn effectively, socialization on a broader scale involving more alternatives, values formation, education beyond college preparation and job training (including continuing education and leisure pursuits), development of skills in evaluating ideas, and education for coping with probabilities and the unknown.[13]

Schooling must be seen as a tightly constructed set of activities designed for optimizing learning within a larger set of supporting activities designed to develop the whole child. Intellectual growth and development are the primary purposes of schooling, and they need to be rewarded, reinforced, and supported by the community at large. In short, we must install learning as a central value of American society. In the new millennium, everyone will be a learner.

As our schools are charged with serving an increasingly diverse student population, the natural tendency of school systems to treat every school the same and to stress conformity to rules and procedures has inhibited school-level creativity and contributed to student failure. More often than not, it appears that good schools succeed despite their district and state systems and not because of them. It is time for school systems to begin to transform themselves from bureaucracies that impede into organizations that actively support and facilitate the development of good schools.

The values and customs of the people in the schools are central to any meaningful changes that may take place. If change is to be sustained, it must have the teacher-student relationship at its core. Judith Warren Little makes a strong case for focusing the effort of school reform on the professionalization of teaching. She concludes that teacher leadership has the potential to change the prevailing culture in schools and, perhaps in a larger way, the teaching occupation as a whole.[14] Professionalizing teaching and building a more collaborative culture in schools can profoundly change the way staff and students in schools grow and learn.

As education is being restructured to create a nation of lifelong learners who are able to thrive in this new world, pedagogy must continue its shift from "teaching as telling" to a more student-centered, constructivist approach. Formal education is no longer seen as the sole responsibility of educators but of the whole community. The educational program involves all of the social and commercial resources of the community working toward a set of common goals. Education is seen as continuing and continuous, sometimes in school, more often in the community or at home. Parents, employers, and service providers are seen as equal partners with professional educators.

Today, it appears that technological change is exponential while educational change seems to be linear. The implication is that the gap between homes and classrooms as information resources is widening at a rapid rate. Unless education adopts and adapts to new technologies,

188

our schools stand to lose their relevance as primary places of learning. Because lifelong learning is a central goal of education, we must be on the lookout for tools that engage all students in the joys and excitement of learning. Schooling is an opportunity to develop essential life skills, including literacy and numeracy. The educational program provides the opportunity to apply and practice these skills both in and out of school by using a problem-centered, authentic context for presenting new content. Problems demand that choices be made; choices require conflict resolution and decision making; and decisions require a moral and ethical context for judging their quality.

Effective staff development must address both the spectrum of available technologies and their uses in a curriculum that honors the notion that every student is capable of learning. Staff development needs to be ongoing, just as it is in industry. The cost of doing this job properly is miniscule compared with the cost of lost opportunity to our nation if we fail to properly equip students for life in the 21st century.

As we look at the emerging images of learning worldwide, common threads become apparent even as we note differences. As we identify emerging pathways to the new millennium, a panoply of perspectives must be identified, analyzed, and synthesized. This synthesis has the potential to infuse public schools with a perspective that will prepare students and staff to address the issues and challenges of the new millennium.

Footnotes

1. Northwest Ordinance of 1787.
2. Richard A. Rossmiller and Edie L. Holcomb, "The Effective Schools Process for Continuous School Improvement," National Center for Effective Schools Research and Development, University of Wisconsin-Madison, July 1992, p. 1.
3. Ralph Tyler, "Education Reforms," *Phi Delta Kappan* 69 (April 1987): 277-80.
4. Seymour Sarason, *The Culture of the School and the Problem of Change* (Boston: Allyn & Bacon, 1971, revised 1982).
5. Nancy Wyner, ed., *Current Perspectives on the Culture of Schools* (Brookline, 1991), p. xv.
6. Michael Fullan, "Staff Development, Innovation and Institutional Development," in *Changing School Culture Through Staff Development*, 1990 ASCD Yearbook (Alexandria, Va.: Association for Supervision and Curriculum Development, 1990).

7. H.W. Stevenson and J.W. Stigler, *The Learning Gap: Why Our Schools Are Failing and What We Can Learn from Japanese and Chinese Education* (New York: Summit, 1992).
8. *Knowledge for All Americans Winning the War Against Ignorance: Empowering Public Schools* (Arlington, Va.: Knowledge for All Americans Center, 1992), p. 36.
9. E.G. Cohen, "Restructuring the Classroom: Conditions for Productive Small Groups," *Issues in Restructuring Schools* (1992): 4-7.
10. Peter Senge, *The Fifth Discipline: The Art and Practice of the Learning Organization* (New York: Doubleday Currency, 1990).
11. G. Wehlage et al., *Reducing the Risk: Schools as Communities of Support* (New York: Falmer, 1989).
12. William Banach, "Top Ten Educational Issues Facing Society, 1990," Institute for Future Studies, Macomb Community College, Warren, Michigan, 1990.
13. J. Pullian, paper presented at the 36th Annual Meeting of the National Conference of Professors of Educational Administration, San Marcos, Texas, 15-20 August 1982.
14. Judith Warren Little, "Assessing the Prospects for Teacher Leadership," in *Building a Professional Culture in Schools*, edited by Ann Lieberman (New York: Teachers College Press, 1988), pp. 78-103.

PART TWO:
THE
CONFERENCE
ON THE
STATE OF
THE NATION'S
PUBLIC
SCHOOLS

KEYNOTE ADDRESS
AND CONFERENCE
DISCUSSIONS

After Harold Hodgkinson's opening address, the Washington Conference on the State of the Nation's Public Schools was an extended Rorschach test. The 56 participants looked at the vast ink blot that is American public education — the whole multifaceted, discontinuous, incoherent, faddish, tradition-bound, decentralized, over-regulated, under-researched, over-analyzed, magnificent elephantine jumble of it — and told us what is right, what is wrong, and what ought to be. Each of these carefully chosen authorities has a past, a personality, and a set of predilections. So it was not unexpected that their five hours of earnest discourse did not produce consensus, though it did produce some well-reasoned recommendations.

The education reform movement in America is a tidal wave with many cross-currents, most of them represented by the participants in this conference. What brought so many leaders together, and what can give all of us hope, was a firm conviction, held by everyone, so far as I could tell, 1) that effective, universal education is essential to a viable democracy and 2) that public education in America has not kept up with the demands of a rapidly changing society.

In what follows I have attempted to extract from the 80,000-word transcript of conference discussions the most interesting and the most significant comments, indicating whenever possible the extent of agreement on matters of special importance.

Communications theory tells us that, more than it should be, the persuasiveness of any argument is a function of the status and reputation of the speaker. That is not the case here, however, because one of the ground rules, known to every participant, was that my report would not reveal the identity of any speaker. The rule was intended to remove inhibitions, and perhaps it did. But its main effect, I think, was to ensure that no statement is buttressed by the status of the speaker or the organization he or she represents. Challenges were frequent in this free-for-all forum. May the best argument win your allegiance.

KEYNOTE ADDRESS BY HAROLD HODGKINSON

Hodgkinson, "America's foremost education demographer," opened the conference on the evening of February 4 with a powerful presentation basic to an understanding of the challenges facing U.S. education. The facts he presented (and some of his opinions) influenced all subsequent discussions at the conference. In his talk, illustrated with numerous graphics, he made some of the points that appear in the paper that opens this volume, but many others as well. Excerpts from the talk follow.

For about 10 years in U.S. public schools, we've been doing things right. We've been concerned with efficiency, tightening things up, and so forth. Now there's a new set of questions that I think the new Administration in Washington is focusing on. All are encompassed in the question, "Are we doing the right things?" This meeting is about that question. And I find it very exciting that we're going to see if there's some common ground underneath the various positions on the issue of the quality of the public schools. Demography can help a little as we look for this common ground. . . .

In demographics, we look at birthrate, mobility, job structure, family types, life expectancy, and other matters that are of immense importance to the society. For example, in West Germany two years ago, it became clear that they were running out of young people because they forgot to have them. The fertility rate is extraordinarily low. The youth population of West Germany represents about a one-third drop from the current work force. The Germans must either bring in new people or get used to a smaller work force.

Consider New York State, which now has 666 abortions per thousand live births. The policy implications of that are extraordinary, if we can separate the ethics of abortion from its demographics. Is it middle-income women who are getting the abortions? Is it poverty women who are not well educated who are getting them? It makes a huge difference to the future of the state. And by the way, I must say, having spoken to both groups, it's my opinion that neither the pro-life nor the pro-choice group is terribly concerned with the children who are born. Once they are born they seem to lose all political significance. Thus there's a very real lack of concern in this country for the quality of life among children ages 0-4, yet we're turning out some very good evidence that those are key years. . . .

Let's consider for just a minute the college freshman class of the year 2010. Some people say, "That's just too far into the future; we can't possibly know anything about a group that is that far away." The answer is, "It's the children who were born last year. It's the only group of people who will become 18 in that particular year." How good a class will it be? Here are a couple of things that happened to the group born last year:

Twenty-three percent were born into poverty; the largest single factor there was the increase in single parents. Thirty percent, if current averages hold, will not get the polio and other shots they need before they get to kindergarten. About half will be raised by a single parent. About 5%, according to the National Institutes of Health, were born with preventable birth defects. If every pregnant woman in America got one physical exam in the first trimester of pregnancy, we could eliminate at least 5% of the children born with handicaps. It's not that they would live with the handicaps better; it's that they would be born without them. The physical exam costs $50. You can spend up to $100,000 per child under the 1975 Education for All Handicapped Children Act. The issue of where we spend our money, therefore, is quite clear in this college class, I think. We were not willing to do what every member of NATO does, which is to say, "It's in our national interest to make sure that children are born healthy."

The first version of National Education Goal No. 1 that emerged from the Education Summit in 1990 was: "To insure that every child enters kindergarten in good health, well fed, and with the support of a good home environment." That's very measurable. And because it was so measurable, it got changed to the idea that every child should be ready for school, which is not quite so measurable.

Demography also tells us what the jewel in our education crown is. We have about 20% of the world's K-12 students, but we have 50% of the world's postsecondary education students — about 14.8 million of them compared with the world total of about 30 million. Although Japan is now graduating a large number of its young people from high school or its equivalent, the percentage who graduate from college in Japan is still very low, especially women. Our postsecondary education system is not only very large but very diverse and flexible in more than 3,500 institutions, each of which has a particular niche. This makes us different from other nations.

Now let's have a quick look at the United States by region. Rumor has it that we've all moved to California, but that's premature. There's still a fair number of us — about 46 million — in Boswash, a huge strip from Boston to Washington. Then there is Cleveburg, or Pittsland, now becoming a metro area that crosses state lines. Chicago covers three states. Detroit goes all the way to Buffalo and across the high-density corridor to Boswash. Atlanta is clearly the Chicago of the South. Forty percent of St. Louis is now in Illinois, moving northeast. Fourteen major metropolitan areas crossed state lines during the past decade, so that the largest metro area in Iowa, for example, is now Omaha; and the largest in Arkansas is Memphis. This complicates things as you begin to think about accreditation and regulation of educational programs. It's very difficult, for example, for the 40% of St. Louis that's in Illinois to figure out who they get their accreditation from.

As we think about population density, let's remember that 52% of Americans live in the Eastern time zone and 30% in the Central zone, so you're at 82% of the country's total by the time you get to the Rockies. The Mountain time zone has about 7% of the population. That means 13% live on the West Coast and in Alaska and Hawaii.

That's one interesting way to think about the country. What it doesn't show is growth. California, Texas, and Florida recently picked up 14 seats in the House of Representatives — seats given up by New York, Pennsylvania, Ohio, Michigan, Illinois, New Jersey, and Massachusetts. These are states that forgot to grow; their populations are going up in average age with extraordinary speed. The new South grew very rapidly. Income levels went up, as did education levels, not so much because people who live there got more education but because educated people started moving there.

It's interesting to think about the South and West as the areas of rapid growth during the past decade. All the predictions are that they will continue for another decade, and the press will focus heavily on the Pacific and Mountain states, ignoring the South Atlantic for reasons not clear to me.

During the Eighties millions of us moved to the 40 largest metropolitan areas — not the central cities but the suburbs. Fifty-two percent of Americans now live in the suburban areas around our 40 largest metropolitan centers. The Congressional Research Service says that by the year 2000 we will have 50 members of Congress from California, 34 from Texas, and 28 from Florida, which will be enough votes, I think, to defeat any legislation introduced from Michigan. The Founding Fathers did not expect three states to have that much power; it's the first time in the history of the census that three states got half the nation's growth. This gives them extraordinary clout. Here, then, is a measure of the future in politics that's going to be interesting to watch.

We now have half the population living in nine states. Forty-one states compete for the other half of the population. It's an extraordinary concentration, with three rapid growers and six described by the census as wealthy but tired. If you look at the six, you get a clear sense of the future, given the fact that California, Texas, and Florida grew enormously. New York went up a little, but the growth rate in Pennsylvania, Illinois, Ohio, and Michigan is simply underwhelming.

Look now at the new South. It is growing fast enough that in the next census there will probably be some eclipsing of the current Big Nine states. As we look at growth in terms of high school graduates to the year 2000, it's very clear that there is no baby boomlet in the Northeast to buoy up enrollments in public schools and later in colleges. Again, if we look at the states that are growing in numbers of high school graduates, we see that the growth is heavily minority. California, for example, with a 41% increase in high school graduates, will find that 52% are nonwhite. Texas and Florida show the same rapid shifts, so that by the year 2010, 50% of the young people in California, Texas, and Florida will be nonwhite. California should be building a new college every week to get ready for this 41% increase. Instead, they've capped enrollments all through the system; and when these heavily minority young people are able to attend college for the first time in their family's history, the door will be shut. What are they going to do? The fact is that we have considerable under-utilized capacity in certain Midwest and Eastern states in terms of college places. Question: Is there some way we can make use of this excess capacity in some sections when there is excess demand in others?

There are great regional differences in the distribution of minorities. And blacks are more heavily concentrated than Hispanics. They therefore tend to lose political clout outside their areas of concentration. Asians now constitute 6% of the total population and are more evenly distributed. This does some very interesting things. For example, Des Moines is supposed to have three of the best Vietnamese restaurants in the United States. Throughout the country, we're beginning to see infusions of Asian culture in a very interesting but not necessarily metropolitan way.

197

Demographic surveys show two countries developing, one (roughly the northern half of the United States) 85% to 95% white, older, without much growth. The other country (the southern half) is ethnically diverse, with increasing jobs and per-capita income and, apparently, growing I.Q. There is some reason to believe that I.Q. data by state will show fairly significant I.Q. differences.

The major drawing in to our 40 largest metro centers leaves states like Iowa with real questions about the continued viability of rural life. How do you get a young doctor to set up practice in Iowa outside of Des Moines, when so many counties are losing population? Without health services, what kind of communities do you have? Those, then, are issues that leap out at you from an analysis of regions.

As we deal with ethnic diversity, the first thing to look at is the way the census asks the questions. In 1960 you could be white or nonwhite. But in the 1990 census, people had many options in terms of their ethnic backgrounds. If you were a Native American you could even list your tribe. And yet, with all these options, about five million people answered the census by saying "other." We learned a lot about the melting pot, because almost three million of those five million turn out to be whites who married blacks, Hispanics who married non-Hispanics, Asians who married non-Asians, and Native Americans who married out of their tribe. We melt by intermarrying the third generation after immigration. We've done that for 100 years. The Italian comes and his children marry Italians, under pain of death. The grandchildren probably will marry Italians, too; but in the fourth generation it's fair game.

We now deal with a large number of high school seniors who are applying to colleges and trying to decide who they are if they have a black mother and a white father or an Asian ancestor. These questions are quite difficult for this generation, simply because the numbers have increased considerably.

So our population growth looks like this: The white population is up a bare 6%, and the baby boomlet that we talk about is basically in three states: California, Texas, and Florida, where about half of the boomlet is non-Anglo. Blacks are up 13%, with no immigration to speak of. So many blacks have moved into the middle class that the fertility rate went down. Every group, as it moves into the middle class, lowers its fertility. There's no point in having eight kids if you're middle class. If you're poor, it's fine, because that's your social security. But if you've got discretionary income, which is what middle class means, and you spread your nest-egg across two kids, it can make a huge difference. If you spread it by eight, the math just doesn't work.

The Native American population went up 38%, about 1.9 million total; but there are some four million people who claim Native American ancestry. That's interesting, because some of these people will reclaim Native American ancestry in the next census. So we could have a very large increase in Native American population with no increase in births if Kevin Costner makes one more movie. Asians are up 10%, Hispanics 53%, and "other" 45%. "Other" includes about three million Americans from the Middle East. We have in this country in 1992 more Muslims than Episcopalians.

There are now 12 states, plus the District of Columbia, in which, by the year 2010, more than half the school-age population will be nonwhite. Among them are Texas, California, Florida, New York, New Jersey, Maryland, and Illinois — big, powerful states. In all of them a new question emerges, "What do we call minorities when they are more than half?" Again, the math doesn't work.

Between 1990 and 2010, the white youth population will drop by 3.8 million while the nonwhite youth population rises by about 4.4 million. That's never happened before, at least in my lifetime. It's a drop, not in percentages, but in actual numbers of white children compared with minority children. There's no point in mourning the loss of 3.8 million white kids. We need to look at the 4.4 million additional nonwhite kids who are here and hope they get a good education and a splendid job, because they fund our retirement when they join the work force. You don't need to be a liberal about these things; being a pragmatist is usually enough.

As we look at blacks, we begin to realize that the suburban black population is going up considerably. That means, I think, that more blacks are moving into the middle class. Bart Landry, who is the best source of information about this, suggests that 40% of black households are now in the middle class and 25% are systematically poor. So the black population, especially, is beginning to show a rich and a poor segment.

Now let's look at the differences between the academic test scores of wealthy and poor Asians and wealthy and poor blacks. Note that wealthy black kids apparently do better at math than poor Asian kids do, even though we're convinced that Asians have a gene that enables them to recite calculus in the crib.

So we're beginning to learn some very important things. One of the most important is that five or six states will move quickly to "minority majorities" by the year 2010, while Maine remains 4% ethnically diverse. Some states will go through an enormously radical change in the next 15 years. Some of the change comes from immigration. We now have a group of immigrants that is about as large as it was in the early 1900s. Although the country is larger, this is still an extraordinary number. But there is a major change in where they came from. Look at the leading countries in terms of immigration from 1820 to 1945, rank ordered by how many they sent us, and look at the current and projected leadership. The sending countries were all European. Now they are Latin American and Asian. When Carl Sandburg and Walt Whitman called us a nation of nations, they were not really correct. We were a nation of Europeans. But we are now bringing the world to this country. This presents us with a different set of tasks. The new immigrants don't have the same old religions, the same forms of musical expression, or even the same diets. Some of these people eat strange things for breakfast. The question for the next generation is whether these people can move through the mobility structure in the United States as immigrants always have. It has taken three generations in the past. The immigrant himself never really made it, felt to be a fish out of water, but got a toe-hold and valued education. The second generation did pretty well, moving into the middle range, going to community college, becoming middle-management and supervisory types, and moving to the suburbs. If you live in the suburbs, you learn that you don't want your children to go to college. You want your children to go to Princeton. It's in the suburbs that you learn to play the mobility game, and the third generation plays it flawlessly.

This has been true for Italians, Poles, Germans, et al., for at least 50 years. These are the people who leap over our great barriers. Their goals are clear. They do not have jobs; they have careers, and they can basically do whatever they want. Indeed, more than 20% of the members of the U.S. Senate have immigrant grandparents. Try that in any other country.

The new question is whether Asians and South and Central Americans can go through the same mobility structure in three generations. It's not clear that they can. So when we talk about multiculturalism, we're really talking ethnicity, age, region, class, and sex, because every one of them has all five of those.

Conclusion: *E Pluribus* is easy and fun. What's hard is *Unum*, the things that hold us together. The problem used to be holding together various European cultures; but now we're talking about Confucianism, Islam, Zen. We're talking about languages we've never heard before.

I think the *Unum* question is one that's going to be worked on by President Clinton for the next four years.

So the issue around ethnic diversity is not an increase in fertility among blacks and Hispanics; the big issue is Methodists. The decline in Methodist church attendance is about 17% in the past 10 years. It's usually blamed on the quality of the bake sales and the theology, but those have relatively little to do with it. It's the inability of Methodists to produce little Methodists.

Let us now look at the United States by age distributions. The oldest state by age is Florida, of course. The second is Iowa, for heaven's sake. Is that because older people are moving to Iowa to retire? For those wonderful mountainside resorts, famous seashores? No, it's because young people leave Iowa as soon as they get a driver's license. So what you have in much of the Midwest is a set of counties that are growing old because young people are leaving. When young people leave and are not replaced by other young people, your average age goes up like a rocket. People in these counties are not much interested in school bond issues. As one gets older, his youth concerns begin to decline.

Every week in the United States, 211 people reach their 100th birthday. If you want a hall big enough to hold everybody who's over 100 in this country, it will have to seat 35,400 people. The idea that you're old at 65 and you should die at 67 to save the country's Social Security fund is an idea that was popular in the Thirties but no longer. The third quarter of human life in the United States is now moving toward 50 to 75. If you make it to 65, your chances of making it to 85 improve almost hourly. And if you make it to 85, your chances of living another 15 years are incredibly good. But as young people become a smaller percentage of our population, it may be that we'll pay less attention to them. We generally do. Native Americans, when we thought they were declining and going away, were not an object of great concern. Now that the American Indian population is increasing rapidly, we're starting to pay a lot of attention to them. This means that youth are likely to decline in political importance. Remember, too, that as you grow older, you vote more often. Today we have 30 million people in the United States who are 65 or older. By the year 2030 there will be 65 million. So we have to face a new political force — people who will do everything to make sure that life over 65 is pleasant. And basically you can forget 18-year-olds; only 27% of them bothered to vote in the last election.

Three other things, briefly: First, note that the population group that increased the most from 1980 to 1990 was prisoners, up from 466,000 to the present 1.1 million. We had a prison epidemic in this country between 1980 and 1990. Drug-related arrests had something to do with it, noncommutable sentences also. If you are looking for an area in which the United States is clearly No. 1, there is no doubt about it. No other country can come anywhere near our prison population total.

There is a very interesting relationship between prisoners and high school dropouts. Some 82% of our prisoners are high school dropouts. Each prisoner now costs us $24,000 a year. Think of the kids we could put in Head Start for $24,000. Think of what teachers could do with $24,000 per student. In addition, 73% of prisoners are back in jail within three years of release, because recidivism is still the name of the game. The best way to reduce the crime rate and prison rate is to give kids the alternative of staying in school and graduating. Here again is a prevention strategy with a lot of potential. But governors are not terribly interested, because it takes about 14 years to demonstrate that Head Start really does work. No governor is going to wait 14 years. But you can prove you are tough on crime in three months by building a jail, although jails have no impact on crime rates. Criminals don't stop a life of crime because the number of jail cells goes up. The research is thin, but Congress has been persuaded, I believe, that Head Start saves the taxpayer about $6 in later services for every dollar it costs.

Now let's look at significant changes in the American family. First, there has been a 17% increase in married couples without children in the past decade, plus a drop in married couples with children. Note the increase in families where there are no married couples. These families are not all headed by women. Indeed, 2.5 million men are raising children by themselves. So day care is not only a feminist issue. There are also large increases in nontraditional households, what the Census Bureau politely calls "people living alone" and "people living with non-relatives." It is very likely that, by the year 2000, for every household with a married couple there will be one household without. At present, roughly one household in four has a child in the public schools. Thus three-quarters of the voters will vote against a bond issue for the schools as a matter of self-interest. The Norman Rockwell or "Leave It to Beaver" family (working father, housewife mother, and two school-age kids) is now about 6% of all households. That's an extraordinarily low figure.

Hallmark Cards is developing a set of cards that will congratulate people for being good single parents. There's no point in panning these people, because they are raising about 17 million or 18 million kids. And we want those kids to do well.

It's all because in the Fifties most women got educated, got married right away, had kids, then years later perhaps got a job. By the Eighties most women, more than half, got educated, then got a job, and a long time later got married. A much longer time later they'll have children, if they do at all. The deferral of fertility and child-bearing from the early 20s to the late 20s and early 30s is one characteristic of the decade of the Eighties. The consequences of that for the future are enormous. Indeed, many women in their 30s are now discovering that it is impossible for them to have a family of six children.

The phenomenon of working women supporting children by themselves has great implications for the schools, because the relationship between family type and poverty is very strong. If the mother and father stay together, 11% of their children are poor. If the father divorces and remarries, it's 13%. If the mother divorces and remarries, it's 23%. If the father raises the kids alone, 20% of the kids are poor. If the mother raises them alone, 50% are poor. If it's "other," 43% of the children are poor. "Other" includes two million Americans who are being raised by neither their mother nor father. More than 450,000 children are being raised by their grandparents.

The current average income for a family with two parents and children is $44,000 a year. If the mother is raising the kids alone, it's $18,000. Would you rather be the $18,000 kid or the $44,000 kid? Poverty is statistically the most important factor behind all dropouts. And if a child is at risk for poverty, he or she is likely to be at risk for two or three other reasons − poor health, for example.

A woman who uses cocaine and who is also pregnant is likely to be a smoker and a drinker. She's very likely to get no medical care in the first trimester of pregnancy because, in several states, if she identifies herself as a cocaine user, she's liable for child abuse. So all these health risk factors overlap too.

Finally, it's important to note the enormous recent shift in the type of jobs available in our economy. Health technology and some other technology fields are growing rapidly. But growth is greatest in the number of clerks and cashiers, waiters and waitresses, nurses, and janitors. Note that high school dropouts can handle three of these top four categories of jobs. The economy seems to be producing a different set of jobs. The number of middle-range, middle-income jobs has clearly declined. Why are we creating so many jobs that pay the minimum wage?

Nobody seems to have a clear answer, but the numbers are quite striking: 14 million minimum-wage workers now compared to seven million in 1979. And we're beginning to see some interesting things about who the low-income, full-time workers are.

We're still basically middle-income as a nation. But if you look at the changes between 1975 and 1985, you see that we created a lot of wealthy households. At the same time, a lot of full-time workers fell below the poverty line; and very few new households appear in the middle of the income range.

We're not creating the jobs that allow people to realize the American Dream. The mobility structure underneath the dream is based on the idea of job production in the middle range. Millionaires, of course, did quite well. We went from 4,000 millionaires to 63,000, a 14-times increase; not bad for 10 years. The interesting thing is their contributions to charity, which were $207,000 on average in 1980 and $83,000 in 1990. So this is a different group of people. Their charitability is not great. That says some important things about our future.

A fair number of college graduates are now taking entry-level jobs that require absolutely no college training. If you concentrated on pre-Raphaelite poetry at Wellesley, how are you going to pay for that degree? At one community college I visited recently in California, 35% of the students already have a bachelor's degree. Nobody will hire them. They are back in a community college to get some skills whereby they can earn a living. That's an odd sort of reversal.

The Carnegie Foundation tells us that over half of future jobs won't require a college education. My conclusion is that most likely we'll have this two-tailed work force of low-skill, low-pay, minimum-wage jobs taken by high school dropouts, along with high-pay, high-skill jobs in symbol manipulation where college graduates make their living with words, like most of us in this room.

So, to conclude: Among the reasons we've had so much stress these days is the nature of change. From 1850 to 1950 there was simply more of the same. More European immigrants, more good jobs, more families with children, more middle-class people, more young people, a melting-pot idea in cities, towns, and rural areas where people knew each other. Today we've got a lot of change at the margins, with more Asians, Hispanics, blacks, and Indians. We have high- and low-pay jobs and only a few in the middle. We have single parents and non-families, rich and poor, more elderly, fewer kids, and a mosaic as opposed to a melting pot. We have self-contained suburbs that are able to totally ignore the city that made them possible. Put that together and you have a pretty tough agenda, it seems to me, for schools. That's the challenge for the next decade. I've not talked about the quality of America's schools or the kinds of work we need to do to make them better. I've simply told you what kinds of people will be in school. Have I raised some questions in your minds?

Discussion Following Hodgkinson's Presentation

Question: "Could you elaborate on what you said about jobs in the future? This conference is directed toward what our schools should look like in the future, and of course that relates directly to the future job market. You emphasized the growth of low-paying jobs. Is there a cause-and-effect relationship here? I've heard people say the low-paying jobs are a result of a decline in the effectiveness of the schools."

Hodgkinson: "I've never bought that argument. I know McDonald's doesn't pay very well because they can hire high school dropouts. But I don't think that creates high school dropouts. It may temporarily, because of the lure of getting a job for at-risk kids.

"What we don't know is how we might structure the economy through new industrial strategies — incubators, for example — to generate more jobs that pay in the middle-income range. Birmingham, Alabama, has an incubator for new small businesses. They've started 250 of them. They have a rule that unless you can show that you'll generate more middle-paying jobs and fewer jobs at the low end of the income scale, you can't get into the incubator to develop your small business.

"I'd love to have economists tell us what to do about the problem. But the economists I talk to suggest that jobs come from storks. However, David Birch at MIT has a wonderful book, called *Job Generation in America*, that gives insights into what we could do to manipulate the system to create the kinds of jobs we'd like."

Question: "Can you give other examples, besides Birmingham, of successful incubators?"

Hodgkinson: "There's an American Society of Incubator Directors you might want to contact. The 10 or so incubators I have looked at are chiefly concerned with starting new businesses and then weaning them. The problem is almost never looked at qualitatively; that is, they don't ask how these jobs can be of strategic use to the community or how job generation can be deliberately manipulated to increase the size of the middle class."

Question: "You didn't mention the dynamics of teacher supply and demand. Nor the new industry of early childhood care. How do these fit into our equation? I'm concerned about the lack of ethnic diversity among teachers."

Hodgkinson: "There's a good set of data from the American Association of Colleges for Teacher Education in a study called *The Teacher Education Pipeline*. It shows that about 12% of the teaching force is ethnically diverse. The National Education Association suggests that this figure will soon go down to about 3%, this at a time when 35% to 40% of our students will be nonwhite. The question is, How much ethnic/racial diversity is enough? Is it important that a black student have every course taught by a black person? Probably not. But it would be nice if that were true of some courses. I also think it would be good for more white students to have black or Hispanic principals.

"At the moment it appears that blacks and Hispanics do not see public school teaching as a viable career. The numbers are not going up very much in undergraduate teacher education programs, according to Dave Imig. That's just one of a number of cases where imbalances will accelerate."

Question: "What you have said is entirely correct if you assume that future teachers come only from colleges of education. But if you look at the 40 largest cities or the 120 largest districts in the U.S., serving 12 million children, most of whom are in poverty, you see that their teachers come increasingly from the alternative certification programs that 40 states now have. This means that, in a state like Texas, 58% of the new teachers are from minority groups."

Hodgkinson: "Yes, and I think that even leaves out returning teachers, teachers who taught and came back 10 years later. That's about 30% of 'entering' teachers. But the data show that even in states that are quite ethnically and racially diverse, the percentage of minorities in schools of education is quite low. We are just not doing that job very well. What I don't know is whether returning teachers are likely to be more ethnically diverse. I doubt it."

Question: "Returning to your earlier thrust, I hear lots of school people say we have to produce more highly trained workers. Are those people just plain wrong?"

Hodgkinson: "Not necessarily. It's just that I don't know what they mean. That is, I think there are some basic skills that we're all going to have to have. For example, the ability to solve problems and to work with other people. If you talk to personnel directors, the two things

206

they want on the part of workers is that they show up on time and can get along socially with co-workers. Now if you talk to the presidents of those companies, they want liberal arts graduates with knowledge of English, Spanish, German, French, physics, and calculus. So there's this big conflict. I'm perfectly willing to say that the skills of 20 years ago are not good enough for the future. That's a viable argument, so long as people will define what they want. I mean, schools are not perfect. But if we want improvement in skills, we do need to say what we really mean."

Question: "What if they're full of baloney? I think they may be. And Harold is himself backing off; he says he's not sure. What I hear convinces me that we're dramatically over-estimating the need for higher-level skills in the future economy. In that case, is there no real need to fix the schools? Is the conference over?"

Hodgkinson: "I think you misunderstood me. We need school graduates who can deal with environmental issues, read pharmacy prescriptions, understand contraindications. I can't work the thermostat in my new house. My VCR says 12:00 all the time. So you have to be smarter in lots of ways to live in this society today. This means our schools need to do a lot better. However, of the four job categories that add the largest number of new jobs, three of the four (janitors, waiters/waitresses, and clerks) can be done by high school dropouts; only nurses require degrees in the top four."

Question: "But you can't use the job market to justify saying that."
Hodgkinson: "We're veering dangerously away from certainty, folks, and we're going to talk about that kind of issue tomorrow. I agree with you; and I think I am backing off because I just don't know."

Question: "Simply projecting what is into the future, which we have done in talking about the growth of jobs in the past decade, does not often tell us about what the future may be. What I'm most concerned about is the question of what jobs we are going to be able to create in the future. If it's low-wage jobs, the question arises, Can we compete internationally with a low-skilled, low-waged labor force? Most economists will say no, only in the tourist industry. So I think we have to look at the high-wage, information-driven part of the economy for hope."

Hodgkinson: "Okay, but you can't neglect the other 40% of the workers."

Question: "I think one of the reasons the whole discussion about the need for technically trained people is so muddled is that everybody is talking about different problems. Obviously, the more skills an individual has, the more likely it is he'll get a job. And this society wants upward mobility for low-income and minority kids. But are we failing to compete in the world economy because we don't have enough technically trained people? Clearly, no. There are 100 other factors that are probably much more important in explaining our international trade problems."

Hodgkinson: "That's true. Let's consider minority kids now in elementary school. They have three choices. They can drop out of high school and take any one of the four million new minimum-wage jobs that come on line annually. They can stay in high school, graduate, and with a little community college education, move into the rapidly expanding health/technology fields. Or they can go to a four-year college and take some of the 2.5 million jobs for professionals — law, medicine, and so forth. It's not clear to me how they're going to play that game. But it will be an important game.

WHAT'S RIGHT,
WHAT'S WRONG,
WHAT'S OUR VISION?

The conference plan called for three sections of the nearly 60 participants, each with assigned leadership, to focus on the same set of three questions, then to come together in a plenary session to compare notes and develop themes that the sponsoring organizations hope will be used by individuals and groups leading America's education reform movement. This movement, now some 10 years old (having received its greatest impetus from the 1983 report, *A Nation at Risk*), may be at a crucial point. President Clinton already has identified new emphases at the federal level; and the states are ready, as the recession fades, to implement a great deal of reform legislation already approved.

The focus questions identified for the conference were: What is right with American public education? What is wrong with American public education? What is our vision of the future of American public education? Implied in the last question, of course, is another: What are the most useful strategies for realizing our vision?

Each session selected a recorder, who took shorthand notes on a chart in front of the group. As conference editor, I have used their notes as the basis for summarizing responses to the three focus questions.

Depending on how one chooses to categorize them, there were 25 to 30 areas in which participants saw strong positives in American public education. One of the interesting aspects of this discussion format was the frequency with which the flip side of a "right" turned out to be a "wrong" in the eyes of at least one participant. This yin-yang phenomenon will be evident to readers who compare the right/wrong lists that follow. Sometimes, differences were only a matter of viewpoint or perspective. (Is the cup half-full or half-empty?) More frequently, they involved different interpretations of the same data, or the use of different data on the same subject. (If data are flawed, this discussion will not reveal where.) First, a summary of what the group saw as positive:

What's Right

On the whole, public education has been true to the ideal of the common school and our founding principles, including the belief that a democracy requires an educated citizenry; that children of all classes, beliefs, backgrounds, family traditions, etc., should mingle, leveling the walls of difference, so that no group is alien to others and all learn tolerance and understanding. In short, the public schools continue to be the engine of democracy, enabling very diverse elements to live together in some harmony.

There is a high level of customer satisfaction, particularly among middle-class parents and the better-educated citizenry. The Gallup/Phi Delta Kappa education polls have documented this fact for 25 years. The 26% of adult Americans who have children in public schools give those schools very high ratings (over 70% an A or a B over the past eight years).

The public schools operate at relatively low cost — lower per capita than in most industrialized countries. (The fact that so many students enroll in postsecondary education — far more of them than in other countries — adds a great deal to the total cost of education in the United States.)

In recent years U.S. public schools have been raising their standards for student achievement, accepting the hypothesis that all children can learn at a high level if challenged and motivated to do so.

A high degree of local control, in most cases exercised by democratically elected boards of education, has enabled schools to be creative and flexible in meeting new problems. Local control also fosters diversity and experimentation.

The public schools have maintained, to a high degree, the ideal of open access to all of the diverse groups in society and have developed a uniquely American characteristic: offering a second, third, or even a fourth chance for education to young persons who, for whatever reasons, do not immediately take full advantage of opportunities for schooling.

Student achievement is rising, particularly achievement by minority students. That student achievement should rise at all is surprising, given the many negative changes in society, among them: disintegrating families, more working mothers, more drugs and crime, more violence and sex displayed in movies and TV, an increase in poverty, growing minorities that are increasingly difficult to assimilate, more permissiveness, more teenage pregnancies and unwed mothers, more one-parent or no-parent families.

There is growing use of technology in the schools, with finance the chief limiting factor.

There is a high level of teacher preparation/education and strong commitment to excellence in most public schools.

In recent years, students are willing to take the more rigorous courses in high school.

People do care about the public schools. Polls show that improvement is widely desired; the citizenry is giving more attention to the needs of the schools.

Many public schools are models of what works.

Except in some isolated rural areas, there are school buildings in every neighborhood.

Most public schools have strong extracurricular programs, enabling students to develop special interests, to socialize, and to sharpen certain nonacademic skills that are of lifelong use.

High school curricula in particular are often broad and diverse, largely in response to public demands that grow with the increasing diversity of school clientele.

The public schools make important contributions to the high literacy rate.

The public schools are an engine for upward mobility, particularly for Third World immigrants.

Public education has produced enlightened unions that have demonstrated strong interest in reform and excellent programs to improve teaching and learning.

More than most other institutions, the schools have fostered racial integration.

The public schools have developed an elaborate and generally efficient transportation system.

Retention and graduation rates have been increasing for several generations.

Many public schools are pioneering collaborative efforts with other youth-serving institutions in the community.

Many parents and other citizens work with the schools and become volunteers.

In the main, the public schools have produced a talented work force.

What's Wrong

We do *not* have common schools; despite all our efforts, segregation by class, race, and economic level continues. The melting-pot metaphor applies in only a limited sense.

The curricula of most public schools are too broad and too nonacademic. They have been "dumbed down," electives have proliferated, and social promotion is the rule. State and locally mandated subjects, such as sex education and driver education, tend to crowd out the basics: English, math, science, history, and geography. Not only are expectations of students too low, but there is a double or triple standard, with certain students expected to do well and others labeled early and written off. Sometimes expectations vary according to parental income.

Parents are unwilling to take charge of their children and insist on academic achievement, and the schools are inept in helping parents do this.

There is ambivalence in Americans' view of childhood, and permissiveness too often wins over insistence on effort and achievement. Many children do not believe that success in school has any connection with success in life.

The public schools generally do not have clear, high achievement goals and standards. In most cases, expectations are pitched at a level that is much too low to prepare students to succeed in today's competitive society.

The public schools lack the resources to help children who come from poverty-stricken and dysfunctional families, in poor health, hungry, and otherwise ill-prepared to learn.

There is a serious equity problem in the distribution of resources within schools, within and among school districts, and among states. Court and legislative efforts to correct these inequities usually have been inadequate and unsuccessful.

Multicultural education is a myth or a fraud.

The public schools have been unable to develop ways of motivating students to accept and meet higher learning standards by making the connection between school and life.

Inner-city schools in particular are disaster areas, without the material or spiritual resources to overcome the handicaps of poverty, neglect, alienation, racial discrimination, and cultural deprivation.

Too many teachers are underprepared to teach, especially in difficult schools. There is a serious shortage of teachers who can meet minimum standards of preparation in such fields as math and science. And the organized profession is unwilling to accept alternative forms of certification that would admit into teaching talented persons who are well-versed in subject matter but without the methods courses offered in teacher-preparatory institutions.

Teachers are not motivated to learn, and many of them do not read their own professional literature or keep abreast of what goes on in the world.

Professional development programs for teachers and staff are haphazard, unimaginative, and ineffective.

The racial composition of the public school teaching force has not kept pace with growth of the minority student population, and many teachers are not familiar with the cultural backgrounds of their minority students.

There are serious governance problems in the public schools, including swollen, inefficient, bureaucratic central offices; top-down reform efforts that stifle teacher/principal creativity; and special interest groups that exercise too much influence over curriculum and intimidate or censor teachers.

There is unclear thinking about, and reluctance to adopt, the kinds of technology that would enhance learning and improve efficiency.

Classroom teachers are protected from and ignore external policy makers, so reforms are often a sham. Too often success in school improvement efforts by teachers is the result of "creative noncompliance."

Many public schools are content to provide only high-quality custodial care; they are boring and uninspired.

Public schools too often are isolated from the community and do not feel the need either to market their services or their needs, nor do they respond to community dissatisfaction. Thus the curricula do not adapt to changes in the larger society.

The organization of the public schools is faulty, resulting in inefficient use of time, facilities, and other resources. Inflexible schedules and calendars and rigid teaching methods ignore what is known about how children learn.

Tracking and ability grouping continue to be used and abused.

Higher education institutions have failed to weigh in and help the public schools.

There is no consistent, widely accepted youth policy at local, state, or national levels.

There is inadequate political will to attack the problems of the public schools.

Educators generally fail to seek coalitions with other interest groups in their efforts to improve the schools.

Educators fail to learn effective strategies from other enterprises.

213

The schools generally do not recognize and do not attempt to nurture the many facets of intelligence and the different forms of talent, sometimes latent, among children.

The Vision

In the plenary session that ended the conference, a set of items that together constitute a "vision of the future" in U.S. public education was drawn from participant contributions and placed on charts in front of the group. However, a study of the discussion transcripts made it clear to me, as conference editor, that there was full consensus on very few of these items. Therefore, in late March Phi Delta Kappa circulated the list among all 56 participants, asking them to indicate, roughly, their degree of agreement or disagreement with individual items. Following are the questions and responses from that poll.

	Avg. Response*	Strongly Agree	Agree	Disagree	Strongly Disagree	No Response
1. The education profession must:		%	%	%	%	%
a) put aside its turf battles and come together to rebuild the constituency for public education,	4.31	69	16	3	3	9
b) clarify what is meant by the term "common schools" and revive interest in these schools,	4.03	34	50	6	3	6
c) find ways to increase respect for all of public education, and establish policies that support better relationships between children and adults.	4.47	66	25	3	3	3
2. The curriculum must be more carefully defined, focused, and strengthened. The curriculum and instructional strategies must permit students to engage in "authentic tasks," i.e., tasks that motivate because they are closely connected with life.	4.44	59	31	6	-	3
3. The system must prepare all children for a lifetime of success in a democratic society and a global economy.	4.25	62	25	-	-	12

*N = 32. "Average Response" is determined by giving "Strongly Agree" a value of 5, "Agree" 4, "Disagree" 3, "Strongly Disagree" 2, and "No Response" 1.

	Avg. Response	Strongly Agree	Agree	Disagree	Strongly Disagree	No Response
		%	%	%	%	%
4. School authorities must wrestle constantly with the problems of the schools' role and function, paying particular attention to the needs of students who are now being lost.	4.38	66	25	-	-	9
5. Everyone involved in education must accept and honor the fact that all students can learn if properly motivated and taught.	4.28	66	22	-	-	12
6. Children cannot learn in unsafe and chaotic schools; therefore, security and order must be given high priority, particularly in districts where life is disorderly and undisciplined.	4.62	72	25	-	-	3
7. a) Teachers are the core of the future; therefore, the recruitment, preparation, and professional welfare of teachers must be given high priority.	4.44	66	25	3	-	6
b) Teachers must have time and incentives to participate in well-planned staff-development programs, including sabbaticals for personal and professional development.	4.19	59	25	3	-	12
c) Teachers must be rewarded for superior performance.	3.97	44	34	9	-	12
8. The profession must challenge the concept that home schools can substitute for the common schools.	3.38	28	25	25	-	22
9. The schools must be dedicated to the proposition that there are no limits on school achievement other than talent and motivation.	4.09	53	31	-	3	12
10. Since the school curriculum provides only some of the services children need from society, schools should establish cooperative arrangements with other social agencies and institutions to provide other services; for example, health screening, inoculations, and dental examinations.	4.12	56	25	6	-	12
11. Educators should: a) engage people in the local community in efforts to reconstruct the school calendar for greater efficiency,	4.03	41	47	-	-	12

	Avg. Response	Strongly Agree	Agree	Disagree	Strongly Disagree	No Response
b) gain support time and schedule flexibility,		%	%	%	%	%
	4.03	31	59	-	-	9
c) link schools to the job market.	3.69	28	50	3	-	19
12. School reform efforts in the future should be targeted on students in greatest need, including the economically deprived, the physically and mentally handicapped, racial and ethnic minorities, and at-risk students in general.	3.69	34	25	28	-	12
13. We should recognize that the wrong kind of tracking equals inequality, and that schools should build on successful models that have eliminated or successfully modified tracking.	4.09	44	41	6	-	9
14. Modest programs of school choice for parents/students should be established to determine whether they can indeed introduce a greater degree of accountability and healthy competition without also introducing inequality and discrimination and other elements that endanger the common school ideal.	3.38	31	19	19	19	12
15. There should be:						
a) near-term focus on improving knowledge and skills for students and teachers.	4.38	56	38	-	-	6
b) a long-term focus on developing instructional technology.	4.09	38	53	-	-	9
16. The system of public education must be transformed in ways that place a higher value on academic achievement than is currently placed on athletic success.	4.28	59	28	3	-	9
17. The profession must adopt policies that will help the public, and particularly parents, sense the value of education.	4.22	59	28	-	-	12
18. Public education should incorporate new programs that open the American Dream to all children and challenge the growing concentration of poor and minority children.	4.09	50	34	3	-	12
19. The schools must develop and establish more rigorous academic and behavioral standards for students.	4.38	56	38	-	-	6

	Avg. Response	Strongly Agree %	Agree %	Disagree %	Strongly Disagree %	No Response %
20. Credentialing and certification of teachers should:						
a) be made more flexible in order to recruit more capable teachers.	4.22	38	53	6	-	3
b) ensure a better match between the proportion of minorities in the teaching force and the proportion of minorities among students.	3.72	31	38	16	3	12
21. The curriculum should be revised in ways that will enhance higher-level thinking as opposed to rote learning.	4.41	69	22	-	-	9
22. The profession should respond to the growing public insistence that the public schools adopt national standards and assessment programs to measure progress toward those standards.	3.88	44	34	3	3	16

THE DISCUSSION
SESSIONS

Small Group I

What's wrong with public education?

"Many decisions that impact on education are being made by noneducators. Often the decision makers are not really aware of what's going on in the schools. They tend to evaluate schools as they existed when they were students and, depending on when that was, they may be quite far from reality."

"I would take issue with that. We're talking about public schools. The citizenry has to have a primary voice in their schools."

"I agree, and I think the schools must be accountable to the public. But what bothers me is that, seemingly, education is the only profession that doesn't make decisions on issues that impact it most. The medical profession has the AMA and the legal profession has its bar association, which have great influence over the decisions that affect those professions. Not in education. I'm not saying there shouldn't be input from the public. That's a different issue. But I think that we as educators have to have greater influence in the decisions that are crucial. I agree with you about accountability to the public. That's critical. We are or should be responsible to the public and the people we choose to serve."

"I think if you ask doctors, they say decisions that affect them most are being made by Congress and state legislatures."

"But these aren't decisions about the practice of medicine."

"All right. I don't agree with you. But let me offer a couple of questions. Why do the schools fail to adapt to the society around them? And why are the schools separated from the infrastructure of the rest of society? I don't know that this is a failure of the schools; it's a failure of the larger democratic system. But there is a serious problem in the schools' lack of integration with health and social services agencies, the agencies required to meet the needs of children today."

"I have a similar concern, the misalignment of the structure and system of schooling with the emerging needs of children and families in the society, a separation of schools from other support systems."

"That is not so much a public school problem as it is a society and governmental problem."

"Well, these other agencies are no more eager to collaborate with educators than educators are to collaborate with them. But the point is that we have a very large group of kids who knock on the kindergarten door with something seriously wrong with them on the first day of school. And the schools have never been able to deal with that set of problems."

"I think Denis Doyle's paper came up with one solution to these problems. They are problems we must wrestle with. How do the schools respond? Do they form cooperatives? Do they change their role and function? Those are pivotal decisions that have been avoided in the last few years."

"There's no youth policy for the country."

"That's a broader issue. I think a lot of the discussion of what's wrong with schools is really conversation about what's wrong with society, including such problems as poverty. But to get to the point, the schools should be doing more to integrate with the rest of society. Given the current level of resources, what can realistically be done now?"

"By schools or by society?"

"Either. Many, many people feel that the schools need to attend to a lot more than the educational needs of children in the traditional sense. They talk about health and social services. On the other hand, the resource constraints are very severe, even to attend to traditional education adequately."

"I'd like to raise the issue of school role definition. Public schools are often mere custodians of children. We focus on sorting and selecting rather than teaching and learning. Thus social and attitudinal changes have to take place, both in the community and in the school. Schools are organized for purposes other than what we want them to do. I think we know enough to teach kids, and yet we use only about 5% to 10% of what we know. And we're told that the reason we don't use more of it is that teachers don't know how to use it. So there needs to be some change in terms of getting teachers to use the pedagogy we know will work."

"The political question is this: Is there a will to do the things that are necessary to educate the kids? What's wrong is that the country hasn't decided there's a connection between public schooling and democracy. It's as simple as that. Until we recognize that connection, we're not going to be able to deal with the issues that confront us. Because it takes resources to do that."

"Lack of political will, then, is one of our most serious problems?"

"Yes, there has to be political will and understanding that the schools have an impact on our democracy — that they can't remain alone, separate, and apart from the rest of the community. There has to be some support for the idea that schools are our first line of national defense in the 1990s."

"Let's emphasize inefficient and inadequate use of school facilities. We've made enormous capital investments, yet we use our buildings and equipment only a small percentage of the time, especially in communities that have desperate need for places in which social services can be delivered."

"Let's define further differences in the quality of education offered to students, specifically on the basis of race and socioeconomic status. These differences are institutionalized within public education through the system of tracking. Unless we deal with the issue of tracking, which institutionalizes different qualitative experiences in school and differential preparation for options when they get out, then we're not going to get at another core problem: the differences in expectations for students, based on such things as race, the language spoken, the kinds of clothes worn, and the like. In fact, when kids enter school, they're placed in tracks."

"The next issue has to do with distribution of resources. I use the city of Baltimore as an example. The difference in allocation of resources between the city and its suburbs is between $40,000 and $77,000 per classroom per year. The issue, then, is that we give the least to those whose need is greatest. And then we blame the situation on students and their parents."

"My comment is related to the point about inadequate political will. I think that underlying our whole view of schools today is a kind of pervasive negativism. We take little pride in our profession, and those on the firing line do a very inadequate job of explaining to the larger public what is right with the schools. People in the schools, even people who defend the schools, seem implicitly at least to accept their low repute. They don't fight back, and they don't seek allies. They do a terrible job, I think, of building the necessary coalitions of public support that are needed."

"I'd like to broaden the tracking theme. It seems to me that there is destructive tracking within schools. But I think the broader problem is the growing concentration of disadvantaged children, poor children, minority children, limited-English-speaking children in urban and oth-

220

er districts. There are districts that have other types of social and family problems on top of a school funding system that denies these school systems what they need to educate those children adequately. So in a sense, it's 'district tracking'."

"To add to that comment, I think there's a growing unwillingness on the part of politicians to address the problem. The courts seem to be the only avenue for change. As the state legislatures become more dominated by the suburban legislators, it becomes much more difficult to address the problems outside of the courts."

"In fact, all of the solutions that we think about for this problem operate under the assumption that children will be left where they are. That's why Governor Lowell Weicker's recent state message was so stunning. He's the first governor who's actually suggested that we ought to try to break down the inner-city system. Everyone else is simply talking about pumping more money into these failing school systems, leaving them structured as they are."

"Bud Hodgkinson is exactly correct. We have no youth policy. But when you think about a youth policy, you usually mean a federally designed policy. While it's important to have a federal youth policy, I think it's equally important to have one at the state level; and each community should develop policies that tie into those."

"When you spoke of the need to sharpen the focus of the schools' role, did you mean to suggest that we're doing everything that the people of the community want and, as a result, don't do anything very well?"

"Oh no, I strongly support the idea of collaboration (and that used to be a bad word). In fact, collaboration with youth-serving agencies at the community level is absolutely indispensable. But when I say sharpen our focus, I mean we have to talk in terms of where the real problems are. The real problems are not just in the inner cities but in rural areas as well. Bud showed us that last night. But we have to sharpen our focus in diagnosing problems. It doesn't make any sense to say the whole body is ill. There are parts of the body that are ill and parts that are well."

"One thing that's wrong is that schools really do not have a clear mission. We have to come to agreement on what the schools are expected to do. Right now I have to teach bicycle safety because a group decided that we needed 10 minutes of bicycle safety in the curriculum. So I think of what is expected of us and then deliver on that. I think the great school curriculum wars are coming. The camps are lining up to divide the time available for instruction."

"Another problem is the inability of schools and school systems to learn from the successes of others. There are many examples of programs that work well and schools that work well in precisely the kinds of populations we have been discussing. But the successes are not copied elsewhere. Somehow there's resistance within the public systems of the country to let anyone from outside the system help."

"No one has said anything about accountability yet. I'm surprised. We haven't said anything about standards yet."

"Okay. The standards/accountability movement has really caught on in a lot of places. It may still be a failure, but a great many states are attempting to install standards and accountability programs."

"The issue of standards is high standards for all students. We have, instead, double standards. With double standards, with the population we have, as described last night, there is no possibility of having excellence in American education. We can't continue to under-educate such a large and growing portion of our population. So we come back to the core issue, as I see it, of tracking. Because it is a system that we use to under-educate poor and minority kids. The problem is not limited to urban areas. It is not even just about money, because in very wealthy school districts where you have minority and nonminority kids, rich and poor, it's like two schools within a school. The poor and minority kids are placed on the lower track, the dead-end track, preparing them for the permanent underclass. So unless that problem is dealt with, even if we do everything else right, we're going to continue to under-educate a large portion of our population."

"What about the reverse side of that coin? Are we doing enough for the extremely bright youngsters who go beyond normal expectations? It's very important to develop continuing education in society."

"I don't think so. I think some of the extremely bright students are in these dead-end courses as well. As a nation, we cannot continue to neglect their brain power and what they could do to help solve problems of the next century."

"The issue is even broader than just tracking."

"But tracking is at the core of it."

"I think the real problem is that our schools are organized around the concept of innate intelligence rather than around the importance of effort and development. If we begin to organize our schools in such a way that we respond to kids as they come, many more kids will do much better. There are many people in our society who, 'are not very bright,' but who yet do spectacular things. What is required is a whole paradigm shift on the part of the teachers."

"I'd rather not see tracking listed as a major problem at all. I think we're talking about two different things. We're confusing tracking and grouping. There are places where you do group people for success. I mean, you don't put boys and girls in the same locker room. I use that as an extreme example to say that there are places where it's proper to group people, but that's not tracking. The important thing is to give people access to the entire curriculum."

"Tracking is a political/administrative decision as it exists in this country. It never was about promoting excellence for all kids. Wherever tracking exists, you know who's going to be in what tracks before you walk into the classroom, whether it's in Washington, D.C., or New York or Tokyo or London. The children that are the most powerful will be in the top tracks and the least powerful in the bottom tracks. The problem here is that we have large and growing numbers of students that we're not educating. That's very damaging. We've got to educate all of America's children."

"Free and fair access to public education by all is one of the real strengths — or should be — of American education?"

"Right. And high standards."

"Part of what we're talking about, I think, is the concept of multiple intelligences and the need to develop different forms of intelligence with individual kids. We can't assume that because somebody can't read he or she doesn't have ability."

"Higher education has always been one of our greatest strengths in America. It's provided a lot of access and upward mobility for a diverse population. In that area we've done a tremendous job. But there are some dangers out there now in higher education. One is rising costs. One is the cutback of public higher education, a cutback of space for students. And the third is that over the past 10 years we've had a growing polarization with regard to students: who goes to which kinds of institutions. There are more very wealthy people in certain institutions and more very poor in others. The closing of opportunities for higher education is a very real problem."

"It hasn't happened yet; but if the trend continues, it's a real risk."

"As a postscript to that comment, I'd like to call attention to the failure of higher education to weigh in seriously and intelligently to help the public schools improve."

"There's a lack of representation of minorities among public school faculties, and the problem is accelerating. This is happening while the number of minority students is increasing. I see that as wrong and in need of correction for a variety of reasons."

"I'm concerned about unimaginative and inefficient use of time in school and after school and through the calendar year."

"Let's return to the inadequate, inappropriate preparation of teachers for an increasingly diverse student population. The teaching population is increasingly *not* diverse; it's mainly white. Not only that, it's increasingly coming from population groups and regions where people have little experience in dealing with others different from themselves before they get to the teacher preparation institutions."

"Probably the whole area of teacher preparation needs to be revamped. I don't think we're preparing teachers to teach students how to do all these higher-level tasks the times require."

"This is a part of the failure of higher education to wade in and help, a point made earlier."

"Now let's see if we can identify about five themes under the "what's wrong with public education" heading. 1) We've talked about the isolation of education from society at large and the fact that schools are not always in collaboration with support agencies. 2) Decision making often is done by noneducators, often on the basis of bad data. 3) There is the problem of low expectations and the related problem of tracking."

"I think inequitable distribution of resources is a central theme."

"There is also the conflict between equity and excellence. When one is emphasized, the other is likely to suffer. And we have been emphasizing equity."

"Don't forget the problem of the school's mission, which is greatly in need of clarification. Many of us think the schools try to do too much by themselves. They should have a definite link with other public and private youth-serving organizations and agencies in the communities. Also at the state and even at the federal level."

"I don't think the schools try to do too much. We just have to do it smarter and work more closely with other youth-serving agencies."

"Instead of saying schools try to do too much, I heard this group saying that school weren't very clear about what their roles are."

"The proper use of time must be one major theme. For all these years, time has been the constant and learning has been the variable in school. It really ought to be the other way around. I think that's crucial. It's been interesting to see the proficiency tests that are given around this country right now. Schools for the first time are deciding that for kids who aren't doing well, time can be found somehow during the day to help them out."

"If you believe in high standards and expectations for all, you can also believe that it won't necessarily take the same amount of time for everybody to achieve those standards."

"Another theme is the fact that we have great difficulty in transferring innovation from one place to another. Perhaps this is related to our inefficient use of time — staff time, in this instance. You can make a broad theme category that we need to become a much more systematic and focused enterprise. We need to be very diligent in changing our practices and skills and behaviors. We're not data-driven in a lot of schools. We don't have a learning enterprise within the school building. We're not taking advantage of what we know in terms of the time allocation, or of what we know about things that work in other places. So for me, the problem's going to be: How do we transform our school sites into learning enterprises that are constantly evaluating information, questioning practice, questioning assumptions, and challenging and taking risks by trying things in different ways? Nothing will happen, it seems to me, until we change our day-to-day routines and the relationships that have been established for schools."

"Our profession doesn't continuously improve itself as the medical profession does. If you look at the way appendectomies are done today, universally it's a lot better than the way they were done 15 years ago. The education field doesn't get better in a uniform way."

"I think public perceptions is a theme, that is, the faulty perceptions of the public about education. Educators haven't done a good job of describing what they are doing."

"Building on that, most people believe that children in low-income school districts get more money than other children. If you took a poll, that is what people would say, that the federal government has poured in all these resources and these kids get more and they haven't shown any improvement. So the public perception is faulty."

"Add to that the perception on the part of a lot of people that we don't have a dramatically changing environment. So this new kind of education being proposed by reformers is really not what people want."

"Can you really say that public perceptions are what's wrong with education? What's wrong with education, it seems to me, is that we don't do enough educating of the public."

"Do we have a consensus that one of the problems of the public schools is that decisions are not made by educators?"

"I would agree."

"Well, we at least have a clear minority opinion that educators need to be more involved in making decisions about education. Perhaps we don't have majority consensus that educators are not adequately involved."

"There's a policy/techniques division here. On a policy question, the public needs to be very much involved. On the techniques side, professionals should make more of the decisions."

"Can I say we have identified as an issue how decisions are made — the extent to which educators are involved — and that the public definitely needs to be involved in decision making?"

"I represent the minority view on that. Let me explain. I have no problem with the public being involved in the decision-making process. But I am concerned about the fact that educators are not as involved as they should be in the process. I believe that if you're going to include all of these other groups, you have to include educators as well. They're the ones who are on the front lines and are faced with the problems of executing policy. Schools get blamed for these wrong decisions, yet educators are not as involved as they should be in the decision-making process."

"Let me summarize what we have done so far. First, we have said that educators are not adequately represented in making school policy. Second, there is a serious disjunction between education and the greater society. Third, we lack adequate vision about or focus on what the mission of the school is. Fourth, educators fail to inform the public adequately about conditions in the schools. Fifth, there is the question about equity and excellence and tracking and how we allocate resources — particularly whether we expend adequate resources on the students who need them most — a very broad category. Next is the issue of the schools failing to get better uniformly. And we have issues in higher education: the closing of opportunity for college for many young people for economic reasons and the fact that higher education is not involved as much as it should be with K-12 education. Finally, there are all the issues involved in whether teachers are being prepared to teach the students we have and whether they are being adequately prepared to teach what needs to be taught."

"Also, preparation is not the end of the support system that's necessary. An ongoing professional support system is not in place."

"I don't think you've included the fact that schools fail to use analysis and reflection, either for staff or kids, and are not changing to accommodate the needs of the kids. That goes back to the whole issue of how our schools are organized and to the question about use of time, to scheduling and tracking, to collaborative practices, to the fact that teachers can't talk to each other, to the fact that there is no extra time in the day for staff development."

"I think you need to break out that resource question from the equity/excellence category, because it just gets lost there. Resources include buildings, people, money, etc."

"On the issue of the exclusion of many students from higher education, I would say this is a risk for the future. I think the situation is still healthy, but we need to be concerned about it."

"Okay. We've got five categories now. To summarize again: One issue has to do with the organization of schools: the fact that we don't make adequate use of time, facilities, the curriculum. The second issue has to do with integration of the schools, or the lack thereof, with the greater community. The third has to do with vision and focus and school mission. The fourth has to do with tracking, whether we are providing equitably for all students and whether we are demanding as much of students as we should. The next one has to do with the differential allocation of resources for schools."

What's right with public education?

"We have the ideal of fair and free access — universal public education. There may be a lot of problems, but that's our approach. It's like peace in the Middle East. We keep working at it and reinvent it every year."

"We have a wealth of knowledge and experience for addressing effectively the problem of educating all students to a high standard."

"We have the best-educated, the best-prepared teacher work force we have ever had, by any objective standard you use. Many of us in this room remember normal school days, when teachers had only two years of preparation after high school. The comments made earlier about not being prepared well enough for a diverse society are correct; but if schooling means anything, we have the best-educated work force in the history of the world."

"All of our data show that, despite tracking, minorities have made amazing academic achievement gains over the last 20 years. Whites have stayed at about the same level as before, but minorities have climbed notably."

"As an enterprise, education has gained status. People believe education is the ladder of success in our society. They are still willing to support public education to a considerable degree. I think we have created a strong public support base for public education."

"We also lead the world in education research."

"The development, over the last decade, of the business community and civic leader interest in and support for education is something we haven't had before. It's a small fraction of the business community, but it is new."

"I would have to put at the top of the 'what's right' list the thousands of dedicated educators – teachers and principals – who daily make big differences in the lives of kids, frequently in working conditions that are less than great. Add this to 'well-educated, well-prepared'."

"Public education is still providing a large, growing, steady flow of marvelous human power to our best universities and to every productive area of society."

"Add the fact that today our schools are open to more people than ever before. There was a time when many of these students would not have been in school. I think that's an important point."

"Isn't that the access issue?"

"It's more than that."

"But you're saying the schools are becoming more accessible."

"Yes, and they offer a second and third chance. This is unique to America."

"People in local communities across the U.S. believe they have substantial influence over the schools. Democratic control is a plus."

"Yes. That's the flip side of one of our negatives."

"I see a slow movement toward greater inclusiveness. We now include handicapped kids, kids who don't speak English, etc. There's an enormous movement in this country beyond multiculturalism. It's inclusiveness when we begin to treat females and males in the same way. Lots of energy is being devoted to this now in every major school system in the country. We're not very successful yet; but we're moving, and we understand the need to do it."

"For me, probably the best thing about the system is that we keep working on it and that there is interest in improvement, which I'm not sure is the case in some other public institutions that need improvement."

"Graduation rates are now much higher than they used to be when some groups were systematically rejected, back in the Thirties and Forties. They're not high enough yet, and that's why we're still complaining."

"Aren't graduation rates still about where they were in the Seventies? Haven't they been flat for about 20 years?"

"We have big differentials. The graduation rate is still very low among some population categories."

"We graduate kids in wheelchairs regularly now. We didn't do that before."

"While we still have a tremendous problem with the Hispanic and the Afro-American population, they're doing better than they did 25 years ago. They're still nowhere near the white population, but we're going in the right direction."

"The point about special education is a strong one. In many ways, we probably are doing better than most countries."

"Oh, no question."

"But we're using special education as a dumping ground for the handicapped."

"That's because we have nowhere else to put them. Regular education programs are not meeting their needs, and we think special education will. But I agree that there's a lot of work to be done. Nevertheless, there is a sense of expanding inclusiveness in the country. I see it everywhere."

"There is growing interest in the public schools in figuring out how to use the incredible technology that is now available."

"That reflects the real efficiency of a local, home-grown system. I was in Japan a few years ago, where there is centralized control. There were no computers in the classrooms. Yet in this country, with 14,000 autonomous school boards, many of them have decided individually to add computers. We moved very quickly. So there's an efficiency in our system that has to do with our form of control."

"I want to clarify what I said about teachers. I said there are examples of teachers who are very dedicated and committed. But I don't want to give the false impression that that is overwhelmingly the case. Moreover, I think that one of our biggest problems is low expectations of students among teachers."

"I think the last two points — consistent attention to improvement and growing use of technology — are part of an important broader issue. There is both a plus and a minus here. We probably do give a lot of attention to innovation, to trying to engage kids intellectually in doing new things, and that's a plus. At the same time, we still have a lot of very routine, mass-production types of schools, which is a minus. But even within these schools, there will be individual teachers who are worrying about whether the kids are involved in education or are growing intellectually."

"This question of low expectations is an interesting one. You've said that teachers have low expectations of kids, but I'm beginning to see that the community has low expectations of the teachers. In the minority community — I could get shot down for saying this, but as a minority person I feel I can say it — the Hispanic community has learned to accept failure and consequently doesn't demand success. It doesn't demand it of the teachers, and it doesn't demand it of the kids. We educators believe all children can learn, and we have to have high expectations for kids. All right, then the community has to have high expectations for adults and say that all teachers can learn. What's the responsibility of the community to provide for the education of those teachers who are there now? I say to my community, 'Look, I want to spend a million dollars in training the teachers. You see, you need to support them'."

"Any kid knows that high school achievement doesn't really mean a hell of a lot unless he's going to go to a select college or university. That creates low motivation to do anything in high school. Michael Kirst's paper says we really have looked at this in the wrong time span: 'Yes, kids aren't doing as well now in elementary and secondary school; but boy, we sure catch up with the rest of the world by the time they are age 25.' So I don't know which side of that issue to come down on. I really think the fact that we give a second and third chance is causing part of our problem in secondary school. So that's a wrong. But if it's glorious that everybody's got a second chance and can catch up by age 25, that's a right. I've really been perplexed about that issue."

"Isn't the issue partly the second chance versus remediation? In many cases, second chance becomes remediation of what the schools didn't do. For example, we have all these remediation classes at colleges and universities because the kids aren't coming out of high school with the necessary skills. That's different from the second chance for somebody to go back to school in order to change careers or get a new set of skills."

"I think it goes further than that, because when a kid in Ohio graduates from high school, it doesn't make any difference what he or she did in high school. He or she knows about Cleveland State or Kent State and about those remediation courses. His or her high school record isn't going to rule out a university. So again we have a right and a wrong, I think. If the universities just say, 'You're not going to get in,' we've destroyed the second chance."

"They could say, 'You're not going to get in without having met a certain higher standard.' Some universities are accepting people conditionally, saying, 'As soon as you meet these skill standards, you're admitted.' There are different ways of skinning a cat."

"How common is conditional acceptance?"

"It's beginning to be quite common."

"I think we need to add higher education and graduate education to this list as well as to the list of what's wrong. After all, it's 'the jewel in our crown,' particularly in terms of quality and access."

"I think our role is to deal with K-12 education."

"Can we really say that our high school graduates are 'a talented work force'? From what I can see and read, they are not. I don't see that as a strength of the system."

"I would agree that we are producing a cadre of people going into higher education who later become a highly sophisticated, talented, and productive work force. But I wouldn't agree that out of high school we're producing that talented work force. I don't believe they can move into society and be productive."

"Just a comment about free and fair access. I have a problem with the word 'fair,' because as one who has been in the inner city of Los Angeles for a long time, I don't see access as fair for all students. I think there's great unfairness for a lot of reasons. For example, in the inner city there is nothing fair about the schools that are grossly over-crowded. In Los Angeles kids may ride a bus two hours a day to get to less-crowded schools. I don't think there is anything fair about that. And they may have 1950-vintage textbooks and no technology."

"But we operate from the theory of free and fair access; our system is based on the theory of free and fair access."

"It doesn't exist."

"I agree, we don't have free and fair access."

"We have universal access, not free and fair access."

"That leaves us with this list: universal access; a public which perceives that it has an impact on school systems, that is, democratic control; the fact that we're getting better despite a lot more variance in the student population; a better-educated education work force, many of whom are dedicated; we are leaders in research on education; we have many examples of what works in education; there is a strong public belief in and support for public education. Does anyone take issue with this list?"

"I think one of our problems is that we *don't* have public support. We have pockets of support; but at this moment, we get lots of rhetoric and not much real support."

"I'd also say I don't believe it is true that we're the leader in research."

"We do a lot of research."

"I would not say we're a world leader in education research."

231

"Strike it."

"There is increasing interest in education, and people see linkages between democracy and public schools. There is public support for public education and increasing attention to education."

"I'm concerned about the research category. If it meant research on teaching, it probably ought to come off our list. But if it meant leadership in the natural and physical sciences, in terms of published papers. . . ."

"No, we're talking about another area."

"The final one is that higher education is the jewel in the crown of our education system."

"I don't know what that has to do with this issue. Why don't we take it off the list?"

"We'll take it off."

"I want to go back to the 'better-educated, prepared work force.' Work force of teachers?"

"Yes, work force of teachers or educators."

"I would agree that we have more credentialled teachers than we've had historically, but I would maintain that that credentialled work force has a long way to go to be prepared to educate deprived children. I would not want to be interpreted in that way."

"I think that the pedagogy that's available to us now is not being used by 90% of the teachers. This is not blaming the teachers; it's just reality."

"Would we like to limit our statement about educators to the fact that there are many dedicated educators?"

"The fact is that teachers are much better educated now than they were in the past. Now whether they are better teachers across the board, that's questionable."

"Third World countries, even small industrialized countries, simply don't have teachers with four or five years of required college preparation. We're just superior."

"Can we say that we have more high-credentialled teachers than ever before? I think the issue here is whether the preparation is better now. Does a master's degree equal better preparation? Are they prepared to teach this new student population to work, learn, and live effectively in a shrinking, interdependent world?"

"We probably have a better base to do it, because there are very few nations that have the kind of democracy we have."

"Do we want to say that we have better-educated, better-prepared teachers? Or do we want to say we have more high-credentialled teach-

232

ers? Do we want to say anything about teachers other than the fact that many of them are very dedicated? I'm going to take your silence to mean that we want to say the latter."

"I think that's useless to say. It's unverifiable, and it's an insult to the rest of the world."

"Do I have your permission to say that we had a discussion about the issue of teacher preparation but no consensus?"

"Our presenter can certainly say that, in terms of degrees and so forth, we have a superior teaching force. I see no problem with that."

Small Group II

What's right about public education?

"I think our founding principles are basically right. They include educating all students; that's the very heart of our public school system."

"The common schools *have* been at the heart of creating a society that works together. But today we're too much into exclusion."

"Even though we tend to malign teachers, I think we need to recognize we have a lot of very energetic, dedicated people in the system."

"I think we have to include customer or client satisfaction. There is remarkable satisfaction among parents who have kids in the public schools. Also, it's a strong plus that our school system is run at relatively low cost."

"Other than rural areas, there's a school building in practically every neighborhood. That's easily taken for granted, but it offers a lot of advantages. For example, the schools are cores around which inner-city neighborhoods could be rebuilt. These buildings could be community-type buildings, so we have the physical structure and network in place."

"We ought to take some pride in the fact that even though the diversity of our students has increased and the number of poverty households has increased dramatically, we still have managed somehow, without much investment in change, to keep achievement levels about the same as they were 20 years ago."

"We're the only system in the world that specializes in second and third and fourth chances."

"I think the ability of the public schools to expand far beyond their original intent is a plus. They've assumed great societal roles that society has not fulfilled: racial integration, feeding children, transportation, for example. These are not strictly educational services, but they are necessary and are performed by the schools."

"Let me comment on the point that we have a dedicated teacher force. I do think we've seen a tremendous improvement in the quality of people coming into the teaching profession in the last four or five years, which speaks very well for our training institutions. But in terms of client satisfaction, polls may show it, but I'd invite you to spend a day in my office and get the phone calls we receive. That doesn't say the same thing as the polls."

"I would point to greater collaborative efforts. We have better business partnerships than we've ever had. We have more people involved in the public policy debates. I think that's significant in improving education."

"Some of the public schools where I live have more than 300 partnerships of various kinds."

"Historically, the public schools have been the great melting pot for the diverse population elements that came to America."

"I was just trying to figure out whether this is something that's right or wrong, but I'm impressed by the breadth of the curriculum; it's astounding in some systems — maybe too broad — but now that we've got a very diverse population, we need to accommodate all these diverse interests, needs, and talents."

"This may seem somewhat redundant, but we have to remember that public schools helped close the achievement gap between black kids and white kids. They also have raised the high school retention level of black children. We forget that 25 years ago, achievement levels and retention rates were much lower among many of the minority populations. The gap hasn't been closed; but we're coming closer, especially in the South. The schools have been an important instrument for integration of the races. That's an achievement."

"The other thing I'd point out would be that even though it's much criticized, one of the strengths of American education is local control, because local control gives much more flexibility to the system. You were talking about your local partnerships in your area. Well, in many parts of the world you can't have them, because you have a ministry of education that has very tight, centralized control over education. Of course, there's a down side to local control, which we are very familiar with nowadays as everybody rushes to national standards. But the strength of local control is flexibility and diversity — many different people approaching things in different ways. In a very large country it makes for better connections between citizens and their schools. People feel that they can vote out boards of education, which they can't do in many of the centralized systems of the world."

"School people do work hard."

"The schools are main contributors to the high level of basic literacy we have in this country, as compared with most places around the world."

"Public schools are an extraordinary agent of upward mobility for people who are able and motivated and lucky."

"That's been true historically, but is it still true?"

"No question. Look at the Vietnamese boat kids who come in. Their achievement is just astonishing. There are plenty of other examples."

"Look at the Mexican kids who are crossing the border to enroll in Texas schools. They obviously see them as a means of upward mobility. I have just come back from two months in the Third World, visiting a number of schools. Do that and you appreciate how much every student here gets. I saw young children working at adult jobs at about age 7."

"I'd call attention to the high quality of leadership in our public schools. There are many John Murphys and Peter Negronis heading up school reform that's really making a difference."

"The public schools are important instruments for socialization."

"I'd like to add the recognition of individual differences, which is a guiding theme in American education. A corollary of that is our investment in special education, which is so rare among nations of the world."

"Add to that the recent thrust toward mainstreaming that's more and more common."

"I think we should mention the extracurricular activities the public schools sponsor — art, music, athletics, special interest clubs, etc."

"There are fantastic physical resources in the schools, including good libraries, great facilities for sports, and elaborate transportation systems. We take these for granted, but in a lot of places around the world they are not required."

"What about something that's often pointed out as the difference between us and Japan — the social benefits that children get in our system but don't get in a structured, rigorous system. I refer to interpersonal skills, getting along with others, leadership skills."

"Visitors from abroad always comment on the extraordinary ways kids are exposed to democratic processes in our public schools. We elect class and club officers, for example, and hold mock conventions. Kids get these very rich experiences in practicing democracy. In some schools they even impose their own rules through student government. This came home to me dramatically when I worked for months with five professors from Poland, who are here to develop a syllabus on schools in a democratic society to be taught to every new teacher in Poland. When I asked them what democratic experience teachers coming into their classes in Poland have, I couldn't get any answer."

"To reinforce what has been said about creativity, people are trying to invent responses to needs in many different ways, instead of waiting for one ministry or one person to tell them what's right or wrong."

"I'm bothered when we talk of the schools creating a society that works together. Are they doing that, or are they contributing to a society that's beginning to fall apart? I say that because of our failure to prepare youngsters to be successful. Are we creating more Los Angeles conditions throughout our nation in urban areas?"

236

"Last night when Bud Hodgkinson was talking about America becoming a mosaic of different peoples rather than a melting pot, I thought, perhaps romantically or naively, that schools were one of the early ingredients of the melting pot. But Bud was talking about the change to a mosaic of different schools with different cultures and languages. If schools lost this function, as places to bring people together, they'll lose public support, I believe."

"The issue of race is never brought into this discussion of mosaic versus melting pot. White people melt; people of color don't melt. The cottage cheese can marry the cauliflower, but the potatoes and the meat don't mix very well, at least in the last several hundred years. The Haitians have better boats than the guys who came over on the *Mayflower*, but they don't mix as well."

"Someone mentioned the relatively low cost of U.S. public schools. It's a good point. It turns out that the U.S. is not investing as much of its gross national product as are many other nations in K-12 education; so if you want to look at returns on investment, note that we're investing low and probably getting a higher return than one has a right to expect."

"Yes, and yet we cater to the desire for athletics and social development among children with elaborate school gyms and pools, etc., that many other countries don't have in their schools. In Germany, for example, such facilities are provided by city organizations, not by the school system. So, in a way, we're paying less and getting more. I'm talking, of course, about K-12, not higher education."

"What about the remarkable range of curriculum materials in the public schools?"

"If we really believe in empowerment and professional accountability, it's important that we have diversity and range. What's missing is agreement on outcomes — where we're heading. Materials aren't the problem. The problem is, we've never had consensus on where we're going. So I think we blame the materials and fail to understand that the schools are a team that doesn't have a goal line. Yet I think it's a strength that we want to create more diversity. We can meet more individual needs. One curriculum isn't going to do it."

"Oh, I agree; but let's look at it this way: A school may have a curriculum that is so diversified nobody comes out knowing anything. But if it's a curriculum where the staff has the option to meet the needs of that community, that's a whole different thing. What are we talking about, broad diversity within the system? There's a difference."

"I just finished a big study for the governor in Ohio on the governance of human services, including education. We have developed, historically, all kinds of structures to provide these services. The human services field is amazingly broad; that's why we have this incredible fragmentation. There's no one in Ohio who can tell you how well we're doing in the human services area other than in education. Education is the most thoroughly governed of our human services. We've got regional structures in education coming out of our ears, designed at a time when needed but never examined since. There isn't any public accountability, and there's never been an attempt to sunset a lot of those structures. But when you go over into the health field, education looks simple by contrast. So we have this fragmentation that is simply out of control."

"We have said we should take pride in the fact that student achievement levels have not declined, despite lots of difficulties and challenges. Any data on that?"

"What happened is that the College Board used to put out its report every year on incoming freshmen, including, incidentally, the average SAT score from the previous year. The report never said anything about scores in earlier years, so I called once and asked, 'Well, how does this compare with the year before that? How about the year before that?' Lo and behold, they discovered the SAT had been going down for 10 straight years. The story appeared on the front page of the *New York Times* in 1974 or 1975, and I was Dr. Frankenstein. Incidentally, scores just kept going down, too."

"Well, there are other measures of achievement (and the SAT is not a true measure of that; it's supposed to be a predictor of future school success) in which scores didn't go down; and we've bottomed out in the SAT, too, though we still are behind the best years. Remember, SAT scores declined primarily because of the increasing diversity of the test-taking population. Many more high school students, including the less able, began taking the test."

"When they are renormed, every achievement test in America — the CAT, the MAT, the CTBS — is up."

"Any data on improving quality of teachers?"

"My personal observation of the last four or five years is that stronger people have been coming into our schools."

"Is that idiosyncratic to your system?"

"I don't think so."

"How about as compared with the teachers of 25 years ago? Or 10 or 15 years ago?"

"Well, when all the best women were going into teaching in the Sixties, quality was probably a little better. Arizona has about 800 people in teacher preparation at any one time. The cut-off GPA is now 3.2 in the freshman and sophomore years to enter the program. That's remarkably high. We have 3.0 students screaming that they've done well in school, why can't they get into education? That's just three universities in Arizona; but I think that in terms of the GPA of entering people now, education is doing much better than it has been for years."

"Looking at all the background papers, with some exceptions there was a lot of comment about the marginal nature of teachers coming out of our preparatory institutions, so they don't support that particular observation. But so be it for the moment."

"Returning to the point about quality of the work force coming out of the public schools, I think we now have in this country the political will and commitment to make it better. I frankly didn't feel that way under the previous federal administration. Now there's the political will; and with the right people in the White House and the Congress and the feeling across the nation that we need to fix this weakness, we have the ingredients for doing this for the first time in one hell of a long time."

"That a very interesting point. Your comment was addressed to the national level. But I think it holds at the state and right down to the local community level as well."

"And it is now a bipartisan commitment."

"Could I add a sidebar to the concept of inclusion we have discussed? I believe we're one of the few countries in the world to concentrate on trying to raise the achievement levels of disadvantaged children as a group and trying to deal with the handicapped as a group. I've had people come over from the European Economic Community wanting to know what the U.S. has done to deal with disadvantaged children and handicapped children, because many of the other industrialized countries don't deal with them. They want to find out what we've done with bilingual education, with Chapter I, and with these other programs. Now I know the down side of all of that — categorization and pull-outs and all of that — but it does seem as if we have recognized our own problems and tried to direct resources to solve them where other countries have not."

"What we have done is create an enormous ripple effect. Other countries follow our lead very carefully. Again, Australia, France, and Sweden are looking at these issues quite deliberately. They do have some very inventive programs of their own. The French, for example, have an extraordinary instrument called a migrant waiver to deal with kids we've never figured out how to handle. In France a migrant waiver is principally for kids who live on canal boats and move back and forth. They get schooling as they go up and down the canals. You're right, we were the leader; but the following is really quite striking."

"The amount of interest in the states of the former Soviet Union in coming here for technical assistance and advice is similar. They are interested in our extracurricular activities, the breadth of our physical resources and investment in plant, and in our elaborate transportation systems. They see our social benefits and personal skills development programs, which are not a high priority elsewhere, and note that our schools are very democratic."

"Let's move on now to what's wrong with our public schools."

"Got four hours?"

"I'd like to add one fact on the last 'goods' point. It just dawned on me, going to France last year, how their science and industry museum was such an important educational endeavor. But then I realized that we have comparable efforts in this country. We just had one in Denver, and the general public is viewing arts and museum big events as an educational opportunity. You have to get a ticket months in advance, as you would for a Bronco game. I don't know where this interest came from, but I hope from the schools."

"Don't forget, we have an extraordinarily enlightened system — actually a pair — of teacher unions in the U.S., when compared with the teacher unions of other nations. In a number of European nations, they are impossible to work with."

What's wrong with public education?

"Okay. Let's try again. What are the problems? What needs improvement?"

"May I speak for Al Shanker, since he's not here now. I think his background paper identified a main problem, which is lack of student motivation. Students don't think they have to work hard for any particular thing. Shanker attributes this to the lack of a uniform curriculum and particularly to lack of standards to get into universities and colleges. It's a key point."

"One of my concerns is that teachers don't read. While teachers are better prepared, possibly, I just don't think they're involved enough, somehow not motivated enough, to learn by themselves, which bothers me."

240

"They don't read their own professional journals, and that's really startling. They don't read magazines. There have been some surveys in this area, and the findings are astonishing."

"They don't even read *Education Week*."

"The University of Michigan has done a report comparing Japanese teachers with American teachers. Japanese teachers spend only half their school day teaching; the other half they spend preparing. Maybe there's something wrong with our structure, in that we have our teachers working so hard doing social things and working all day in class that they don't have time to prepare."

"Absolutely."

"We have a serious attitudinal problem within the profession, too. There's still a lack of understanding or belief that we can effectively meet the needs of all of our children. Also, the kind of resegregation that's occurring in many schools is a serious problem."

"The fact that we vary our expectations according to the race or income of the child is another way of saying it."

"Right. There is no community in schools. There's not even a community in individual buildings, as a rule. The gangs and the absence of safety just reflect what's going on in the society at large."

"Piggybacking on the 'no community' concept, look at the problem of high schools. They're just too large."

"Let's examine a little more closely this issue of motivation. We have this terrible problem of low expectations for poor kids and kids of color and for girls. All too often, the expectation levels of teachers, guidance counselors, etc., are too low. But I see two sides of this problem in New York City. Kids have a terrible time relating what they're doing in school to the larger world. They don't understand that there is indeed a connection between what they study and what they will do in jobs or in what gives meaning to life or in their ability to take care of children. So schools have got to do a better job of linking — particularly for kids who have lower or shorter horizons — the world of schooling with the world of work and life outside school. On the other hand, we have this wonderful system that offers a second, third, or fourth chance. In New York schools and colleges, you see adults who are working full-time jobs and desperately trying to get an education, maybe having discovered this connection later in life. My God, are they motivated; and, God, do they work hard to get what they need to improve the quality of their lives! So I think it's more complicated than Mr. Shanker's background paper suggests. We need to look at it more carefully."

"One of the themes that struck me in the papers we read was the number of people who talked about raising expectation levels, which has become trite. But the form that now takes is setting higher academic standards and trying to achieve them. I think there is almost a consensus that we have to shoot higher for everybody. And I think the form any solution takes — standards, assessment, or whatever — remains to be worked out."

"Where we're going wrong here is in failing to see the other side of the equation, which is some way of building the capacity to meet higher standards. It's fine to say higher standards are needed, and let's assess and hold people accountable, and all of that. But I think there are too many critics, particularly in state legislatures, who are ignoring the investment we have to make in our schools and in our human resources. When we look at California and the cutbacks there, we realize how many citizens don't want to support schools. We need to build up this other side. I mean, higher standards are great, but we need resources to achieve them."

"This is a remarkable consensus among so many people. Here's one thing we really all need to do better. I would like to take a different approach, however. We've been thinking about the number of dysfunctional families and dysfunctional neighborhoods we have to deal with. I hesitate to say it, because of Denis Doyle's paper in which he said we're on the border of blaming the victims, and I don't want to do that. But it is really hard to educate kids from dysfunctional families and neighborhoods. Unless we talk about fixing those problems outside the schools, it's very hard to talk about fixing what goes on inside the schools."

"May I put a rider on that? I think one of the great problems facing schools is children having children, which really is our failure to care for our children while they are away from school. The task is almost impossible for the school to deal with. And consider our inability as a society to take care of the size of the needs of our children before they enter school. The size of the readiness gap that so many have when they arrive at school makes it almost impossible for teachers to close it."

"Going back to motivation. Do we have a problem with motivation among *school* personnel as well? And do we as educators have a problem communicating to parents why it's important that their children are in school?

"We do have dysfunctional kids in the schools, but the system itself is dysfunctional. I mean, it's a larger context."

242

"Add lack of adequate resources to the list. I know that's always a debatable question; but when you look at English teachers in California having 40 kids in class and you expect them to teach youngsters how to be better communicators — that's an impossible task."

"While we're on dollars, I think we should add that we don't distribute the resources we have correctly. Not enough money is getting into the classroom. A lot of it, I think, is getting picked off by people who check to see if the 'inputs' are right and that kind of thing. American business doesn't always do this right, either; but I think the fact that some businesses are taking a hard look at their layers of bureaucracy sends us a message. That really hasn't happened in education."

"We haven't told the inequities in distribution story well. I visited a New Jersey high school recently where science teachers had only three classes. Labs had no more than eight students. The top of the salary schedule was $75,000."

"Bet that wasn't in Newark."

"No, that's right. But the point is that it was in New Jersey; and Newark is in New Jersey, too, right?"

"But when we talk public schools, we talk about Princeton, Camden, and Newark. The differences in resources among them are just incredible. It's not a homogeneous system."

"We haven't put the spotlight on inequities. Even though we've written about school equity court cases, it's always in an abstract kind of way."

"Texas has spent five years trying to equalize funding among districts and still doesn't have a formula."

"There are some states that do. They did it 18 to 20 years ago when nobody was looking. Nevada, for example, distributes all school funds at the state level. Otherwise there would be absolutely no schools in some areas where there are 50 children and no property tax base because of federal lands. Yet they're supported equally with the urban areas."

"I would like to say, regarding the problems with motivation and everything else, that somewhere along the line, public educators started being reactors and not actors. Therefore confidence among the public in what educators do to change is shaky, because educators don't seem to lead anymore. That's a real problem. Educators talk to themselves a great deal but don't talk outside very often. They're not revered in society as leaders. We revere professional athletes and CEOs of the Fortune 500, we revere physicians, but we don't revere educators in this country. And that's because educators have been tar babies, taking it but not hitting back."

"But there's another interpretation: that educators have been so successful that we no longer revere educated persons; they're no longer unusual. We're all educated now. At one time the only educated people in a neighborhood might be the priest and the teacher."

"That's true. But educators *should* be smarter and better educated than I."

"Does this attitude problem of educators not go back to the unionism of education?"

"There's a credentialling problem involved. I have just come from the North Carolina School of Science and Mathematics, which has no credential requirement for its teachers. It's the only school in North Carolina with any Ph.D.s in it, because Ph.D.s won't go back and get a teaching credential. But they will teach in this school, because there's no credential barrier to keep them out."

"There are no text requirements either. Teachers can use their own books."

"They also have a group of kids who are highly motivated; they're self-selected. There is a whole set of factors at work there."

"That's right. But when you combine them all, you get some really exciting activity — when you have a group of motivated kids and you don't force the school to use credentialled teachers. There are only 11 teachers in all of North Carolina certified to teach college-level physics."

"State legislatures put credentialling laws on the books under pressure from the teacher unions."

"That didn't happen in North Carolina; there wasn't a union problem there. But elsewhere there's plenty of blame to go around. It's certain that legislatures have been induced to fall for the credential routine. But that has been the fault of the professional education associations and educators themselves who've created the problem. And they've created low standards. I mean, it was once thought to be a floor, now it's a ceiling. And it's a nightmare."

"Joe Doe and Joe Sixpack don't know that. They stereotype educators. They say: You're an educator, therefore this is your fault. And therefore public schools have lost respect within the society. The public doesn't know that a union group was responsible. They just know that educators allowed themselves to be degraded."

"Could I add a twist to this: I wonder whether teachers will be respected unless they are full-time, full-year employees on the same type of work schedule as regular employees. And I wonder whether schools shouldn't change so that they go from 8:00 in the morning until 6:00 at night, the regular work day, instead of having this strange work day that doesn't fit in now with two-parent working families."

"It's a remnant of the agrarian society. There's no reason for the U.S. to be on a farmer's schedule anymore; not too many kids work in the fields now."

"Most people know that teachers don't work for two months in the summer and know that they're off at 3:00 p.m. They're not willing to pay teachers better because, they say, 'I've got to work all day. I'm not home until 6:00. Why should I pay the teachers better?' I wonder whether we don't have to reconceptualize schools and put teachers on a regular work schedule."

"Would you add to that the nature of the reward system?"

"Yes, exactly. They would tie together."

"The best and the worst?"

"As you know, teachers spend and ought to spend an awful lot of time in the summer in institutes and inservice training programs. We can structure the full year so there's an opportunity for teachers to continue to grow intellectually and grow in the knowledge of their fields. That's fine. If they're teaching 12 months of the year, they will be no damn good, I assure you."

"Well, if any of us were in the situation of teachers having to handle kids from 8:00 in the morning until 3:00 in the afternoon, we would be pretty tired and want to go home. So we have to change the demands we put on teachers during the regular school day, so they can grow differently. The whole structure has to be rethought. The good thing about the Edison Project is that private money is supporting the rethinking. I'm not sure about having proprietary schools do it, but at least it's private money that supports different thinking about how you should structure schools."

"As you suggested, the school day has to be reconfigured. But then within that, we have to come to understand that teachers are working even when they're not with children. That will be easier for people to understand, perhaps, in a reconfigured day. Teachers have to have more time, even the best teachers. You can't expect teachers to do anything in school-based management or other reforms if you don't give them time."

"I think one of the key problems I've seen in my recent tenure is that we want simple answers for a very complex institution. I think the main issue is none of these we've mentioned. It is, How do you build a coherent system whose parts reinforce each other? I haven't heard that discussed. I've seen us wanting to tinker and do incremental things. We need to do the hard work, to have a sense of what coherent means and how you achieve coherency. All these suggestions are great, but they won't change the system. On the positive side, it's refreshing that we are willing to look at this problem deeply. I hope we can maintain the moral and political will to sustain the effort."

"Our list is more of a wish list than a reality list. I was impressed with how diverse it is, covering social, academic, community, economic factors. One of the problems the list highlights is how many different expectations we put on the schools. By emphasizing setting standards, perhaps we're saying, think about academics first. That may allow us to start restructuring the schools, because then we'll know what they're being restructured around. You can't start restructuring and rebuilding the schools unless you know what their mission is. If you're only socializing kids, maybe you don't want all-day, all-year schools. Maybe they socialize better on the playground, not in the classroom. I think one of our problems is that we still haven't really, consciously, come to an agreement. What's the point of all this? How much is it going to cost? Then, how are we going to do it? But begin by deciding what's the primary goal."

"John Murphy has done that in Charlotte, as his paper says. In Charlotte we raised those issues exactly, directly, frontally, and then worked on them. And standards are everything. Mastery of those standards is what's expected. Everything else yields to that, and the whole system is transformed."

"I see in all the meetings I go to this growing consensus favoring standards and some type of assessment system. I worry that something is happening akin to what happened when we deinstitutionalized the mentally ill. The theory was that people would be cared for better in the community. We were going to have a system of drug clinics throughout the country. Everyone would be cared for. And then we did away with the state institutions, and ill people *weren't* cared for. Now we have the homeless and psychotics on the streets. We have to understand that standards development is one thing, but resource allocation and this reconfiguring are all integrated. You can't just wash your hands once you have the standards and once you have the tests. It's a long, bloody business involving, probably, consolidating schools and districts and changing the basic structure of schools. It's all going to take money.

246

Even though we're spending a lot of money now, we're spending it extraordinarily unequally. In Illinois, one district has $2,000 and another has $14,000 per student. So we have to rethink the whole thing, not just pin everything on standards development. I believe that is a starting point, but it's certainly not an ending point."

"I'm sure Charlotte has taken your counsel to heart."

"The advice was given and received. John should speak to it, but he isn't here. It's been quite an extraordinary process to watch unfold. But to address the issue, yes, the standards and the measure of standards and mastery are simply the first step in the process of renewing the whole school district."

"Then you can begin to focus on every child to make sure you do have the growth that you need. That is the beginning point."

"Something running through all of these examples — dare I say it, it's such a dirty word these days — is deregulation. You're talking about standards, longer school days, about the ability of teachers to have time for planning. How can they do that if they've got a dozen mandates from the state or federal government requiring the filling out of all these forms, etc.? And then they mandate from the local government. Somehow all of these things have to be localized so that schools can say, We'd like to attempt this on our own. We'd like to give a teacher an hour-and-a-half planning time during the day to grade papers so she's not doing it at 9:30 tonight after she's put the kids to bed."

"I think attitudes are shifting very rapidly at the state level. In Ohio, for example, you can get waivers on almost anything now. It's a very simple process. And that has happened very rapidly."

"We have to be very careful. Let's not duplicate the national airlines fiasco. We can't deregulate in the absence of standards. We've got to have some way to ensure fairness and equity to our kids. I worry when we get these simplistic responses like: Deregulate. Another point is that you don't shrink-wrap standards like the test packages we get from ETS."

"What is shrink-wrapping?"

"You get the test in, you give it, you don't know what's in it, you don't know why you have it, and then you start saying the results are important. The key with standards is: I have to build them. I have to endorse them. I have to be able to teach them, to assess them, and to help students learn them. Standards building requires professional development. And that's what we've never invested in in this country. I view this whole movement as a great opportunity to get people to build the capacity of our teachers to do their job better. I could never sell staff development before. I could get accountability — man, they'd give me all the tests I wanted — but I could never deliver on building our teaching force."

"It's always been kind of a mystery to me. Why is it so hard for you to sell that concept? It would seem so obvious, and yet it seems to be the most difficult thing to do. Look at Congress. They have this grand, elaborate total in the Higher Education Act, and yet you can't get a penny for teacher/staff development. At the state level, I see the same thing; it's the first thing states cut when the budgets need balancing."

"Why is that?"

"We've failed to make connections again. We haven't related staff development to student needs. We've got to start showing how staff development relates to student productivity. That means we've got to have an agreement with the teacher unions on what the mission of the school is."

"We're used to politicians wanting an easy answer. Then they wash their hands of it and say, 'Let's go on to the next problem.' Standards development is relatively cheap. So they'll say, 'Let's have national standards development and put up $10 million.' Then they walk away and deal with health care or something. They don't deal with everything else that has to follow standards development. So there's a danger that people will perceive standards development as an easy answer and move on to another social problem."

"An emphasis that impressed me in this conversation is that standards setting is a systemic process and not a product. That distinction is crucial."

"It's not being well made. It's an ongoing process. There are 30 pieces that fit into standards setting. It's not simply: 'The student will know and be able to do the following.' That's not what we're about. This is not writing objectives for eighth-grade math. It's a whole different process."

"I'm not so sure. I mean, writing objectives is part of it. I've been very impressed in watching educators do this kind of thing, putting the pieces together grade by grade. That is the beginning of a process."

"There are a few things we haven't mentioned. One is the terrible failure of the schools in general to teach higher-level thinking skills. That fact is revealed repeatedly by NAEP reports in almost every discipline. And look at the level of remediation that colleges are forced to do. Something like 20% of all students have to be remediated. Why don't we raise students to higher-level thinking in most areas? One reason is that there's too much curriculum to cover. I think that the Coalition of Essential Schools is on the right track with the notion that 'less is more.' Also, I think the schools are handicapped by societal values that affect the schools, that is, the anti-intellectualism in our society. It takes its worst form in inner-city black schools, where it's said that it's 'acting white' to want to be a serious student. (Little do they know that most of the whites don't want to be serious students, either.) The climate in so many schools also contributes to anti-intellectualism. Add in violence, which is a real problem. Finally, I think the biggest problem in education in this country — one that wraps together some of those other problems — is the total failure of inner-city schools. And I've had the opportunity to spend days at a time in inner-city schools of big cities throughout this country. I can guarantee you that you can go into classroom after classroom where they're operating on about a third- or fourth-grade suburban level in what are supposed to be high schools. You can't imagine how bad it is."

"Down-sizing would be one way to attack the problem."

"It's certainly a factor because of the anonymity in the big schools."

"One of the major problems as we move into reform is to get away from blaming individuals — whether they be teachers or students — for failure, rather than creating shared accountability. Exit tests and teacher tests have divided us, not led to collegiality."

"Have you found a way to create shared accountability?"

"I think the state of Delaware is beginning to do it. Schools shouldn't be chartered if they can't be successful. You don't have level playing fields; but criterion measures and showing progress, I think, is a way to begin. It's certainly not easy, because people want those simple knee-jerk answers: Take the student's diploma away or decertify the teacher when neither is at fault."

"You've been using the ward 'systemic,' and I applaud that. I think we've got to have a systemic picture and understand all parts of the system, their interconnectedness and interdependence, and move away from the legislative turn of mind, which is to impose a process through legislation. We've got to take a hard look at government at the state and local levels, how their work is done and how they approach their tasks."

"Do we want some identifiers here that would be useful in reporting back on our session, some ways of characterizing points that we've made? The first point would be the ideal of the common school. We need to be faithful to it. There's consensus that we need higher standards, higher achievement levels. I hope, along with that, that we hold to the belief that all students can learn."

"That's a new belief, I think, that we have never shared deeply: that all kids can learn at high levels."

"We're having trouble here, I think. We want to go back and identify things that are right with the public schools, and I'm hearing you say things that are still in the future."

"What's good is that there's a fairly decent basic system of public education in this country."

"Another of the things that are right is the fact that the resources the schools provide are close to the citizen within the community. I'm thinking of physical and personnel and financial resources. There's a great investment in public schools, and there is one in practically every neighborhood. The potential for usability is great."

"I appreciate the sentiment, but over the past decade resources have become more and more remote from the school. The states, with only a few exceptions, have centralized funding. California's the world's worst example of everything, of course. Thanks to Proposition 13 and budget scarcity and the *Serrano* decision, about 85% of all spending there is state-generated; and the balance is controlled by state statute. It is virtually a state school system."

"I agree, but we're talking of good things, and that's a bad thing. The good thing is that the potential is there. The buildings are there. I strongly agree that the negative is there, too. I'm one of the group having a hard time finding any good things, but this is one."

"We didn't stress the negative that schools haven't connected to the human social service system. The question is, Will we be able to do that? Do we have the will?"

"Do you mean integration or coordination?"

"Well, the integration of social services — doctors, health care, that quonset hut outside the school where you get all those inoculations before you come into the schools."

"I need some help here with our mention of flexibility as a plus. Somehow, that's not what I think of when I think of our public schools. I understand their local nature and that you said it increases flexibility. I just want to question it."

"There are some school districts that have done away with ability grouping. We have some school districts that have passed bond issues that have changed their schools so that they have completely integrated interactive technology systems. You have flexibility that you don't have in many industrialized countries with a centralized ministry of education that prescribes everything: the salary schedule, the curriculum, the types of building, etc. There's a down side to this local flexibility, and that's what we're grappling with, trying to find some way to nationalize standards and curriculum in a very decentralized system. Nevertheless, local control is a strength."

"I think local control is more the word we should use, not flexibility."

"I don't think, as an institution, our education system overall can be characterized as flexible."

"Let's make sure of our first three 'rights.' First, the idea of the common school. A lot of discussion centered around that. Number two, we're reaching for higher standards, although we haven't necessarily achieved them. And three, we have a fairly decent basic system. It's sophisticated in many respects."

"Does the ideal of the common school include the mobility ideal, being able to move up in society?"

"Right. Diversity also. Civic-mindedness, possibly."

"Let's go now to the down side. We've almost a reverse image of the up side."

"The public schools' curriculum is too broad and too nonacademic."

"There's too much garbage."

"How about our failure to be really systemic in our reform efforts? There's probably a better way to say it, but we look for the quick fix and tinker with one piece, but we fail to pull all the right pieces together."

"We have the myth about multicultural education. There's a lot of rhetoric and very little's being done. A Black History Month and a corn-soup day and teaching about Indians the week before Thanksgiving doesn't weave multicultural education into the fabric of the curriculum. So we don't really have a common school, do we? One that will make us both civic-minded and tolerant citizens?"

"The strength of what was said leads me to list the myth of multicultural education as a 'what's wrong'."

"Let's list lack of motivation. Shanker's position on motivation is that we must make students realize there are bad consequences to poor school performance. But I think we should accentuate the positive; people ought to understand the up side of doing *well* in school, that is, that there are rewards."

"It's not just a matter of negative reinforcement. First, it would be wonderful if kids loved learning. But if they don't, they ought to understand that good things happen when you do well in school and graduate. I'm still preaching that to my own kids. I haven't gotten very far with them, either."

"I'm not sure if this is a right or a wrong, but one of the things I've been thinking about is the ambivalence of our vision of childhood. On the one hand, we want our kids to relax, take it easy, have summers off. And on the other hand, we want them to work hard, go to school, do homework. It strikes me that we have this incredible ambivalence about what the nature of childhood ought to be. Part of the problem is not knowing quite what we want but wanting all of it simultaneously. I remember watching little Japanese kids working very hard. But we Americans want kids to sit around and relax because life is tough later on."

"We don't have clear, high standards for student achievement. There's too much variation in what we expect of different kids."

"We've mentioned the problem of resource distribution within states. I am concerned about resource distribution within a school, not necessarily lack of resources, but inequitable distribution."

"There are so many inequity issues wrapped up in that comment. I mentioned that Columbus, Ohio, has 300 partnerships. They're very unevenly distributed across the system. You have a hustler, an entrepreneur, in the principalship; and that produces inequity in other places."

"I have three things to mention. Maybe they're already included. One is the failure to teach higher-order thinking skills in general. Two is the failure to create a climate for learning in so many classrooms, particularly at the secondary level. And third, the failure of inner-city schools serving minority kids. It seems to me that this third problem is in a class by itself. When people talk of an education crisis, they're papering over the fact that there really are two educational crises in this country. One is that all schools are not doing something about their systemic problems; but the inner-city crisis is so bad that, in not too many years, our democratic structure is going to be overwhelmed by it."

"We just cannot overestimate the problem."

"But the problems aren't just inner-city schools. I think the same problems exist in a lot of suburban schools, too, when we resegregate those kids. There are just more of those at-risk kids in the inner city."

"Low-economic-level minority students. Maybe I should rephrase it to say that."

"Let me ask a terrible question. How many of you have been in the worst schools in Memphis? Or the worst schools in St. Louis? Or the worst in Baltimore? The problems get worse by the hour. You can't put the brakes on."

"That leads to something that hasn't quite come up yet: all the troublesome cultural values and the social problems that walk into the school each day. These are not, strictly speaking, school problems; but we face them, from anti-intellectualism to sheer vulgarity to antisocial and even criminal attitudes. All these things certainly contribute to the schools' inability to meet their goals, as do dysfunctional families and dysfunctional neighborhoods."

"My single concern to note here is with the quality of teachers. I think too many underprepared teachers are teaching."

"Absolutely."

"There are ways to get rid of them."

"They don't know the field. They don't know how to teach. It is a serious problem. I have a surrogate son who teaches in an inner-city Baltimore school with Teach for America. He's Phi Beta Kappa at a fine university, and he has worked for a year just to survive in this school. He's very smart. What finally won for him and his students was their realization that he knows math and science. He is a very good teacher. And after he struggled for months with criminal behavior and every other problem, the kids finally said, 'Dude, you're smart and we want what you know.' A connection has been made; and a classroom has been turned on to learning because this young man is, number one, dedicated to teaching. He's not antagonistic to the kids; he wants them to learn. And they realize he really knows his subject. Something has happened because this kid knows his field and they want to learn what he knows. So I think the quality of our teaching force is crucial. And generally it's not so good."

"I assume that your surrogate son also looks like the kids he's teaching and can relate to them better. I think we've got a real problem, not just in preparation, but in who's coming into teaching mismatched with the student body."

"If we can say all kids can learn at high rates, I hope we'll also have the courage to say all teachers can teach."

"If they know their subject. . . ."

"They all can do it, and we're going to help them to do it. But there's an unfulfilled promise on both sides. Kids aren't learning, and teachers aren't teaching well. But if we have this vision, we've got to remain faithful to it."

"One thing we haven't talked about is school governance. There was a time when superintendents got together and talked about board/superintendent relationships. You know what they're talking about now?

The special interest groups. The far-right groups, the stealth groups that are controlling education and battling Sizer's and other reformists' programs of systemic change. Governance and special interest groups constitute a major issue. As you go farther west, you see that they have a strong, strong influence on what's going to happen in public education."

"You want to talk about governance? In New York City the third superintendent in five years is about to be fired. The system is going down the tubes. There is a hissing match over someone who is recognized as one of the best superintendents in the country. I'd say the governance problem is much broader than influences from the far right."

"To follow up an earlier comment: If kids aren't learning and teachers aren't teaching, then leaders aren't leading. So it's not just the teacher problem. We've got a leadership problem at the district and building levels as well."

"I think one of our problems is that educators are not marketers. We live in a world of marketing, and education is not being marketed to the public. That's why you're getting the fringe groups who speak up. The average person can't find a way to be heard, and school boards are a part of the bureaucracy of school districts. There's no real tie-in between the citizenry and the schools. We need to learn to be more articulate about what we're trying to do, to offset some of the special interest groups."

"No one's said a word yet about technology. I'm not sure what to say, except that it needs to be talked about. I've come up with a new spin on it. I've been working with a software company in northern California, and I've discovered a really dramatic growth in home schooling. It's no longer just a matter of religious fanatics dropping out of public schools. The computer nerds have suddenly discovered that they have extraordinary opportunity to do home schooling, and it's a lot cheaper than sending the kids to a private school. In California, at least, a number of districts are now collecting their ADA; but mom and dad are doing the home schooling. These parents will show up for two hours a week to pick up the crayons and paper and demonstrate that they have a lesson plan and so on. The number of such home schoolers is still not very large, but it is growing. Technology is going to offer an explosive growth opportunity to home schoolers."

"I think the inability or unwillingness of some parents to take responsibility for the development of their children has to be on this list. The schools pay a price for it. Children are having children now, but they aren't the only families I have in mind."

"I think we need to pair that point with the fact that most schools aren't good at helping parents to understand why doing well in school is important or what they should do to help their kids in school."

"And you could add, the ineptness of schools when it comes to working with families."

GROUP SUMMARIES — PLENARY SESSION

Group I

"We started off with a set of statements about the 'goods' of public education and very soon came to the realization that each of our statements had a yin-yang quality, that each of the 'goods' could be followed by a 'yes, but' and the presentation of the negative. For example, continual access. One of the background papers said we are a great second-chance nation, where unlike the situation in most countries, you can change your mind, pick up where you left off, and find new opportunities. Someone pointed out that this is a result of failure to motivate and guide earlier in life.

"Another good: A large percentage of people in this country cares about schools, and a large minority wants the schools to do better. It was felt to be a good that improvements would be made largely as a result of nongovernmental efforts.

"We also noted a great deal of faith in this country that education improves opportunities for a better life. We asked the question Bud Hodgkinson asked last night: Will the new immigrants take the same path to success? Our faith seems to be that they will.

"Another 'good' was that many people try to make significant improvements in schools, that many parents are eager to work with the schools. Millions of young people will work hard and contribute to communities as a part of going through school. It was felt that it was a remarkably good thing that, in the face of disincentives for achievement, there has been an increase in the number of students who take rigorous courses in school and take Advanced Placement exams.

"Another 'good' was that the system is open to change. Whether it *would* change or not generated a great deal of discussion.

"It is good, someone also argued, that we are shifting toward assessment of outcomes in education, as opposed to inputs, because this will fundamentally challenge the schools. It was said, for example, that third grade is fixed but nine-year-olds are not. They differ wildly.

"It was even good that we could have a dialogue about the purpose of schooling.

256

"One of the big negatives we kept harping on was that resources for public education are not equitably distributed and that the schools are not financed in a proper way.

"I got concerned that we weren't saying anything about what goes on *in* schools. We were talking about things around schools. So I said schools are often boring, but nobody wanted to talk about that.

"We then debated ways to get reform going. Someone said we can't agree on the purpose of schooling. Someone who actually works in a school said, 'All the teachers in my school know why they are there.' Another said, 'Yes, but now schooling is too often defined in terms of getting a job.' We couldn't do much after that."

Group II

"We suspected that all three groups would arrive at the conclusion that there is a flip side to almost everything we talk about. We decided that number one among 'what's right' is universal access and democratic control of the schools in this country. Number two: The schools are getting better in terms of minority achievement and the trend toward greater inclusiveness, which encompasses mainstreaming and Chapter 1. There is growing use of technology, but there is a down side: Not enough is being used. Teacher preparation and education are a 'good,' and there are many highly dedicated teachers. We had a tough time with this point, because we believe not enough attention is paid to teacher preparation and staff development. We spent as much time on this topic as on anything. We asked: 'Are today's teachers, particularly those just coming out of institutions of higher education, just better credentialled? Or are they better educated and prepared for teaching?'

"There are many examples of 'what works,' and we see increasing attention to public education.

"On the negative side, we lumped a number of things under the heading of poor organization and the inefficient use of time. We examined the whole issue of time as a constant and learning as the variable. We noted the need to make better use of facilities, the unequal-resources issues, and the wrong-curriculum issue. We noted the failure to integrate the schools to a sufficient level with the larger community, to adapt to societal change, and to collaborate with other child-support systems. We kept coming back to the lack of clear goal focus in the schools. We said that while there are many examples of 'what works,' there are also lots of examples where people aren't employing 'what works.' Finally, we discussed the equity/excellence issue and deplored the fact that there's still a lot of tracking and still a lot of low expectations and a differential allocation of resources."

Group III

"We talked about the ideal of the common school and the ideals of equity and *e pluribus unum* as the foundations of our possibilities in American education. We agreed on higher standards and the belief that all kids can learn at high rates. Later, we added our belief that all teachers can teach. Neither is a reality now, but they are what we're pursuing. We agreed that we have a fairly decent basic system. The structure and infrastructure are there. Today we have to have all kids ready for school, and that's not going to happen with just kindergarten as the starting point; it's got to happen earlier. But we felt that the infrastructure is certainly a resource. The resources at the community level are what we regarded as important. There was a debate over the term 'flexibility.' We decided that perhaps that's not the best word for our public school system and that we should go with 'diversity' and 'creativity.' It was pointed out that a lot of our clients feel good about our schools and care about them. We agreed that the second or third or fourth chance we offer students is one of the great 'goods' of American schools. We mentioned that our system can be fixed; people really believe this, and it's a wonderful belief.

"When we looked at the negative side, we said we don't really have a common school system. There is not a shared curriculum and shared beliefs. There's a lot of variance in what's happening to kids, and this is probably a product of the fact that the curriculum is too broad and nonacademic. There's no focus, and kids are meandering through. Some kids get a good education, but a lot of them don't.

"There's one theme we kept coming back to: that what we have is a systemic problem and a coherence problem. How do you make teacher standards and student standards and delivery standards all fit together so that, in fact, they work? The myth of multiculturalism goes back to the first problem: no common schools. We decried the lack of motivation in our students, parents, and teachers. We discussed the ambivalence in our view of childhood in America. We noted that while inner-city poverty and school failure get most of the attention, there is one poor rural kid for every poor inner-city kid."

Plenary Session Discussion

"When we talked about customer satisfaction with education, one participant suggested that ignorance is bliss. I remember that the automobile industry decision makers once thought they knew what the American people should have and should buy. And they kept producing that car. Then one day, they woke up and saw we had a lot of Japanese names on our cars. Hundreds of thousands of people in Michigan were out of a job because of these very intelligent people who were making General Motors, Chrysler, and Ford cars. We lost the outboard motor industry completely for a similar reason. So sometimes the experts are ignorant of what the people want, which is the name of the game.

"Now for the balance of the plenary session, which has to do with our vision of the future. That's a very general phrase, and obviously we cannot create a vision within the amount of time we have. But we may be able to identify some parts of a vision and leave it to the genius of the people who are listening to the tapes and reading the notes to give it coherence. What, in your judgment, is an initiative, an idea, a concept that might be a part of this newly constructed vision?"

"I'll suggest modest voluntary choice to help bridge the gap and return to the common school system, because right now we have segregated school systems in cities and elsewhere. Perhaps we can follow the magnet school model that John Murphy has described, or the Joe Nathan model, where voluntary choice might bring different races, different nationalities together again."

"My concern remains: How do we best re-energize the general population, insuring an interest in the future of the public schools and building a constituency for the common school across the country?"

"My concern is about the process by which we include people in the community who have a stake in education, so that we rebuild a community and a consensus on the importance of education."

"I'm concerned about how we can support, through policy, creation of strong, respectful relationships between adults and kids in schools. We must build learning communities where kids and adults are working together."

"We need to transform the culture in this country so that it prizes academic and artistic achievement as much as it prizes athletic achievement. We need to create a system that encourages and assists rather than frustrates and inhibits people with vision, talent, and energy."

"I would hope that the education community comes together and puts aside turf wars so that communities, the public, and parents can latch on to the real concept of public education and can identify what we mean by common school. There would be less bureaucracy, so that school policy is not so far removed from the citizen. We must have more re-

259

spect for education in this country, and I would hope it can be achieved quickly."

"I want to second the comment about modest voluntary choice. Second, I'd like to see Chapter I used very broadly as an after-school rather than a pull-out program, using the Murfreesboro, Tennessee, model. Third, I'd like to see schools begin to understand technology as a productivity-enhancing tool rather than just bells and whistles. I hope the schools begin to enter the mainstream of modern life and use technology wisely and well."

"I'd like to see educators define, focus, and strengthen the academic curriculum and create sound courses of study for children of all backgrounds."

"I'd like to see schools establish a sense of community by becoming smaller. These schools should communicate their vision, encourage ownership of the school by students and parents, demonstrate high expectations, allow for autonomy, and focus on learning and outcomes."

"I think teachers are the core of the future, and we have to place very, very great emphasis on staff development and the teacher pipeline."

"We talked in our group about the fact that we know what teaching strategies work but that we don't learn from the successes of others. I'd like tighter focus on the way we train and then develop staff so that we model those good practices."

"I think we have to have a system that prepares all children for a lifetime of learning and success in a diverse democratic society and an interdependent global economy."

"We must insure that parents value the intellectual development of their children and are helped to do so, to the extent that they need that help."

"Let's develop curricula and models of instruction that permit students and teachers to engage collaboratively in authentic tasks that mimic the way people learn through the rest of their lives."

"I want to see behavior on the part of government — local, state, and federal — that demonstrates a belief that all of America's children are equally important."

"We need to wrestle with this issue of the role and function of schooling in society and to have a concentrated federal, state, and local effort to reach those students who are now being lost in the system."

"We need to agree on clear, high goals for what students should know and be able to do; and we need an absolute, unequivocal commitment to reorganize the system and the resources within it — people, time, materials, dollars, incentives — as necessary to enable all students to reach those standards."

"What we're doing here is trying to identify ideas that can be incorporated in a total vision. That is, a vision that might lead to improvement in public education."

"I'll only repeat what I hope we believe collectively, that we build in the assumption into whatever we do, whether it's new legislation or new reform efforts at the local level, that all children can learn."

"I'll second a lot of things, but *all* children *can't* learn in unsafe schools. We have to concentrate some of our effort in the redesign of neighborhoods and schools so that they're safe. I think we need to equalize funding up and down. In states that do not have equalization formulas, we have incredible disparities in funding; and it's not fair to kids. Also, if we're talking about systemic reform, we have to talk about funding the technology needed for schools of education to pull their weight in the preparation of teachers for the schools we're trying to create."

"I would expand our conception of time for schooling and learning so that all children and all teachers have the time they need to grow and develop and to meet high standards, on the presumption that they're not all going to need the same amount of time."

"Overcome isolation of the schools from the family and the community. Invest in programs that work."

"We need to accept the vision that there should be no limits on how far you can go in education, except your talent and motivation."

"In realizing academic excellence for all students, it's the system of tracking that maintains unequal quality of education for large groups. Tracking should be eliminated. We can build on successful models of what works to promote excellence for all students. We should expect to see no differences in performance based on socioeconomic status, race, and ethnicity."

"The schools should be part of a comprehensive delivery system for children so that the whole of children's needs are met. Second, there should be motivation for both children and teachers to achieve at the highest levels."

"Let's attack the growing concentration of poor and minority children. The educational consequences of that concentration are enormous, and we need to stop accepting the situation as the status quo."

"We need to come to grips with the tension between two values that we seem to hold very dear. One is the idea of the second chance and all that means. The other is the value of desiring early academic achievement. The one is causing a problem in the other."

"I propose something that may sound a bit reactionary, and that is that American schools need to incorporate new Americanization programs, not for immigrants and not for minorities but for the majority populations, so they can begin to understand the meaning of democracy and how we keep democratic institutions functioning."

"For the near term, focus on the knowledge and skills needed by students and teachers so that the school becomes a learning community for all. And for the long term, come to terms with technology before the schools become the Sears catalogue of the year 2020."

"Establish rigorous academic and behavioral standards and an accountability system that allows us to focus our energies on each child in the school."

"Look at the total development of the child and find better methods of controlling some of the factors that influence educational achievement that are beyond the control of the schools."

"I'd like to focus the public policy discussion so that we separate out some of our most important problems from our suggested solutions. On our important problems, one is the vast differences in resources available to different districts. Another is the link between societal problems, including poverty, and the education system. We must separate them out and stop blaming the problems of society on the education system."

"As a country, we must not be obsessed with being right or wrong. We must build a community with the fundamental principles of respect and honor for all Americans."

"I would wish that people responsible for schools would design them in such a way that they themselves would be willing to work in them and be willing to send their own kids to them."

"I'd like to see the schools reflect what research tells us about how much learning takes place the first four years of life. We now pick children up at kindergarten age when they have very diverse backgrounds and opportunities. Doing so delays their ability to take real advantage of what's in the schools. So I'd like to see us get into pre-kindergarten care for all children, rather than neglect those whose parents can't pay for early care and may not have the cultural resources to give it themselves. Also, someone spoke about the need for schools being part of a comprehensive delivery system of services to children. Again, what we know about the effects of health in those early years and the impact it has on the learning that takes place tells us we need to tie schools to other community youth service agencies."

"We must strive to engage all students in the achievement of non-trivial intellectual and artistic and cultural objectives. That can be accomplished by connecting their success and achievement to clear and visible stakes. Second, we must involve professionals in the system in a relentless quest for the most effective ways to ensure that achievement on the part of students. Again, do it through the development of significant stakes for the adults within the system. In short, reward teacher success."

"Link staff development to clear and high standards. Second, link teacher standards, student standards, and delivery standards in a coherent and systemic manner."

"Get better teachers. Many of us have commented on the cancer in the system: not reaching kids in poverty situations, whether urban or rural. I think the most immediate and most effective strategy is already being tried in many areas around the country, and that is recruiting and keeping better teachers."

"What I'd like is to have every single child find an adult in school who deeply cared about that child, had high standards for him or her, and was both capable of and willing to be an advocate for that child."

"I just want to offer one caution. Before any vision can be built or any vision realized, there has to be a real coming together of the profession to respect the differences as well as the similarities among us. In building any vision for the future, I would like to see us involve those people who are affected by it. I'm talking about the practitioners in education as well as others."

"I would add to the point about staff development that those who lead American education at every level — superintendents, chief state school officers, school board members — should have the same opportunity that their peers in other fields have to engage in sabbaticals, in executive training workshops, etc. They need the same opportunities to stay up to speed as leaders in the military, business, and industry do."

"We must monitor school ties to job market changes, because the schools we are designing may not fit the market for kids when they graduate."

"I'd like to emphasize engagement of people of the local community in support of advancing their public school systems. It's easy to talk about federal and state initiatives, but what really counts is how the local community supports and nurtures its educational system. That is a basic responsibility of citizenship in the local community. We can never take the emphasis off the responsibility of people in the local community to foster both excellence and equity in their schools."

"Schools serving concentrations of economically deprived kids or minority kids who perform at the lowest levels ought to be first in line for reform efforts instead of always at the end of the line."

"Test question: Can any of you recall a document in the history of American education that contains a lot of what has been said here? A single volume that has said it all? It was the Educational Policies Commission report of 1938, *The Purpose of Education in American Democracy*. Almost all is there in beautiful prose."

"Another kind of question: Given the importance of these observations, who should take the initiative? What leadership populations ought to be energized in this respect? What responsibilities do all of us in this room have in regard to these notions about the future and vision and improvement? We said a lot of important things. But they're just going to be said or they're going to be on the printed page. Who takes the first step? Coalitions, broad-ranging coalitions. Several of the successful reform efforts we have heard about should be involved in those broad coalitions of stakeholders to make it happen. I don't think if any one group takes leadership, you're going to get huge success."

"I think if each of us in this room individually took the responsibility for pushing this message, it might have great impact."

"One of the points made was the relationship between the schools and other segments of the society that have to interact in order to improve services for all youngsters. Typically, at meetings like this, those other elements are not represented. So there probably needs to be a broader effort. Maybe it goes back to the idea of coalitions, formal efforts made to draw people together who serve children and their families in direct ways."

"Idealistically, the profession of education would take the initiative, and then form these coalitions we are talking about."

"In our group we felt that change would probably not come as a result of action by the federal government. I think to a certain extent that's true. But I do think that the role of the President is significant in galvanizing public support among all the constituencies that we've identified today. I think that still needs to be emphasized. We have a President who's made a commitment to public education that will be difficult to live up to because of a tremendous number of other pressures, economic and otherwise. But I think the President, in many respects, is the controlling influence."

"We need to listen to the voices of the community and not solely to policy makers or people who sit in this room and have written 200 reports in the last 10 years — most of which are gathering dust. We need to figure out how the top meets the bottom in terms of development. They say it takes the entire village to educate the child. Now, the village can be Detroit, and it can be Pine Ridge, South Dakota. But I think you need everybody engaged in some way, rather than reports and policy statements."

"John Dewey argued that whenever we had these big transitions — from agriculture to industry, now industry to high tech — we needed to re-establish the town meeting, dialogue, conversation at the most basic level to incorporate increasing numbers of people in a civic sense. Other people here have said the same thing. The communitarian movement is based in part in that sensed need. How can we convene the community at various levels? And who ought to do it? Who says, 'You all come'? One of us said that 'for education the professionals ought to take the lead.' Someone else said that there are other services significant in the lives of families and kids that ought to be represented around the table as well. Where do those convenings take place? One of us said that maybe we ought to put the E back in HEW. We knocked it out some time ago."

"Eliza Doolittle in *My Fair Lady* shouts at Henry Higgins, 'Words, words, words!' I somehow think we're at that point. If I had my druthers as a foundation executive and I could find five of the best community organizers in this country, I'd drop them into Cleveland and organize some support for the public school system. If I wanted to produce lasting change and incorporate any one of the number of good ideas about how to improve education that have come out of a meeting like this, that would be my answer. So I think we've got a political problem here with a smaller P than the presidency, although I agree that the bully pulpit is a valuable asset, and I hope it's utilized to engage the nation's interest."

"I really think that we have to build constituency in a very primary way. I'm not sure it'll make changes in the most distressed places in this country. But I don't think anything will happen in those places unless the communities become democratically involved. The education establishment is so isolated and is so self-isolating in many ways that I'm not sure that leadership will come from there. Nor do I think it's the best use of their time, nor do I necessarily think they have the talents for it."

"As states get more different from each other in terms of their demographics, both the style and substance of participation may well shift.

That may be highly appropriate. The different states have different ways of getting people to the table."

"I think we need to start at the local school level. I think that the principal and the teachers and the community need to get back to the town meeting concept. Professionals have to abandon their wars. We've got to find a common thread that is articulated to all the groups. Then at the local school level, building by building, street by street, we begin to reinvest in our schools again. Trickle down doesn't do it. It's got to be bubble up."

"I agree that the leadership for convening the community has to start with the school. I doubt seriously that principals or teachers are necessarily the ones who are skilled at doing that. I don't think that's generally part of their training. So in the meantime, until we can prepare a new cohort of educators who know how to work adequately with the community, I think there needs to be some partnerships with community organizers, people who do know how to mobilize the community. I think three things need to happen with the community. It has to be informed, because communities don't always know what the issues are. Communities need skilled organizers, so someone needs to work with them to develop some skills. Once they're mobilized and trained, they can help professional educators make changes in the schools."

"In the question of who, I hate to be the one who has to raise this subject. But the people who teach children in America are not represented at this meeting. There are no classroom teachers here. Two days ago I attended a meeting in Denver sponsored by the Education Commission of the States, discussing the future of teacher education and the induction of young people into teaching. Not a teacher was present. I embrace the idea of convening communities. But as long as the community concept that is bought here is top down from the President to the top of the teacher bureaucracy so well represented here by all of us, the people who teach are not represented and are implicitly voiceless in these conversations. We see the vision and presume it will trickle down in the old bureaucratic way. They — the practitioners — are told what to do once we figure the vision out. But nothing will happen. Nothing. A waste of time. A different concept needs to be thought out."

"Who's going to do it? If I am the one who's going to do it, then I'm the one who is going to have to make these changes. If you are writers, say, 'I'm the one that's going to have to write it to see that it gets out.' If you are a superintendent, say, 'I'm going to have to initiate something.' I don't think we can pass and let somebody else tie this bell around the cat's neck."

"In addition to that, who do we go to for help? There's not one community in this country where you don't see this enormous banner that has sometimes three, sometimes as many as 23, little signs saying Lions, Kiwanis, church groups, civic groups of all sorts. They're often overlooked. When you go to them, they often want to help. Those people volunteer. They want to do something besides sit there and listen to someone."

"Local school boards are the natural convenors of the community to address local education issues. They need, though, to see the need to do that. They need training to do it. And they need some resources to carry it out. This is one of the principal initiatives of the National School Boards Association during the coming several years. We believe that one of the major functions of a local school board is to establish a vision for education in the local community. Now this isn't something they do in a locked room; this is something they do throughout the community. They follow that up by insuring that there's the right infrastructure present in the school district to achieve the vision. The extent to which they do that is, in my judgment, the extent to which the whole system of American representative governance of the public schools works and achieves its mission in our country."

"I think that the issue is not either/or. The magnitude of the challenge we face in American education is such that it's going to take all of us working together. Grassroots involvement is absolutely necessary. Leadership at the top is absolutely necessary. And everything we are doing in between is also necessary. I think that the strategies that can be effective will be different for different ones of us, depending on what it is that we bring to the table. Different states and different places require different strategies. There's not just one answer. What we in this room must do in addition to advocating academic excellence for all students, high standards for all, is put down our buckets where we are and do all that's within our reach."

"In Ohio our achievement was a cascading out kind of process where first we looked for natural allies or people who ought to be with us. The Business Roundtable folks, the educational organizations in the state, others. We used them to galvanize the state vertically and then went back out horizontally to the local communities. But the real key was the people who were interested, our natural allies who were already motivated. We all had to start moving in the same direction, following the same musical score."

"Maybe we're making something more complicated than it actually is. First, I think we ought to distinguish between two kinds of coalitions. One type is where you know where you're going and all those people who want to go to the same place get together. An example is the voting rights bill. Everybody wants to push it and engages in a march on Washington. In such a case you don't bring people together to throw in a lot of different ideas. The ideas are already there. Those coalitions are very effective.

"On the other hand, if you have 20 or 30 ideas and you try to bring people together in a coalition to add to the ideas and modify them and everything else, you'll only get good committee work. We all know where that goes. You'll get a report and it's filed and maybe somebody will read it.

"I want to suggest that maybe there's a lot more agreement in this country on a vision for education than people in this room think. There are men and women out there who, if you ask them what schools are for, will say, 'We want our kids to be able to read well and to write well and to know mathematics and science and know about the history of the country and the world; we want them to develop a decent set of values and to learn how to live with other people in our society.' You don't have to convene anybody for that. These people also know they're not getting some of these things from the schools.

"So I don't think we need to convene people to develop a vision consisting of 20 or 30 different pieces. Nobody is going to engage in an effort to reach 40 or 50 goals. It's too difficult, it's too diverse. There are trade-offs. I think the question is, Are there one or two or three points of leverage that, if you do those things, other things pull together. Then you can develop a coalition, if you can show people the need. And I think, by the way, that's what the President is going to have to do on economic policy. He has to say, 'If you swallow a few painful medicines, here's what's going to happen to our country in the future.' He's going to have to do it on health care. And we've got to do that on education, too. I think we can lay out a simple vision. It's not only accepted by parents in the U.S., but by parents in every industrial country in the world. If you ask them, 'What's your vision of schools?' they'll all give you the same one. Why are we trying to give them a vision that's different from the one they already have? Is there something wrong with theirs? I don't think so. I think the problem is not that there is no vision or agreement.

"By the way, that vision is common even with all the diversity in our society. The interesting thing is that if you look at recent polls of Hispan-

268

ics sponsored by a couple of foundations in this country, polls taken in New York State on curriculum issues, in minority communities, there's very little difference. There may be a great deal of diversity on all sorts of other issues, but not on what parents want from schools and on what they expect of their children. I think that this is one of those cases where people in high places and people who are intellectuals and culturally sensitive tend to create problems that are not there for the overwhelming majority of people in this country."

"What has just been said is absolutely true. The differences that divide Portland, Oregon, from Portland, Maine, are essentially very modest."

"That long speech scares me a lot as a noneducator. If we all know what the people want, why haven't we achieved it? That's very frightening to me as a consumer and supporter and lover of education."

"Part of the reason we haven't done much is that we haven't been able to get a broad-based, common set of stakeholders who are willing to make that vision become a reality. It's so incredibly politicized at all levels; even if we agree that that's where we ought to go, we can't make it."

"Remember, we're achieving a lot of that vision in most of our schools already. We're talking about a huge system, about 110,000 schools, some of which have remarkable success at providing what their communities want for their kids. We also have schools that are clearly failing. We've pointed to them a number of times here. Some are in rural areas, some in inner cities. Nobody wants to defend what's going on there. But I don't think we want a blanket statement that we haven't achieved good goals. It isn't true."

"But we do have schools doing driver education and drug education and other things like athletics that seem constantly to get in the way of what we need to do."

"Referring back to the long speech, the speaker mentioned the things that parents all say they want, and he said there's public consensus on that. But what they want doesn't end with his list. People also want choirs, football teams, and 40 zillion other things. When John Goodlad published his study of schools, he titled one chapter, 'They Want It All.' When Ernest Boyer did his high school study, he wrote a chapter titled, 'They Want It All.' It's simplistic to say we know what they want."

"One can draw a parallel between wants in education and wants in health care. People want everything in health care because some insurance company is paying for it. They want it all in education because there's no visible cost for having all these extra things. But suppose you didn't have a system that said every youngster could enter a college whether or not he can read, write, or count. Suppose you had the same standards for entering higher education in the U.S. as exist in most other industrial countries. Now suppose as leader of a school system, you told the people who wanted the choir or wanted you to invest three times as much in football that the price was likely to be that fewer of their kids who want college can enter college. The reason our system doesn't work is that we've hidden the consequences of nonachievement. We've made believe that if you don't work and don't achieve and you put your money into all sorts of things that are extraneous to the central mission of the institution, there's no failure in it. Of course there's failure down the road. People fail then, but we leave it to employers and to society to confirm it. We don't give information to parents and kids, and we omit any good system of rewards and punishments. Other countries don't do it that way, because they know what the school's mission is. They know what the consequences of poor achievement are.

"We have a lot of discussion now about providing funds for youngsters to go to college. I think that's great. I don't think we should have a single youngster capable of a college or technical education or a work experience or whatever who should not get it. But I don't hear a single voice saying, 'We ought to attach standards to every one of these opportunities.' And we ought to say, 'You work for what you get. You get nothing for nothing.' Until we do that, we'll have no educational system, no matter how much 'vision' we have."

"Those remarks reinforce the importance of local discussions and control. If we ask a higher level of government to do everything, we'll continue to want everything at no cost."

"There is massive disagreement in this room about a number of things. Some of us have looked carefully at national standards and tests and have a very different view of them than others have. Some of us have spent 15 or 20 years developing public school choice systems that really disturb other people in this room. And so on. One thing that occurs to me that Phi Delta Kappa could do is to sponsor a series of meetings around this country on specific subjects that we have identified over and over. For example, equity funding and national standards. What are the trade-offs? What can we learn from countries that have a different approach? Pick three or four other issues and get not only educators but parents and young people together. I think we should declare a moratorium on meetings about education that do not involve students and teachers."

"Part of what we're talking about here is: How do you manage change? The world is changing. America is changing. And the schools need to change. The issue is how we are going to manage the process of change. Thank you all very much."

EDUCATION, PRESIDENT CLINTON, AND THE 103RD CONGRESS

At the close of the plenary session on the second day of the conference, Michael Usdan, president of the Institute for Educational Leadership, introduced Jack Jennings, general counsel for education for the House Committee on Education and Labor, U.S. House of Representatives. "Jack," he said, "is celebrating more than 25 years as a very respected staff member. We thought it would be very valuable to hear his perspective on the 103rd Congress, which recently convened. There's no one better equipped to do this than Jack Jennings." Jennings' remarks follow:

I cannot tell you, of course, exactly what Congress will do about every issue affecting education in this session, although there are indications of general themes. However, it would be useful to step back for a minute and look at the overall political situation in Washington.

As you know, President Clinton had a rather rocky beginning, with Zoë Baird and gays in the military as the first issues he had to deal with. In fact, when Governor Carroll Campbell came to town last week, he said, "Well, if President Clinton keeps going in this direction, he must be getting pretty bad advice from his staff."

When I heard that, I thought of Liz Carpenter, who worked for President Johnson. She liked a certain Biblical quotation:

"And Jacob leaned on his staff and died."

She used that quotation to warn people in public life that ultimately you have to take the consequences of your own actions; you cannot blame your staff all of the time.

But I do not think you will find President Clinton and Hillary Clinton, this dual team we have at the top, relying on staff in the area of education. It may be true in other areas; but we have been dealing with the Clinton transition staff and the Clinton political appointees in the last couple of weeks, and I know that all the decisions these teams and Governor Richard W. Riley [the new Secretary of Education] are making are brought to the White House. A Clinton, one or the other, tells them whether they are right decisions or wrong decisions.

So I think we are going to have a very activist President this time around. People ask me what that means for America 2000, which the last Administration spent so much time on. Are we going to wash it out and start over with something new?

Well, one of the reasons I am talking to you now is that I have collaborated in an effort with Mike [Usdan] and Lowell [Rose] to publish something called *National Issues in Education: The Past Is Prologue*. It tries to depict what happened in the last couple of years at the national level in this debate on school reform, in the debate on postsecondary education, and on other issues. Former Secretary Lamar Alexander, Senator Ted Kennedy, Senator Jim Sasser, and former Representative Leon Panetta, now Clinton's budget director, as well as Diane Ravitch of the Department of Education under Secretary Alexander, are among the contributors. The book outlines the long-term context of policy decisions in education at the national level. We do that because the new policies we will have in the next couple of years will grow out of the policy debates of the last couple of years.

In Washington, we do not just wash everything out and start over with a change in the Administration. To give you an example of that continuity, look around this room. Many of the same people you see here today are going to be involved in the policy debate of the next few years as they have been in the past, but they may change their jobs.

So what will happen, I think, with America 2000 is that part of it will live, part of it will die, and part of it is going to be superseded. The parts that are going to live are the National Education Goals and the push toward national content standards and some type of national assessment system. The parts that are going to die are any national push for vouchers for private school tuition and any national push for federal money for New American Schools. The parts that are going to supersede America 2000 include more interest in federal assistance to encourage systemwide reform in education. The push will be to set standards or outcomes for what programs should achieve, and then rigid requirements will be loosened. There also will be more interest in using the White House positively to help public education.

One of the more intriguing ideas Clinton will advocate is the youth apprenticeship concept. I will not dwell on it; but if this idea is implemented correctly, it can reform American high schools in several important ways. For instance, many at this conference have emphasized motivation for learning. Apprenticeships do that. Kids have much more motivation to study when they know there will be some conse-

273

quences for their actions, as when the subjects they study in school relate directly to their paid work. But the apprenticeship proposal may be a way off, because it is very difficult to move from a broad concept like this to creating a national system to implement it.

So, Clinton will keep some ideas from the past, some will be washed away, and some will be new. What is going to happen in the Congress? Well, in this Congress I think most of the Democratic chairmen want to be very cooperative with Mr. Clinton, with a few exceptions. The Democrats, who now control both the presidency and the Congress, realize that they must cooperate for the good of the country or face the consequences at the polls.

Now, let me give you some idea of the testimony we have been hearing this year on education. This testimony will give you some indication of the policies the Democrats may create. We have had hearings in the last couple of days on elementary and secondary education, and we tried to bring in a variety of people to talk to us. Let me tell you the three themes that emerged from those hearings.

One is a push toward a standards-driven system instead of a system that is framed around particular programs or particular interventions. The second is a push toward deregulation, in the sense that if you have a standards-driven system, you can deregulate federal programs. Third, there has been a great emphasis on the need for better coordination of education programs, and also coordination – with education programs – of all the social and health services that impact on children.

In the last two days, half our testimony must have been from business people and from education leaders about coordination of services. It will take leadership from the President to effect this coordination, because the President is going to have to tell these different federal departments to get together, to mesh their programs, to create common definitions, to provide services at common sites. But I think all this can possibly happen.

This reminds me of Denis Doyle's paper, in which he quoted the late, unlamented Lester Maddox, governor of Georgia. Maddox said, when asked about the miserable condition of prisons in Georgia, "We can't improve the prisons until we get a better class of prisoners."

Well, one message we are hearing constantly is that the schools can not improve the education they are providing unless the kids are ready to learn when they come to the school door.

Is this merely an excuse for the public schools, another case of "blaming the victim"? I don't think so. We *all* have responsibilities for chil-

274

dren. Part of the responsibility the federal government has is to mesh its programs better than it has been doing. Government has to find some way to make all these social services more readily available.

So that is where we are going. It is very early in the new Administration. But I have a feeling that the political alignment is correct this time. I have been in Washington a long time, and I have not seen the sun and the moon and the planets lined up quite as propitiously as I see them now. You have a President who obviously knows education. He has sat in meetings like this for countless hours, not only in Arkansas but nationally. He and his wife know these issues backwards and forwards. You also have a President, I think, who wants to spend some money on these issues and is willing to think a little bit differently.

In Congress, the last two years have been very frustrating; actually, it has been the last 12 years, but the last two especially. We were dealing with an "education" president who proposed a program that had some merit. But we could not get beyond politics, and we could not get beyond the private-school choice issue. However, many of the issues Bush brought to us — standards, assessments, etc. — were issues that were useful for us to grapple with, because in a way it prepared the ground for Clinton's program.

So I think, as a result, the Congress is going to be much more agreeable with ideas that come from the Clinton Administration. Sometimes in the beginning of an administration your hopes are high and you wind up being disappointed. But this time around I think things are going to go the right way.

I know, of course, that the federal government does not provide much money for education. But I also know that it is the President who dominates the news media. If the President talks about education, and if the federal government, with the money it does have, tries to assist more positively, I think you are going to have a better system of education in this country. Thank you.

EPILOGUE: PRINCIPAL CONFERENCE THEMES

What features of American public education drew the most passionate attention and earnest advocacy from participants in this conference? Immersion in the 80,000-word discussion transcripts and review of the background papers lead me to these observations:

• Systemic reform — massive change from top to bottom, not mere tinkering — is required to produce a system of public schools capable of meeting the needs of a new era characterized by growing racial, cultural, and ethnic diversity and rapid social, demographic, and economic change. High-level thinking, lifelong learning, and the capacity to make frequent career changes will be required in an increasingly competitive, high-tech, knowledge-driven, worldwide economy.

• All youth-serving agencies, including the public schools, should concentrate and collaborate on giving very young children a good start in life to overcome the effects of unstable, dysfunctional, and one-parent families; the deterioration of traditional values; and the increasing number of children from economically and culturally deprived homes.

• Savage inequalities in the distribution of resources have produced disaster areas in education not only in the inner cities but in rural America. Policy makers at every level must attach a very high priority to overcoming this scandalous and long-standing disequilibrium.

• Curriculum revision is at the heart of reform; and the new curriculum must be rigorous, focused, and trimmed to the essentials, with clear and attainable goals.

• Higher standards of achievement, with appropriate assessment techniques, must be developed to drive the reform movement nationwide, bearing in mind that all children can meet these standards, given the time and the resources to do so and teachers who have mastered both subject matter and teaching techniques through better preparation and higher-quality staff-development programs.

• The question before America now is whether the public consensus and the political will can be mustered to achieve the reforms that will produce a more effective public education system. The profession is challenged to end its turf wars, seek partners, build coalitions, and persuade the public to make the investment of time, thought, and money that will guarantee success.

Stanley Elam, Conference Editor
March 31, 1993

CONFERENCE PARTICIPANTS

Jeanne Allen, Director, Town Hall, Heritage Foundation, Washington, D.C.

David Bergholz, Executive Director, George Gund Foundation, Cleveland, Ohio.

David Berliner, Professor of Education, College of Education, Arizona State University, Tempe.

Richard A. Boyd, Executive Director, Martha Holden Jennings Foundation, Cleveland, Ohio.

Gerald Bracey, Education Consultant, Alexandria, Virginia.

Nancy Braham, Executive Assistant to the President and Director of Development, Institute for Educational Leadership, Washington, D.C.

Louise Clarke, Chief Administrative Officer, Institute for Educational Leadership, Washington, D.C.

Emeral Crosby, Principal, Pershing High School, Detroit, Michigan.

Christopher T. Cross, Executive Director — Education Initiative, The Business Roundtable, Washington, D.C.

Luvern Cunningham, Partner, Leadership Development Associates, Gahanna, Ohio.

Denis P. Doyle, Senior Fellow, Hudson Institute, Indianapolis, Indiana, with offices in Washington, D.C.

Stanley Elam, Editor Emeritus, *Phi Delta Kappan*, and Conference Editor, Daytona Beach, Florida.

Chester Finn, Founding Partner, The Edison Project, Washington, D.C.

Sy Fliegel, Consultant, Sy Fliegel Associates, The Manhattan Institute, New York City.

Pascal D. Forgione, Jr., Superintendent of Public Instruction, State of Delaware, Dover.

Keith Geiger, President, National Education Association, Washington, D.C.

Milton Goldberg, Executive Director, National Education Commission on Time and Learning, Washington, D.C.

Pauline Gough, Editor, *Phi Delta Kappan*, Phi Delta Kappa, Bloomington, Indiana.

Sandra T. Gray, Vice President, Leadership/Management, Independent Sector, Washington, D.C.

Martin Haberman, Professor of Education, University of Wisconsin-Milwaukee.

Betty Hale, Vice President and Director, Leadership Programs, Institute for Educational Leadership, Washington, D.C.

Andrew Hartman, Education Policy Coordinator, U.S. House of Representatives, Committee on Education and Labor, Washington, D.C.

Kati Haycock, Director, Education Roundtable, American Association for Higher Education, Washington, D.C.

Norbert S. Hill, Jr., Executive Director, American Indian Science and Engineering Society, Boulder, Colorado.

Harold Hodgkinson, Director, Center for Demographic Policy, Institute for Educational Leadership, Washington, D.C.

Sol Hurwitz, President, Committee for Economic Development, New York City.

John F. Jennings, General Counsel for Education, Committee on Education and Labor, U.S. House of Representatives, Washington, D.C.

Vinetta Jones, National Director, Equity 2000 Program, New York City.

Anne Kahn, Director, Organization Relations, National Research Council, Mathematical Sciences Education Board.

George Kaplan, Education Journalist, Bethesda, Maryland.

James A. Kelly, President, National Board for Professional Teaching Standards, Detroit, Michigan.

Sally B. Kilgore, Senior Fellow and Director of Education Policy Studies, Hudson Institute, Indianapolis, Indiana.

Jack Kosoy, International President, Phi Delta Kappa, Granada Hills, California.

Anne Lewis, Editorial Writer, Glen Echo, Maryland.

Anne Lynch, Immediate Past President, National Congress of Parents and Teachers, Las Vegas, Nevada.

Arturo Madrid, President, Tomas Rivera Center, Claremont, California.

Gene Maeroff, Senior Research Associate, Carnegie Foundation for the Advancement of Teaching, Princeton, New Jersey.

Phillip Merchant, Program Officer, Exxon Foundation Corporation, Irving, Texas.

John Merrow, Executive Officer, Learning Matters, New York City.

Richard A. Miller, Executive Director, American Association of School Administrators, Arlington, Virginia.

Linda Moore, Senior Associate, Leadership Programs, Institute for Educational Leadership, Washington, D.C.

Frederick Mulhauser, Assistant Director, Program Evaluation and Methodology Division, U.S. General Accounting Office, Washington, D.C.

John Murphy, Superintendent, Charlotte-Mecklenberg Schools, Charlotte, North Carolina.

Joe Nathan, Director, Center for School Change, Humphrey Institute of Public Affairs, University of Minnesota, Minneapolis.

Peter J. Negroni, Superintendent, Springfield School Department, Springfield, Massachusetts.

Chris Pipho, Division Director, Information Clearinghouse/State Relations, Education Commission of the States, Denver, Colorado.

Lowell Rose, Executive Director, Phi Delta Kappa, Bloomington, Indiana.

Iris Rotberg, Senior Researcher, Rand Corporation, Washington, D.C.

Ted Sanders, Superintendent of Public Instruction, State of Ohio, Columbus.

Esther F. Schaeffer, Senior Vice President, National Alliance of Business, Washington, D.C.

Gilbert T. Sewall, Director, American Textbook Council, and Editor, *Social Studies Review*, New York City.

Albert Shanker, President, American Federation of Teachers, Washington, D.C.

Thomas A. Shannon, Executive Director, National School Boards Association, Alexandria, Virginia.

Donald M. Stewart, President, The College Board, Baltimore, Maryland.

David Tatel, Partner, Hogan & Hartson, Washington, D.C.

Michael Usdan, President, Institute for Educational Leadership, Washington, D.C.

Sandra M. Weith, Director, Administrative Center, Phi Delta Kappa. Bloomington, Indiana.

Gene Wilhoit, Executive Director, National Association of State Boards of Education, Alexandria, Virginia.